TO VISITORS
Please ensure that all birds
are out of the house before leaving.
Deny

KING OF THE WILDERNESS

Christobel Mattingley is an award-winning
author who has written over forty books
for children, many of which have been
translated and published overseas. She
researched and edited the acclaimed
Aboriginal history, *Survival in Our Own
Land*. For services to literature she was
made an Honorary Doctor of the University
of South Australia and created a Member
of the Order of Australia.

KING OF THE
THE LIFE OF DENY KING
WILDERNESS

CHRISTOBEL MATTINGLEY

TEXT PUBLISHING MELBOURNE AUSTRALIA

ILLUSTRATION SOURCES

Grateful acknowledgment is made to the following for permission to reproduce the illustrative material in the picture sections:
Section 1: plates I, II, III, IV, V, VIII, IX and X, King Collection/Queen Victoria Museum; plates VI and VII, Bob Mossel.
Section 2: plates XI and XIV, King Collection/Queen Victoria Museum; plate XII, Sally Fenton; plate XIII, Dr Gregory Jordan; plate XV, Geoff Fenton; plate XVI, Bob Mossel; plate XVII, Roger Archibald; plates XVIII to XXII, Trevor Waite, plate XXIII, Dave Watts.
Section 3: plate XXIV, King Collection/Queen Victoria Museum; plates XXV and XXVI, Geoff Fenton; plate XXVII, Bob Mossel; plate XXVIII, courtesy of the Mercury; plate XXIX, Norton Harvey.

The Text Publishing Company
Swann House
22 William Street
Melbourne Victoria 3000
Australia
www.textpublishing.com.au

First published 2001, reprinted 2001 (twice)
This edition 2002, 2003, 2004, 2005

Maps by Tony Fankhauser, with map on p. xii based on a drawing by Janet Fenton
Painting on p. i by Hilma Tyson, photograph by David Mattingley
Designed by Chong Weng-ho
Typeset in 12.3/16.5 Minion by Midland Typesetters
Printed and bound by Griffin Press

National Library of Australia
Cataloguing-in-Publication data:

Mattingley, Christobel, 1931– .

King of the wilderness : the life of Deny King.

Includes index.

ISBN 1 877008 41 9.

1. King, Deny, 1909-1991. 2. Naturalists - Tasmania - Melaleuca - Biography. 3. Melaleuca, Tas. - Biography. I. Title.

994.6204092

For Mary and Janet,
a bunch of Deny and Margaret's forget-me-nots,
gathered with love

Contents

A myrtle tree of strength, you stand
and gaze upon your windswept land.
Your sun-streaked hair, the raindrops bless,
and walnut back, the winds caress.
Far deeper than the sun-seeped skies,
and swept with stars, your silent eyes.

Time's tales mark hands too rough to bless
but tell of love's unselfishness.
The years have gathered, page by page,
they cannot move your spirit's age.
These rainbow tears are spilt in joy
too great to speak, for words destroy.

Janet King, late 1960s

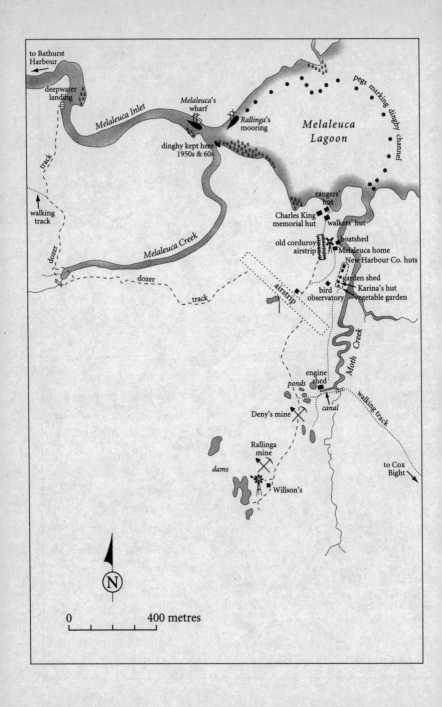

to Bathurst
Harbour

deepwater landing

Melaleuca Inlet

Melaleuca's wharf

Rallinga's mooring

dinghy kept here
1950s & 60s

pegs marking dinghy channel

*Melaleuca
Lagoon*

track

walking track

dozer

Melaleuca Creek

dozer   track

rangers' hut

Charles King
memorial hut   walkers' hut

old corduroy   boatshed
airstrip   Melaleuca home
                      New Harbour Co. huts

airstrip   bird   garden shed
              observatory Karina's hut
                           vegetable garden

Moth Creek

ponds

engine
shed

Deny's mine

canal

walking track

Rallinga
mine

dams

Willson's

to Cox
Bight

N

0   400 metres

Meeting the man at Melaleuca

I met Deny King in the last seven weeks of his life. In March 1991 my husband and I spent two weeks as honorary wardens on a survey monitoring the highly endangered species, the orange-bellied parrot.

These beautiful little birds, numbering less than two hundred, migrate from coastal Victoria and South Australia each spring to breed in remote south-west Tasmania. Deny King's concern for their diminishing numbers led to the establishment of the program at Melaleuca, where he lived, at Port Davey.

Five days before our stay ended, we met Deny at the airstrip as we collected an injured parrot returning after treatment in Hobart. I'll never forget the image of him, checked shirt, baggy trousers tied with string, sockless feet in lambswool slippers, sugar bag slung over his shoulder, striding up the track, an indomitable old man overjoyed to be going home.

Deny had taken the trouble to learn our names beforehand, and as we carried stores to the house for him and he unobtrusively reset the fire I had laid for his homecoming, he asked if my husband was related to A. H. Mattingley, the ornithologist (which he is). He recalled having read an article by him in *The Emu*, the journal of the Royal Australasian Ornithologists' Union, in 1926!

Later, when he invited us in his soft slow drawl, for 'a cuppa cawfee and nice fr-resh bun', it soon became obvious Deny's reputation as a storyteller was well-founded. He had an unlimited fund of anecdotes and stories, and a rich treasury of local lore to share, garnered through a lifetime of patient observation. With our mutual love of nature study we had much in common and Deny seemed to enjoy our company. He invited us to stay to help him eat a big stew he had made and went off to fetch 'a nice caw-lie', while I scrubbed his homegrown 'taters', and stewed apples from his trees. It was nearly midnight before we left his fireside and the warmth of his hospitality.

We had a second wonderful evening with him, and now felt that it was not too crass to comment on the ingenious construction of the house he had built and the finishes and furnishings he had contrived. I told Deny how in his absence I had guided two visitors, more sensitive than most, through his garden. They were so delighted with it that I had decided on the spur of the moment to take them into the house to sign the visitors' book, one of Deny's traditions.

As they entered, the man had been spellbound, reading the life of the creator and occupier from every detail, down to the hat thrown on the floor, the boots by a stool at the door, the torch, the lamp, and the bough suspended from the curved ceiling, a favourite perch for the dusky robins. He asked if he might take some photos and when I demurred, he confessed that he was an architect and had been building houses in a somewhat similar style for twenty years. He asked me to pass on his compliments and tell Deny that he had preceded him by more than two decades in his achievement. He signed the visitors' book and his name was Glenn Murcutt!

His wife, a librarian at the Mitchell Library in Sydney, asked me if Deny's oral history or a biography had been done. I didn't know. That night I woke with her questions humming in my mind, and lay in the quiet Melaleuca darkness unwillingly turning them over. After our third evening with Deny they again disturbed my sleep.

I had some experience in collecting oral histories and knew how important they could be as the most appropriate and sometimes the only way of recording memories and information which would otherwise be lost. But surely it would be presumptuous to think that after such a short acquaintance with Deny and brief experience of the South-West, that I was the person to do an oral history, let alone a biography?

The next day Deny seemed dispirited, and confessed to having had another bad night. He was finding it increasingly difficult to sleep and spent long hours recalling the past. I suggested he get a little tape recorder and think his memories aloud. He looked very sad and told me he had been trying to write his story for some time. He had already written about his father's life and his stories, but was finding it very hard, partly because of failing eyesight, to do his own.

I told him I was a writer and shared with him tips and practicalities of writing and advised him of publishing pitfalls. Deny listened eagerly and asked me to read some of his work. With some misgiving I took the proffered half-dozen handwritten pages and left him searching anxiously for the remainder.

I knew Deny had had only one year of formal schooling and I began reading with some apprehension. I need not have worried. His integrity, his love of life, his keen powers of observation and phenomenal memory for and appreciation of detail gave his writing strength and a unique flavour.

The last morning I went to say goodbye and found him quietly sad, sitting on his stool by the stove, suddenly looking his eighty-one years. He asked me if I would come back and help him write his story. 'We could get through it quite quickly in the winter, when there aren't all the visitors,' he said. I agreed and he looked happy again.

When we trundled our gear to the airstrip that afternoon, we were surprised to see him standing by the plane. He gave me two plastic bags. One contained some of his sweet freshly pulled carrots he knew I loved. 'To eat on the plane.' The other was full of little plants. 'Look after my forget-me-nots for me,' he charged. He was crying as the plane took off. So was I.

Deny had told me with quiet pride that his younger daughter Janet was a school librarian. He urged me to phone her, saying he knew we would get on well together. He was right. Janet was delighted her father had asked me to help him with his story and that I had agreed. When we hung up after a long conversation, we felt as if we had known each other for ever.

I wrote to Deny when we got home, and also sent him a card from Kangaroo Island which he had visited and loved. And he wrote to me.

He flew to Hobart, as he usually did for Anzac Day, and stayed with his older daughter Mary at the family home at Sandy Bay. We had several good phone conversations, discussing plans for my return. We had a great sense of urgency. A date was fixed for late May and I booked my ticket.

Then Janet rang to say Deny was in hospital with pneumonia. We waited for better news and a few days later, I spoke with him again. He was so eager for me to come that my husband collected my ticket on Saturday morning. The next evening, on Sunday 12 May, Janet rang to say that her father had just died after a massive heart attack.

Mary and Janet still wanted me to come and to carry on the work. But helping Deny to tell his own story, with him as source and authority, was very different from undertaking a biography. I felt many other people who had known Deny much longer were probably better qualified to write his story.

His daughters didn't see it that way. They saw me as their father's choice and urged me to come to Melaleuca. I flew in alone on 10 June, just ten weeks since Deny had farewelled me. Mary and Janet and their children Kylie, Tony and Sally were waiting at the airstrip to greet me. It was as if I was already part of the family.

The next morning was frosty cold and as I walked up the buttongrass ridge above the house to look on the encircling mountains in the early light, an amazing sight awaited me.

A great white rainbow arched across the southern sky. It seemed like a message. For three successive mornings it was there. How Deny would have loved to see those rainbows and how I wished he was there to talk about them and share his immense store of observations, amassed through a lifelong passion for weather lore.

Mary, Janet and I spent three days talking, laughing, crying, looking through old photos, letters and boxes of mementoes, my tape recorder competing for memories against the sound of the children's games and songs and music from the historic piano. Then everyone went back to school and I was alone in Deny's home for another nine days, poring by lamp, candle and firelight over the diaries in his spidery hand, sorting through boxes of jumbled letters dating back forty years and earlier. As I read his diaries and correspondence I realised that, growing up in Hobart in the late 1940s, I had lived close to the King home in Sandy Bay and I knew many of the people and places mentioned.

Deny had loved the company of birds, as I have always done, and this had been one of our special affinities. In the daytime as I worked, the house was full of the little visitors, twenty or more at a time—dusky robins perching on the Aladdin lamp, blue wrens chasing blowflies on the windows, olive whistlers, firetail finches and little brown scrubwrens. Deny's favourites had always been the grey shrike thrushes and he called generations of them 'Richard', after the famous singer Richard Tauber.

The Richards had always shown an awareness or prescience of the highest and lowest points of Deny's life, and they showed it for me too. At my worst moments of self-doubt about the undertaking, I would look up to see the grey thrush watching me from the casuarina outside the window, or calling from the porch, coming to my hand as soon as I opened the door. It was Richard's trust, complementing Deny's, Mary's and Janet's, which helped me to accept this task.

Since then I have interviewed people in every state of Australia and corresponded with many others, some overseas. Often interviews had to be suspended for the tears they prompted as people shared their memories. Everyone has been very generous with time, personal papers, photos and hospitality. Deny knew so many people and all were proud to claim him as their friend. Even now, ten years after his death, people still speak of him in the present tense.

I hope my work is worthy of Deny and his remarkable life, and the expectations of his family and friends. I have made a number of visits to Melaleuca, absorbing its natural splendours and the intimate atmosphere of Deny's home, getting to know some of the creatures which were part of his life—bush rats rustling in the pantry, pygmy possums sleeping in the knife drawer, wombats, wallabies and pademelons in the garden, and the quolls, whose nightly droppings on his doorstep were so distasteful to him.

To remain faithful to Deny's voice I have used many of his terms and kept his names for the native fauna: 'roos' are Bennett's wallabies, 'wallabies' are pademelons, 'native cats' or 'nady cats' are eastern quolls, 'tiger cats' or 'ger cats' are spotted-tailed quolls, 'tigers' are thylacines.

I retraced Deny's strides over the button-grass plains to and from the coast, explored the mine workings and old campsite at Cox Bight and followed some of the waterways of Port Davey. I have written sitting on the window seat where Sir Edmund Hillary slept; on the waterfront with *Scamp* and *Blue Boat* resting on the reflective waters of Moth Creek; and up in the studio looking across to Mount Counsel in all lights. And Richard was always there.

CHAPTER 1

Nature's gentleman

'I am a lucky person. I have met Deny King.'

Deny King made an indelible impression on everyone fortunate enough to know him. Observant blue eyes far-seeing as the horizon and often twinkling with fun gazed from under maned eyebrows. In a weather-brightened face scored by the seasons, from a wide mouth always ready to smile, words came slowly in a distinctive husky drawl, greeting, welcoming. Work-strong square hands stretched out in friendship and help to others. Broad shoulders never shirked a burden. Warmth, wisdom and disarming humility revealed a man at one with himself, at home in the domain he loved to share.

This was the wild and rugged Tasmanian South-West, and tales of Deny King's exploits on land and sea abound. His phenomenal strength and stamina, his ingenuity, humour, kindness, his unparalleled knowledge of the bush and its creatures, and exceptional ability to foretell weather, all combined to make him a legend in his own lifetime.

His sturdy self-reliance in such magnificent isolation stirred the imagination of many and he became affectionately known as King of the South-West. Even people who met him only briefly have an anecdote, always ending, 'Deny King was an amazing fellow!'

The world came to Deny by land, sea and air—on foot, often blistered; under sail, often seasick; in small aircraft, sometimes airsick. And the world returned later, in envelopes crammed into a canvas mailbag marked in black: D. KING—PORT DAVEY. Deny was friend to everyone and his mailbag's contents reflected that friendship.

Envelopes addressed DENY KING, PORT DAVEY, TASMANIA always found him, judging by numerous boxes of letters stowed in cupboards. Sometimes hand-decorated, or on cards selected to appeal, they expressed appreciation of his kindness and readiness to welcome and help those who made the effort to discover his realm. People thanked him for so freely 'sharing his kingdom' and expressed their hope of returning to 'his paradise'. Many recalled with gratitude his gifts of homemade bread and jam, homegrown fruit and vegetables, fresh and extra welcome after days on the track had depleted rations.

Sometimes there were gifts in return for hospitality and transport: books signed by their authors, or selected with Deny's wide-ranging interests in mind; little sketches and paintings; tea or favourite foodstuffs; socks or woollies; even a ticket in a Wilderness Society raffle. A group who had enjoyed substantial hospitality while weatherbound, sent in a side of lamb. Leonard Long inscribed a book of his paintings.

Nevil Shute, who visited in February 1953, later wrote from London. 'I saw some little gimballed kerosene lamps and remembered Mrs King wanted something like that for the children in *Melaleuca*. So I ordered a couple to be sent as a souvenir of all your kindness and hospitality when we came in *Saona* last summer.'

People wanted to show their gratitude for bandaids and bread, fruit and philosophy, but most of all for the pleasure of Deny's company. One recorded simply, 'I am a lucky person. I have met Deny King.'

Another, from the US, wrote after fourteen years, saying he would name his forthcoming baby, if a boy, after Deny. 'You will always be to me one of the greatest and most natural men I have ever known. I have not forgotten a single thing you taught me and the close rapport you have with nature and all living things will always be to me the prime example of how men should live.'

When the Kings featured in the media, it always brought responses. Hazel Hassett wrote from Western Australia:

> Ever since seeing the TV interview I've been meaning to write, but felt rather shy. I actually stayed in from square-dancing [to watch], to make sure you were the same soldier billeted at Meadows with the Smith family many years ago, and sure enough that low voice and painting ability was unmistakable. I can still hear your favourable comments about Mum's melon pie and cream!!

As Deny became increasingly sought-after at home and overseas, the range of correspondents increased. Comments in Deny's visitors' book by a French film crew were euphoric. 'An incredible country, an incredible man, an incredible story,' Denis Chatelain enthused. 'Touching hospitality and what humour. I am overwhelmed! The reality, the truth of this life spent turned away from the beaten track. I shall take away this feeling of quietude, of happiness and I shall keep it forever.'

Claude Regnier said, 'It is difficult to express the joy of return-ing to Melaleuca, the surprise is not so strong, but the emotion is unchanged. Melaleuca is unforgettable. Deny is always the same.'

Letters came in French, Christmas cards in German and Spanish and visitors from the US, Canada, England, Wales, Scotland, Ireland, Holland, Switzerland and Spain all wrote to him. Travellers sent postcards from Argentina, Indonesia, New Zealand, Nepal, Pakistan, Japan, China, the Falklands and the Hebrides. After Deny's 1985 South American trip at the age of seventy-five, a Chilean guide corresponded frequently, sharing his travels and memories.

Deny's correspondents also included numerous scientists and naturalists, requesting his help in collecting specimens of flora and fauna, including insects, fish and molluscs, many unique to south-west Tasmania, and asking for his observations. Through his field work species new to science were discovered and described, and much new knowledge recorded.

Anthropologist Therese Belleau Kemp, in thanking Deny for his help on a field trip to Port Davey in 1964, wrote:

> Words are almost useless to express how I feel about my trip to your corner of the world. May I say you have made history. By your sincere and wide interest in the world near and far, you have made it possible for research to proceed along new lines, new horizons. I thank you, not only for myself, but for science.

After Deny's death in May 1991, condolence letters flooded in from all over Australia and beyond, even from people who had never known him personally, but to whom he had endeared himself through the media by his transparent goodness and quirky humour. Others shared memories going back a lifetime. Carefully chosen cards depicting birds, animals, flowers, seascapes and mountains reflected Deny's love of nature. Photos and poems bore tribute to Deny's influence on countless people. Everyone who knew him loved him.

More than two hundred people from all walks of life came to Deny's funeral at Judbury beside the great Huon River. The scent of gum leaves from a glowing fire, a Richard thrush melodiously calling from the bush, and Beethoven's *Pastoral Symphony* evoked Deny's spirit.

In her eulogy an old friend, Karen Alexander, said Deny was extraordinary, 'because he thought of himself as ordinary, and accepted people for what they were. He leaves a legacy of fantastic richness and inspiration', she declared, a statement with which everybody who was privileged to know him would agree.

CHAPTER 2

Early years in the Huon

'Challenge—the sap of life.'

Deny King was born on 12 September 1909 at Clifton Grove, his maternal grandparents' home, near Huonville. Buds were swelling on the apple trees in his grandfather's orchard, daffodils danced like stars in his grandmother's garden. On the hillsides grey thrushes' rich notes resounded through the bush where wattles billowed yellow.

He was baptised Charles Denison, after his father and the river flowing wild from its headwaters in the rugged Snowy Range into the Huon. He was Denis to family and friends, Den for short, until World War II when army mates called him Deny and the name stuck. He was the third child and only son of Charles George King and Olive Skinner, both of strong moral fibre and adventurous spirit.

Olive Skinner, Ollie, was one of ten children, daughter of a well-established Huon family engaged in apple production, whose forebears came to the district in 1843. Her mother, energetic and forceful, kept a guesthouse popular with visitors from Hobart and beyond. Even the governor was a guest.

Members of visiting musical companies who sometimes stayed at Clifton Grove commented on young Ollie's beautiful voice and musical talent. She was invited to join one company for training and travel overseas, but her parents would not have it. She remained organist at the Congregational Church, gave music lessons at home and played and sang duets with her brother Herbert.

Ollie was attractive, with searching grey eyes in a smooth round face framed by thick curly chestnut hair. Her serene dignity concealed a free spirit, lively intelligence and deep determination. She did not lack local suitors, but none appealed enough for her lifelong commitment. Then handsome, independent Charlie King with his endearing sense of humour returned from the Boer War with her brother Harold.

Charlie's parents had migrated from England in 1876 to Toowoomba, Queensland. Charlie was born a year later in Brisbane, the first of four children. His mother's ill-health caused a series of moves southwards, to Melbourne, then to Lilydale in north-east Tasmania. Ultimately they settled at Huonville, where Charlie's bootmaker father established himself.

Charlie left school at twelve. His parents, keen he should continue in an educational atmosphere, found a position as errand boy at a Launceston bookshop. But commerce and city life did not fulfil Charlie's longing for adventure. Seeing an advertisement for a rouseabout at a tin mine on Flinders Island in Bass Strait, he begged his parents to let him apply. As the only applicant who could harness a horse and set a snare, skills acquired from an old north-east bushman, he won the job.

When the mine was abandoned, young Charlie was left as caretaker with only a collie for company. He soon moved to a farm on Robbins Island off the north-west coast, where he learned new skills with stock and crops. Later he became a farmhand on the coast, and then went south looking for work.

He found employment clearing land for the expanding Skinner orchards. But the outbreak of the Boer War promised more excitement and in 1900 Charlie enlisted with Harold Skinner in the First Tasmanian Imperial Bushmen.

Ollie's family, particularly her mother, disapproved of Charlie's unsettled life as bushman and prospector, and discouraged the courtship. But at twenty-seven Ollie knew her own mind. She married the man of her choice in a quiet ceremony at Clifton Grove on 17 April 1906.

The couple went first to Robbins Island, then moved to the west coast. At Tullah Charlie worked for the North Mount Farrell silver lead mine, sometimes in the bush cutting timber, but mainly underground, where he had some narrow escapes from detonating charges and rock falls. His luck became a byword. 'You can't kill Kingy. He's been to the South African War.'

Their first child, Rosemary, was born in May 1907, and their second, Olive, in July 1908. Then Ollie's mother came to visit. Shocked by the mining town's rough conditions, worried about underground accidents and long-term effects of lead dust inhalation, she prevailed on Charlie to bring her grandchildren and pregnant daughter back to a more civilised, healthy environment. So Deny was born in the Huon.

Charlie and Ollie acquired a small property at Judbury, with a comfortable four-roomed house they named Home Burg, and Charlie planted its orchard. The family soon became part of the little community. Charlie had established a Sunday school at Tullah, and now he took charge of the Judbury Methodist Sunday School. Ollie played the church organ and enlivened the singing. Winsome, their third daughter, was born in September 1911.

As the children became old enough to walk the four kilometres, they began attending Judbury school under Miss Creese. Denis's first encounter with an outside authority figure was not a happy one. Miss Creese did not suffer dreamers gladly and, by Deny's own admission, he *was* a dreamer. A cousin remembered her as a good teacher, although very intimidating. 'If she had her grey flannel suit on, we were in for trouble.' Young Denis was frequently rapped over the knuckles with a ruler and more than once his ears were boxed so hard that he saw stars.

In those impressionable years Deny had another unfortunate experience of authority figures. On Sundays the minister preached thundering sermons. The concepts of judgment and damnation he presented were utterly alien to Deny's experience of firm but loving parents who lived by the golden rule. He remembered church as 'a dark place, full of doom and gloom'.

His sisters loved acting 'church', thumping an apple-box pulpit, playing on a box-and-board organ with stones for pedals. Denis preferred soaring on the swing their father had rigged in the stringy-bark tree, or romping with other boys on the huge sawdust heap at the mill by Judd's Creek. On summer nights he loved to watch bats and cockchafer beetles flying, and to experiment striking sparks from quartzite pebbles.

Young Denis had learned long division by the time the family moved again. For him it was a miraculous escape from institutional education and religion, and thereafter he avoided both, learning from and finding his inspiration in the world of nature and its laws. In the new environment there were three formidable factors which shaped his character and future: weather, vegetation, isolation.

Charlie was a frontiersman and his heart was not in farming. After six years he felt confined living in such a close-knit community, near his more affluent in-laws, whose values and viewpoints were so different. To the great annoyance of Ollie's brother Herbert, who employed him to attend the horses so necessary for farm work and transporting apples to the local port, Charlie began to absent himself. He was drawn to 'the outback', as locals called the area beyond the settled lower reaches of the Huon, where the Denison, Weld and Arve, rising in the Snowy and Jubilee ranges and Hartz Mountains, pour their waters into the untamed Huon.

Here Charlie made numerous expeditions on his horse Sam, south-west towards the Weld, prospecting and investigating farming potential. 'Out the Denison' he found a small property for sale, with the unlikely name of Sunset Ranch and, impressed by its soil, he arranged to buy it. It was the last selection on the track which disappeared 'up the Weld'. The only human habitation beyond was the cabin of lone prospector Charlie Fletcher, eight kilometres further out.

Sunset Ranch sounded a magical place to the children, who delighted in gifts their father brought home: a feather or flower on a bed of moss; a strange insect in a matchbox; sometimes a little bush animal; or some delicacy—wild honey in the comb or a freshly caught trout.

The property consisted of two adjoining blocks, eighty hectares each, fourteen kilometres beyond Judbury, nearly five beyond the Denison and three up from the Huon. It was in a valley two hundred metres above sea level on the south-east slopes of a massive mountain over 650 metres high, heavily timbered Barn Back, where, as Deny remembered, 'the tall trees stood in bold relief against the sky'.

On Christmas Day 1915 their father borrowed a horse and dray and took the family to see the place. It was a long day's journey, the bad road deteriorating to a worse track. The dense bush and towering gums were awesome. 'Tallest trees in the world,' Charlie announced with proprietorial pride. Young Denis was excited to spot wallabies feeding on regrowth among the ringbarked giants.

Olive remembered how her father handed down their mother like a queen from her box seat, beside the two-roomed slab and shingle hut. With regal calm and her practical acceptance of reality Ollie surveyed their domain. If she had been depressed by the miles of ghostly eucalypt skeletons and the acres of burnt-out debris with engulfing bracken taller than a man, she said nothing. If she was daunted by the sight of the primitive little dwelling, stark in the westering sun, she gave no sign. Opening its door, wrinkling her nose at the stale smell, she showed no dismay, simply remarking with characteristic pith, 'Dogs and bachelors', and set to making the future family home habitable.

Sensing his children's apprehension, Charlie sent them to gather sticks and fill a billy with water from the sparkling, fern-fringed creek running down the hillside only a few metres from the hut. He fetched water in kerosene tin buckets and put them to heat in the deep fireplace built of local stones set in clay mortar. Ollie, with the resourcefulness which Deny inherited, contrived a mop from a stick and an old shirt and washed the floor with boiling water dosed with caustic soda. The transformation had begun.

In the spring of 1916, when Denis had just turned seven, the family moved to Sunset Ranch. Children, mother, possessions, were all crammed onto the dray for the marathon journey skirting the Huon River, then crossing the Russell and Denison. The narrow road was rough and muddy, deeply rutted, steep and tortuous, often blocked by fallen trees. On uphill stretches the poultry, plants and chattels stayed aboard, while the family walked to ease the strain on the horses.

For the last seven kilometres the track degenerated even more, petering out at Sunset Ranch's southernmost boundary. The last pinch up to the shelf where the hut stood was the worst, a hazardous fifty metres with rocky outcrops, burnt logs and stumps.

'A shattering finale to a trip with all stops out,' organist Ollie described it in later years, though she did not even murmur a protest then, so determined was she to exchange what she called 'parochial mediocrity' for 'pioneering challenge'.

'Challenge was the sap of life at Sunset Ranch,' Olive wrote:

> The early years were just about all challenge. The raw land we coaxed into providing a living was challenge. The very size of the trees either standing or recumbent was a challenge. Holding back the rampant regrowth was an endless challenge, so too coping with the all-devouring

game. The enticing unknown-ness of our vast hinterland was a challenge. Communication via the thing called a road was constant challenge. Getting some form of formal education when so many excuses cogent to survival distracted application was challenge.

That night—and every night for eight years—the girls slept in a tent on stretchers Charlie made from saplings and sacking, while Denis curled up on the kitchen couch. Rosemary, practical like her mother, was undeterred by the lack of basic amenities. When her siblings inquired for 'the dub', she directed them matter-of-factly behind logs.

At first the children were overwhelmed by the wildness and isolation of their new home. Its aura of romance evaporated before the raw reality. Even Denis, who loved nothing better than spending hours alone in the Judbury bush, did not relish the prospect of being alone in this strange place. The immensity of the unknown outside in the all-enveloping darkness, full of secrets and mysterious sounds, stimulated already overactive imaginations. But in the light of the new day the children caught their parents' infectious pioneering spirit.

After breakfast, cooked in the camp oven, Charlie was eager to start on the work confronting them in every direction outside. Ollie, born homemaker, had different priorities. The first job to which the whole family was set was lining the rough slab walls with scrim and paper to shut out any creatures which might creep through the cracks and the wind which had whistled through the slats in the night.

The children held old chaff bags taut while Charlie slit them open. They then stretched and held them up against the walls while Charlie tacked them firm. Ollie boiled flour and water into a paste in a bucket over the fire, lacing it with alum to deter rodents. From the dray Denis and Win fetched bundles of old newspapers brought for the purpose, from which Rosemary and Olive, being readers, were allowed to select the pages for wallpaper, and to slap on the paste.

The walls of the kitchen-cum-schoolroom became aids for reading, spelling and world history, and Gainsborough's *The Blue Boy* and Rembrandt's *The Syndics of the Drapers' Guild* inspired the children's artistic efforts.

Olive and Denis were next sent to collect red clay from the roadside to ochre the fireplace with a brush Charlie made from tough native grass. He split a sawn length of blackwood and fixed it, rough bark out, as a mantelpiece.

Rosemary put down the hearth mat and laid a bag stencilled CERTIFIED RYEGRASS in bright red at the door. Curtains were hung at the two windows. The fresh-scrubbed table was spread with a cloth and Winsome placed an enamel mug filled with pink clover blossoms in the centre. Suddenly the little hut was home, an oasis of security, a sure sanctuary of loving warmth and familiarity, which Ollie in her wisdom knew they all needed to face the uncertainties beyond its threshold.

CHAPTER 3

Sunset Ranch

'Where is that dratted boy?'

The whole Sunset Ranch area had once been covered by a forest of mighty blue and swamp gums (elsewhere known as mountain ash). From the track below the hut a belt of virgin forest stretched for kilometres down to the Huon River, like a great green undulating sea. On the southern horizon the Bermuda Hills and Hartz Mountains gleamed snowcapped for many months of the year. Behind the hut, ridge upon wooded ridge rose to the summit of Barn Back, and on either side green walls of scrub 'thicker than a possum's fur', as Charlie described it, advanced relentlessly on the patchwork of clearings so hard-won by the slash-and-burn efforts of the original selectors.

Deny remembered thirty-five fully grown tree stumps, all one to two metres in diameter, within a radius of sixty metres of the hut. The landscape was spiked by stark bleached forms of giants killed by bushfire and the ground was littered with fallen trees of massive length and girth, 'blackened logs like stranded whales on a grassy shore'.

Falling limbs from standing trees were a hazard even on still days and the tempestuous westerlies which swept in from the Roaring Forties brought them down with devastating speed and force. In such conditions Ollie kept the children near the house, only allowing them to venture further to bring in the cows.

Over the months the children explored the new terrain. They used logs as paths when they went after the stock and as vantage points when searching for newly dropped calves or hunting for hens' nests. There they were out of the mud, cutting grass, Scotch thistles and wet bushes, and had more chance of avoiding snakes.

Logs were used for fences too, and even shed walls. Hollow ones which had not become kennels or sties, Charlie used for smoking bacon or storing potatoes. The children took over unoccupied ones for cubbies and storing their clay models. The horses and cows also sheltered on the logs' lee-sides and loved rubbing against them.

With fertile imagination, the children named features of their new realm, including trees, dead and alive. They were always sad when one of these venerable landmarks finally succumbed to the rampaging westerlies. Bee Fat House, a mighty swamp gum 'as fat around the base as a house' was a bee tree. After it fell victim to a September gale, Charlie paced its length, 'two hundred and seventy of my number eights'. An earlier victim, now the cowyard's side fence, was over 200 feet (fifty-seven metres) without its crown.

The children, self-styled 'the Sunset Ranchers', began developing their own vocabulary, with names and descriptive words for local sounds and conditions. Soon they had peopled the lonely landscape of their new world with characters they observed, as poultry had to adapt to new freedom, while pigs and cows became more domesticated.

I Am, the rooster, became I Was when he lost not only his tail but his confidence in an encounter with a Tasmanian devil. Someone had forgotten to close the coop and the devil grabbed him from a low perch, but unwisely went under the house to consume its supper. Awakened by the dogs' barking and I Am's frenzied squawking, Charlie tried to drive out the marauder with the clothes prop, adding to the commotion. Ollie's quick thinking saved the night and I Am's life, if not his dignity. Seizing the kettle from the hearth, she poured hissing water down the cracks onto the skirmish. I Am escaped from the snarling devil, which emerged to meet dogs and Charlie's gun.

The forest included blackwoods, musk, sassafras and stringybarks, and a dense understorey of tree ferns, shrubs and ferns. In more open areas pomaderris, prickly wattle and stinkwood flourished. Pomaderris was good stock-feed and the cows used prickly wattle as medication. Stinkwood, however, could be lethal. Three precious heifers, cut off by a sudden snowstorm, died of stinkwood poisoning.

Yet such fatalities did not deter the children from investigating other foods for subsistence. They noticed the pigs thriving on bracken rhizomes. When neighbour Charlie Fletcher told them the roots had been a staple for Aborigines, they tried them both raw and roasted, but found them tasteless.

The pigs had a good nose too for blackman's bread, a subterranean fungus also relished by bandicoots. The children dug walnut-sized ones around stringybark saplings where bandicoots had been scratching, and occasionally their father unearthed ones as large as turnips when he ploughed. With a nutty flavour, they were reputed to be high in food value. The children found no acceptable greens among the native vegetation, but foraging in introduced pasture sometimes produced cress.

An important product that helped the family live off the land was honey. Charlie sometimes brought back billies of delicate leatherwood honey taken from bee trees on his outback trips. A single swarm of bees the children encountered on an early bush foray was to become the nucleus of over sixty hives. The deep amber eucalypt honey took the place of sugar for everything except jam-making, and was also a steady income earner.

Winsome had spotted what they thought was an enormous bunch of blowflies behaving strangely and Denis, who had no time for them, hurled a lump of wood at the bush where they hung. It was a painful run home, beginning 'the era of the blue bag and swollen features'.

During the swarming months, December and January, Charlie made the children responsible for collecting any bees, if he was working beyond cooee. To hear 'the sultry roar', the signal of a hive swarming, was a welcome interruption to lessons. The children donned their father's voluminous work clothes and old hats, enveloped faces in butter-muslin, and thrust hands into socks before pursuing the bees, banging kerosene tins with sticks as they went and squirting the stirrup pump to simulate a thunderstorm.

Working in pairs, one would shake the branch where the swarm had settled, to dislodge the bees into a box held underneath by the other. It was all part of the teamwork and courage Charlie and Ollie had dedicated themselves to fostering.

Wax was a profitable bee by-product. Spent comb was sold and even the water in which it had been boiled had its use. It was excellent for plants and, on one occasion, for pigs. They broke into the garden and guzzled the fermenting contents of the kerosene tins. Finding the pigs sprawling in blissful abandon evoked Charlie's favourite utterance of amazement. 'Well, I'll be jiggered,' he exclaimed. 'Drunk as lords! That water's turned to honey mead!'

Many outdoor tasks vied for priority. Establishing a vegetable garden for subsistence and breaking in the cows for milking to build up a source of income from cream sales were both matters of urgency. But before they could be undertaken, a fence to protect the vegetables from voracious marauders, and a dairy to comply with health regulations had to be built.

Young Denis, at his father's right hand to fetch and pass tools, learned many of his skills in those early years. He watched as Charlie tested logs for splitting qualities and measured them before proceeding to apply axe, crosscut saw, maul and wedges, paling knife and mallet to produce a pile of neatly split palings, even in width and length. After the family carried the palings to the site, Charlie, with help from Charlie Fletcher, built the dairy and later roofed it with stringybark slabs.

The triangular cowyard had been formed by felling three tall gums. Charlie installed saplings as sliprails for extra security at the entrance and constructed a sturdy bail bolted to a log, where recalcitrant cows could be tied. It proved a necessary addition as the herd was gradually broken in. The children soon became adept at milking, but Denis always disliked cows swishing their muddy tails round his neck and in his face.

The milk had to be scalded and the cream churned into butter, which was taken to Huonville, over thirty kilometres away. Charlie astutely used return journeys to pack out supplies for other selectors, thereby supplementing the family's meagre income. He later bought a separator and made a weekly trip by dray to Huonville with the cream in cans to be shipped to Hobart. When Olive and Winsome had learned to ride bareback they delivered the cream to Judbury where a motor truck collected it.

Charlie was a hard worker. He was not big, but he had immense strength and stamina, a physique inherited from his father and passed on to Deny, and he tackled the vegetable garden with vigour.

He fenced a patch of good volcanic soil with palings then attacked the all-invading regrowth with mattock and muscle. The children dragged roots to burning heaps and rolled rocks downhill. Ollie laid a path to the creek with flat stones. They used round ones to reinforce the excavated walls of the larger pool, forming a dam. Although Sunset Ranch had a very high rainfall, copious water was needed for the vegetable crops vital for subsistence and sale.

Seeds were sown in the warm ashes to hasten germination and soon pumpkins, peas, carrots, broad beans, swedes and potatoes sprouted in the rich red earth. But even Charlie's regular snare setting and vigilant night-patrolling could not always protect the plants from possums which swarmed in from the scrub, tempted by a succulent change of diet. Once when Ollie and the children had worked all day setting out over 1000 cauliflower seedlings, only six remained next morning. Olive remembered it was one of the rare occasions her mother allowed her discouragement to show. She had already planned to spend the proceeds from their sale on luxuries like books and flower seeds.

Charlie's next onslaught was on clearings which had reverted to bush. His brush-hook was rarely idle and needed frequent honing, while young Denis pulled slashed growth to burning heaps. He found the regrowth beautiful—silver wattles with soft grey-green ferny foliage and eucalypt saplings with shiny young leaves tipped bronze, gold and ruby red—and cutting it down saddened him. From 1920 to 1924, however, he had to do so, as Charlie, keen to be as self-sufficient as possible, wanted to grow oats for feed. They had now acquired a half-draught horse, Old Doll, which at least made breaking the new ground easier. By 1923 the land was at last beginning to yield a worthwhile return—over ten tonnes of potatoes and several of small fruits.

Snaring was another activity distasteful to the whole family, though necessary for their survival. Wallabies and possums had increased to plague proportions. No longer hunted by Aborigines or their natural predators, thylacines, the marsupials denuded new pastures and crops overnight. As there was a good market for their pelts, Charlie took out a licence when open seasons were declared. For weeks Charlie, Ollie and Olive sat making the hemp and copper wire snares by lamplight.

When the season opened Charlie went off to set them, sometimes taking young Denis. The snares had to be checked daily, necessitating camping out overnight and longer for more distant rounds. A good haul meant heavy work, resetting snares, then skinning louse-lively carcasses and carrying skins home for pegging out and drying. If the catch was poor, carcasses, bloody and heavy, would be carried home slung across the shoulders, the meat to be used as well. Skinning, pegging out and drying were special skills and if not done properly, the value of the pelts was considerably decreased.

Young Denis loved being in the bush with his father, but disliked the killing of the beautiful little animals he enjoyed observing. Looking back he said, 'I hated snaring. But times were hard, so something had to be done, like it or not.' Denis had no stomach for killing of any kind. Once when in Charlie's absence he was deputed to slaughter a pig, he was unable to carry out the task.

Winters were hard and long, with cold snaps even in summer; sharp reminders of the frosts which devastated garden and fruit trees. Although the Snowy Range shone pink at sunrise for much of the year, snow rarely fell at Sunset Ranch. However, in the winter of 1921 it was heavily blanketed for days.

The westerlies swathed the mountains in cloud and sometimes brought sleet or hail, but mainly rain. Heavy and frequent through much of the year, the rain often turned the already boggy track into a complete quagmire. It also encouraged the dense vegetation and rapid regrowth, the bane of selectors.

Young Denis was fascinated by the weather and set his mind to understanding its mysteries by careful observation of all its signs and patterns. At first no-one took his forecasts very seriously, but soon they proved right too often to be dismissed and by 1928 they were accepted by the family. Olive ended one diary entry, 'Den predicts rain for tomorrow', and concluded the following day, 'Den's rain arrived sure enough'.

Because of the rain and mud, Ollie expressed to young Denis her wish for a verandah. At first he was daunted by the request, but when he realised his mother only wanted some wooden flooring outside the door, he tackled the task with help from Rosemary. It was eventually roofed with shingles he helped split.

Ollie and Rosemary also planned house extensions and felled a good tree for splitting. However, with all the other work on hand, Charlie had little time for building. It was not until his brother George came to stay, that building commenced. George helped split timber for rafters and studs, as well as weatherboards and shingles. Bearers were laid on blackwood logs and George helped erect the framework. After he left no further progress was made and when he returned several years later in 1926 the building was still far from completion. By now Denis was useful with the adze and worked hard trimming the rough split timber. Still, it took a further two years before the extensions became habitable, when carpenter friend Charlie Helm took over and sawn timber was bought to finish the flooring.

It was a red-letter day when Ollie's piano was finally brought to its new home. A gift from her brother Harold, it had been left at her parents' when the Kings moved to Sunset Ranch, and had survived the fire which destroyed Clifton Grove in 1922. The piano became a focal point in family life. Everyone gathered around it on Sunday evenings for hymns, and at other times when they were 'in an unworking mood', sing-songs and piano-playing were favourite relaxations. Although Denis did not learn to play, he always enjoyed music. Another regular family entertainment was reading aloud. Greek myths and legends and Henry Lawson were favourites.

Sunset Ranch was too remote for the children to attend school. But Ollie ensured that formal education was not neglected and rounded them up for lessons while she did housework. Denis never stayed inside a moment longer than necessary. When the girls were dutifully seated at the kitchen table, pen or slate pencil ready, he was not to be seen. Then Ollie would exclaim, 'Where *is* that dratted boy?'

Even the informal lessons at Sunset Ranch could not compete for his attention against all that awaited discovery outdoors. Although young Denis learned to read, write and reckon, he never acquired Charlie's beautiful penmanship or even the smooth rounded flow of Ollie's or Olive's. His writing was awkward, his spelling often phonetic, with random capital letters, and his punctuation almost non-existent. 'I wasn't a very good pupil,' he admitted, 'and I had to be dogged along all the time.'

Unlike Denis, Olive was heartbroken to leave school. She wanted to be a teacher and practised on her siblings. Her unpublished memoirs provide a valuable insight into her parents and the unconventional upbringing they gave their children. Charlie and Ollie were a loyal pair, strongly independent, running against the tide of convention.

Olive believed their parents decided their children should grow up in a setting where they could develop all their senses to the utmost; where their powers of observation and deduction would be honed by the demands of survival; where characters would be built by the need for self-reliance and living in harmony with all things—weather, plants, animals, people; where their sense of awe and wonder would be stimulated and nurtured by the mysteries of the unknown terrain surrounding them; where they would learn to appreciate solitude and beauty.

Charlie and Ollie knew the value of education but did not set much store by formal qualifications. They had none themselves yet were natural teachers. Charlie always said, 'Learning isn't only what comes out of a book. Seeing with your mind what your eyes are looking at is an education on its own.' He frequently admonished, 'For goodness sake, use your eyes!' and 'There's no such word as "can't".' He always made light of difficulties and exercised patience and perseverance finding ways of overcoming them.

Ollie inspired her children with the excitement of discovery, fostering their natural sense of wonder. 'We'll find out no end of things for ourselves,' she promised before they left for Sunset Ranch.

Young Denis, with a naturally inquiring mind, was always experimenting:

> I always wanted to be something I wasn't, some animal or bird, and I'd go around mimicking them, always imagining where I would fly if I was a bird and what tree I would perch on next. I made wings with thin ends and a handle.

I would get on a log or stump, jump off flapping vigorously to see how far I could go. But the results were not encouraging.

Birds fascinated Denis from an early age. He had abundant scope for his passion at Sunset Ranch where seventy-seven species were recorded over the years. He took what his sisters considered an inordinate pride in trying always to be the first to spot a new species. His mother liked birds too, but found they disrupted schoolwork.

'One day we were doing lessons inside,' Deny recalled. 'We heard some white cockatoos in the valley below and of course I tore out grasping my slate and tripped over, shattering it! Mum rounded on me soundly about running out every time a bird squeaks!'

He tamed a flame robin, digging up cockchafer grubs for it, and spent time in snowy weather when he should have been studying, cutting grubs from logs for the currawongs. When birds of passage or the occasional vagrant from the mainland were spotted, Denis became intensely curious about migration. Ollie, always quick to nurture her children's interests, encouraged them to write to the Hobart Library for relevant books. Those the librarian supplied did not satisfactorily answer the children's questions about migration, so speculation continued.

One of Denis's own most prized books was J. A. Leach's *An Australian Bird Book*. 'I was beside myself with excitement when it arrived. I treasured it'. He pored endlessly over illustrations and text. The standard botanical reference, Rodway's *Tasmanian Flora*, which they always took on expeditions, was also a precious work in the family collection.

Another exciting acquisition was Denis's telescope. It cost £11, a substantial amount of money he earned from selling pelts. When a visitor, whose values differed from the Kings', suggested the money would have been better put to use if invested for interest, Denis's mother sprang to his defence. 'There are more important interests than financial,' she snapped. 'That telescope will ensure compound interest for life.' Later, when the same man committed suicide after business enterprises failed, she couldn't resist driving the point home, remarking, 'His sort of interest hasn't done him much good.'

The children kept a joint nature diary of discoveries, which they illustrated. Fascinated by the mysteries and miracles of life forces they saw in action around them every day, they pondered on the hidden power in seemingly inanimate seeds and bulbs. They dissected a precious pumpkin seed to try to find out its secrets. They marvelled that the minute swamp-gum seeds contained the beginnings of such mighty trees. Genetics enthralled them and they liked to conjecture future developments.

From their first day at Sunset Ranch they were conscious of the shift in balance their arrival caused, noting with keen interest how different species, wild and domestic, adapted to changing conditions. Denis and Olive were intrigued how nesting birds used new materials including poultry feathers, knitting-wool scraps, cow and horse hairs carefully pulled from scratching posts and even substituting more pliable introduced grasses for tougher native grasses.

The children deliberately stretched their senses, trying to communicate with animals and birds, working out their behaviour patterns, responses and instincts. Encouraged by their mother who maintained intuition was of the spirit, they attempted to transcend normal limitations.

In 1926 Denis rigged up a rain gauge and began his lifelong personal diary habit with a little notebook in which he noted the movement of the seasons—first wattle blossom, swallow, cuckoo, daffodil, plum blossom, etc. A British handbook, *The Story of the Weather simply told for general readers*, which his parents gave him, laid the foundation of his deep knowledge and understanding of meteorology, and he frequently quoted its rhymes. His father also gave him a pocket aneroid barometer.

Despite its isolation, or perhaps because of it, Sunset Ranch was a fertile field of learning about human nature too. Over the years the young Kings encountered a wide range of characters, from city men of authority and influence to experienced bushmen. Professionals, educated men in senior positions in Hobart, like explorer Major Lyndhurst Giblin, appreciated the qualities in this unusual household and took the children's activities seriously. They encouraged their aspirations, sending helpful books and information, or putting useful words into appropriate bureaucratic ears.

Bushmen like kindly Charlie Fletcher shared their knowledge and taught practical skills. There were selectors who battled on, as the Kings did, and others who gave up. They got to know entrepreneurs, such as fur-farming Frenchmen, who came to exploit without compunction the resources of the area. When the osmiridium rush up the Weld began, hopefuls included drunkards and down-and-outs, as well as honest toilers. They knew the kindness and concern of some neighbours and relations, and experienced the enmity and malice of others.

There was always a tradition of hospitality at Sunset Ranch and Ollie ensured that everyone was made welcome. Living 'outback' did not mean social graces were forgotten, and a starched white cloth, polished silver, good food and good manners were part of the welcome. Guests remember Ollie as a dignified, gracious hostess of great kindness and humour.

From their parents Denis and his sisters learned love, loyalty and commitment. They gained not only self-respect but respect for others. They learned to get along together as a family, conscious that survival depended on co-operation and each responsibly doing their share to the best of their ability.

All the children took part in the household routine. Young Denis was not exempt from domestic chores, just as the girls were expected to work outside helping with stock, crops and garden. Denis was responsible for the 'morning sticks', to kindle the fire before breakfast. He also fed the dogs and the cat they had for keeping down mice. Despite his affinity for birds, he liked the cat, which accompanied him checking snares. When he got his bullock team it would sit on the dray with him.

At the end of the Great War and for years after, times were tough and market prices were low. So when Charlie had the little farm established, he took outside jobs as they were offered, to augment the family income. He had a solid reputation for reliability and conscientious work and received many approaches.

Young Denis was released from his lessons more and more frequently to accompany his father. He could not have had a better tutor for his education in bushcraft. Sunset Ranch gave Deny his primary education. In the following years he was to gain his secondary schooling 'up the Weld'.

CHAPTER 4

Up the Weld

'A valley of forest and unknownness.'

'Up the Weld', remote and mysterious, was both'a challenge and a promise. Over 1300 metres, Mount Weld, often sheeted in cloud or mist, sometimes quilted in snow, dominates the rugged terrain and dense vegetation of the Weld River valley. All through childhood, climbing Mount Weld was the pinnacle of ambition for Olive and Denis. 'It's never been climbed,' Charlie told them. 'When you're big enough, we'll do it.'

Beyond Sunset Ranch the track continued into the Weld Plains, bronze with button grass and in spring purple with melaleuca. It extended eight kilometres along the northern bank of the Huon, between two major tributaries, the Arve and the Weld.

The Weld, rising between Mount Anne and the Snowy and Jubilee ranges, rushes noisily out of the forest from its narrow valley in the Bare Hills. Home of wedge-tailed eagles, these spectacular hills rise hundreds of metres above the river. For the avid young botanists the steeply sweeping peat and white quartzite slopes were fairylands of many small wildflowers. Every so often the children helped Charlie fire the hills, thus preserving their upswept contours and preventing the track which scalloped their base from becoming overgrown.

Each spring when the Weld Plains were 'a pageant of colour', and early summer when the Huon's banks were splashed red with waratah and blandfordia, Ollie asserted, 'Botanically we have a lot to thank the Aborigines for. Unfired, the Weld Plains would soon be shrouded in thick tea-tree, and orchids and such small plants would be lost.' After fire had cleared the bracken, Denis discovered Aboriginal millstones on the Huon bank.

In Olive's words, 'the Huon hailed more deep and dark from out Lake Pedder way, beyond Mount Anne, beyond the ken of ordinary men. In its dark waters we fished at dusk for its bountiful blackfish and eels, while the horses munched in their nosebags in the belt of scrub up the bank.' By contrast the Weld was a trout stream, where released fingerlings grew into beauties 'in amber, bustling waters hailing from a valley of forest and unknownness'.

Charlie and Ollie took every opportunity for picnics along the Huon, fishing and swimming. Fresh-caught blackfish and trout grilled over the coals or pan-fried, made a welcome change from wallaby and bacon. As the children grew older, these trips often extended into overnight camps further afield.

A favourite place was The Eddy, a big pool upstream of rapids where the Weld meets a dolerite outcrop some distance above its confluence with the Huon. Deny fondly remembered the green banks and little beach under spreading blackwoods and myrtles, where the silvereyes made 'such a lovely warbling whistling song which still lingers in my mind'.

Because of its rugged remoteness the Weld Valley had remained largely unexplored and unexploited. Steep and narrow, with forested spurs rising to Mount Weld on the west and the Bare Hills and the Snowy Range on the east, it was a tough challenge to prospectors and loggers.

Not everyone had such passion as the Kings for this wild country. In 1920 and 1921 the Hydro-Electric Department investigated damming the Huon River. Letters from the survey foreman to his seniors snug in their Hobart offices, describing it as 'this vile country', declare:

Young men *will not* stop down here for any length of time, they do not like the place. Men swear this is the worst country they have ever been in. It has been an awful battle to get round, dense jungle the whole way, bauera and cutting-grass 12 and 14 feet high, and miles of horizontal [scrub]. It's quite common for men to get lost coming home of an evening.

Charlie King was engaged to cart supplies to the camps. He brought the stores from Huonville, then packed them out on horses to the Huon River, where they were taken across in a special transport cage. It was sheer slog, especially in the wet, trudging along the boggy tracks, and very hard on horse and dray. Young Denis, absolved from correspondence lessons, was often dispatched on horseback with the camp mail, for which the cook would reward him with an enormous slice of mince pie or jam tart.

Soon after the Hydro team left, an osmiridium rush into the Weld provided Charlie with a Mines Department contract, to blaze a prospecting track. He was to re-open an old track to the Seventeen Mile Peg, extending it through wild terrain and dense rainforest. He considered Olive and Denis sufficiently experienced to be initiated into the trials and the wonders of the Weld. 'Time and spartan living by then having hammered enough stamina and nous into us, Denis and I were allowed to accompany Father.'

They cut down bags for knapsacks and greased their boots with mutton fat against blisters and wetness. It was a memorable journey. 'We twisted ourselves in and over, round and under labyrinths of horizontal scrub, straddled slippery logs and poles over rushing streams, and found the Seventeen Mile Peg was all Father had promised—the ultimate in beauty and tranquillity.'

Charlie had a prospecting licence and taught them to pan a creek and to test the weight of a likely rock. They outstayed their week's rations and faced the last day's long tough tramp back on almost-empty stomachs. Crossing a sunny spur where leatherwoods were still in flower, Charlie spotted bees streaming from the butt of an old musk tree. They quickly made a fire, and under cover of smoke chopped out enough prized honey to satisfy their hunger and to fill their billies.

Snaring trips in 1925 and 1927 up the Weld were not so happy. The work filled Denis with revulsion and the rough track was littered with fallen trees. But he got to know the country and loved the beautiful ancient moss-draped myrtle forest along the river, although he named one flat thick with horizontal scrub The Place of Gloom, because it was so dark and dank in winter. Nevertheless, ever practical, he noted the wallabies were always fat and very good eating, whereas those from open country and pastures were not. Sometimes they found a thylacine had been caught but the powerful animal always chewed its way out of the snare.

It was a closed season in 1926, but with the osmiridium discovery at Adams River, Charlie and Denis had another job, clearing and cording the Weld track to the Nineteen Mile Peg. It was heavy work slashing back overgrowth, cutting out logs across the track with the crosscut saw and fixing small bridges. One over the Eddy Creek involved cutting logs to span it, which had to be dragged into position by Old Doll. The bridge enabled them to take the horses eight kilometres further into the forest. But from there it was too rough.

In 1927 Charlie and Denis, now seventeen, were asked by the Huonville Council to look for an alternative route via the Huon and Weld to Adamsfield. Denis was sceptical when it was suggested he would enjoy such an undertaking. 'I was not so sure,' he recalled, visualising the true situation, 'scrounging through horizontal in pouring rain and tucker running short.'

His forebodings proved well-founded. Around the Fork and northward the dreaded horizontal scrub was almost impenetrable, consuming inordinate time, energy and supplies to traverse. Beyond the Fork it was unknown country.

Charlie, always resourceful, made a couple of packs from canvas, but Denis just had a sack with ropes attached to its corners and top. Olive, Rosy and Win accompanied them with the horses to the Bare Hills, where the girls would return in ten days to assist the last homeward stretch.

For two days, Charlie and Denis skirted the steep slopes of the west side of the Jubilee Range down to the Weld River. It was tough going, rough with sassafras roots, slippery with sticks whose sodden bark peeled off treacherously under the tread of hobnailed boots. 'On such a steep slope it was hard to keep on our feet. If we had to take our eyes off the ground, down we would go.'

They were trying to pick up old blazes or cut-off limbs, as well as keeping a grade and measuring the distance, while getting over the big fallen logs down the slopes. 'I would go ahead with the tape,' Deny recalled:

> Dad would sing out when I got to the end and I would make a mark on the ground and go on. Dad had a compass and corrected my course if I veered too much one way or another, which is easy to do in scrub. Although the tape was only one chain long, we did not often see each other and sometimes Dad seemed miles away.

At first they covered close to four kilometres a day, but on the limestone river flats they managed only one. They battled on, mostly in rain, through the horizontal scrub, hazardous with sinkholes and caves, finally reaching more open forest on rising ground. In one shallow cave they found a thylacine's nest, the dry leaves still warm, and they could see where the pups had been playing.

Charlie and Denis discovered an archway over the river with a creek emerging from an opening further up before disappearing again down a sinkhole, and were unsure whether this was a branch or the main stream. Over thirty years later Deny described the Weld River caves in an article in *The Tasmanian Tramp*, concluding: 'Now you young cave-men, there lies some real exploring on what I hope is still new ground. I wish you every success.'

As Denis had feared, 'tucker was getting short', so after cooking the last of their rice and drinking the washing-up water, they decided to stop taping and make their way to the Port Davey track back into Fitzgerald.

After about thirteen kilometres, seeing smoke from a farmhouse chimney, they paused for running repairs. Screened from view by a dense sassafras, Charlie, always careful of how he presented himself, took out needle and thread and sewed up the numerous rips in their clothes. Respectable again, they went and asked for food.

Deny gratefully recalled the young wife's welcome. '"Come in, you poor men!" She put on a great pan of fried spuds and what a feed we had!' Her husband told them of vacant huts at the nearby sawmill. Here they were given shelter and food by the mill foreman. Next morning he brought 'a great pan full of fried bacon so we had another good tuck in', before setting off for Fitzgerald.

Charlie knew the local storekeeper, a skin buyer, and asked him to send a message advising the family they were safe. He also arranged a food order for the return trip.

After another night at the sawmill, they set off 'with well-laden packs' to a hut at the Twelve Mile on the Port Davey track, before venturing again into the unknown. Measuring and blazing as they went, they eventually reached the limestone country, picked up the end of their outward route and headed homewards.

Still their misadventures continued. Negotiating crumbling ridges and gulches, Charlie slipped and fell, badly hurting his hip and thigh. Denis set up camp on the spot. No bones were broken, so Charlie bathed the painful area, rubbed it with ointment, rested for a day, then stoically pushed on.

Denis carried most of the gear and cut away obstacles as they proceeded slowly along the Weld Valley, encouraged by thoughts of home and plenty of tucker. When they finally reached the Sassafras Camp, they found a note from the girls written weeks earlier and, much to Denis's disappointment, a packet of mouldy tomato sandwiches!

When they failed to appear at Bare Hills on the given day, Olive and Win climbed to the top, hoping for a smoke signal.

Tobogganing down the slopes on boughs, the girls reached the restless horses. When cooees brought no response, Olive made a daring decision to ride further into the forest than she and Win had ever done, to the Twelve Mile. Still there was no answer from the engulfing green. 'Haunted by spectres of other intrepid men who'd gone into this unknown and never come out,' Olive was anxious to get out before dark.

Ollie, in a rare vulnerable moment, admitted to having had uneasy feelings. Then the next day, an uncle arrived from Huonville with a telegram, assuring them of their men's wellbeing and arranging another rendezvous in a week.

Again Olive and Win trekked out to the Bare Hills. This time blustering winds in the forest tops prevented their venturing further. Instead of abating the wind increased and the journey home was a nightmare of hurtling sticks, limbs, bark, and deep anxiety.

Lessons and chores were neglected a second and third day as they returned to wait. On the fourth, Rosemary was saddling up to organise a search when the dogs' joyous barking alerted them to look down the bank. 'Appallingly thin, tattered, pale as though they hadn't seen the sun for weeks and on their last legs, they came over the brow, Father leaning heavily on a stick and Denis carrying both packs. Denis said, "I could eat non-stop for a week, Mum."'

Charlie was laid up for several days, but soon resumed his usual occupations. In his report to the council, which included careful charts of topography, rock formations and timber, he advised a secondary route to Adamsfield by the Upper Huon and Weld valleys would not be feasible.

Months later the council sent a cheque for £13. Ollie was incensed. 'Furious at such parsimony and underestimation of the work, she told the council so. Evidently abashed, they sent out their road inspector to peg the worst spots on our road for metalling, something she had been writing to them about for a long time.'

In 1928 Charlie and Denis were up the Weld again prospecting, this time on Mines Department sustenance. It was an unproductive trip. Denis, however, observed a species of boronia new to him, and discovered a spectacular waterfall coming from the southern end of the Jubilee Range. He had already been to Gallagher Plateau near Mount Anne in 1924 with Major Giblin's South-Western Expeditionary Party, trying unsuccessfully to reach Lake Judd from the Weld River side.

In the summer of 1929 they made the long-awaited expedition to Mount Weld. The byline on an account published in the *Mercury* is D. and O. M. King, but style proclaims Olive's mind and pen:

> Mount Weld at last! Not in dreams, but in reality.
> The reaching of the pinnacle, the possibility of lakes, the lure of an objective in country largely unexplored! It all acted like a magnet on us—the North Huon party.

Charlie, Denis and Olive set off with packhorses and were already rain-drenched when they reached The Eddy. Bright bells of late blandfordia and the scent of white waratah cheered them across the Weld Plains. At the foot of the Bare Hills they took their swags, containing telescope, camera, pencil, paper and the much-travelled Rodway and Leach, and turned the horses back.

At the Ten Mile they encountered a massive landslide, over a hectare swept clean of even the biggest trees, 'leaving the hillside furrowed like the trail of a giant's plough'. The slip had hurled tonnes of yellow earth and trees into the river below, crushing the timber to splinters, accounting for the river's sudden discolouration downstream.

They entered magnificent forest, on hills and in gullies: 'huge old beeches, gnarled old sassies, stringy-barks with ten-inch bark which has never felt the scorch of fire; leatherwoods, laurels, musks, and giant manferns, and beneath them all, over earth, logs, limbs and roots, a carpet of moss that a king's ransom could not buy.'

After a night in the Fifteen Mile hut, they located a fording place on the Weld, discovered a beautiful clear creek with an underground course, then crossed a swampy plain with rushes and coral fern up to four metres tall and a formidable quantity of horizontal scrub.

Bearing south-west they climbed a narrow limestone spur dense with eucalypts. Soil then became richer, growth more luxuriant. But there was no water. Hearing a rushing sound below the cliffs, Denis tackled the steep descent and returned with a welcome billyful.

By evening after scrambling through tea-tree, bauera, pandani and clattering shield ferns, they reached the small plateau between Mount Weld's two peaks. Surrounded by mountains torn and rugged, smooth and rolling, they camped at about 1000 metres, among sheltering beeches and pandani, with armfuls of fronds for beds.

Investigating a gleam of water, Denis and Olive discovered a beautiful little tarn, warm and shallow, teeming with tadpoles. Denis then found a much larger lake fed by two rushing streams, where they observed many small fish and disturbed a large platypus. It was an idyllic scene with rose-tinged cumulus clouds, the last glow of the setting sun on the mountains, and a glimmer of the river in the Weld Valley far below.

After a chilly night, with weather closing in rapidly, they started for the summit at dawn. Before the low wind-twisted scrub gave way to rocks Denis, in the lead, cut a stout gum pole to place at the pinnacle.

When the cloud lifted temporarily, he spotted two more lakes, and Charlie saw a fourth at the base of the peak they were about to climb. By consensus they named them King's Lakes. A less spectacular but equally pleasing discovery was colonies of a plant they had not seen before, the rare mountain geum found only in a few places in Tasmania's southern ranges, here in full exquisite white flower.

Although dark clouds threatened, they were rewarded with views of the Arthur and Frankland ranges, Mount Picton and Mount Anne. By the time they reached the true summit on the second peak a grey wall of mist obliterated the scene and bleak winds whipped round them. Nevertheless the pole, carried so laboriously by Denis, was duly fixed.

Making a triumphant descent, sliding down snow in the gully between the two peaks, they were jubilant when the mists broke and bright sunlight revealed the panorama beyond. By midday they were back at camp, enjoying well-earned food, when sharp showers blew up with a strengthening wind.

Fearing weather would prevent them crossing the river, they hastily began the downward push through pandani and prickly richea scrub. In teeming rain and thick mist they failed to pick up the previous day's trail, so chose the hazards of following steep spurs rather than risk being engulfed in horizontal scrub which filled the gullies.

Six strenuous hours later 'our leader [Denis] had brought us with unerring exactness to the place where we had crossed the morning before. The wading sticks lay on the bank at our feet.' After another night at the Fifteen Mile hut, they walked eleven hours next day, reaching home 'weary, but elated', their ambition fulfilled.

CHAPTER 5

The outside world

'The beginning of a new way of living.'

In the early years at Sunset Ranch Denis had several holidays with Ollie's parents at Clifton Grove. 'A visit to Grandma's was a real highlight in our lives.'

Apart from marvellous roast-beef dinners, candy, horehound beer and the intriguing soda fountain, there were other delights. He was fascinated by Grandfather's acetylene plant, providing gas for house lighting, and intrigued by the telephone, forge, and apple-packing shed with all its carts, spray pumps and implements. The children were always invited in autumn, to help carry apples and walnuts up to the attic.

Denis enjoyed birdwatching on the hillside or lying in the sun on cliffs above Clifton Grove, surveying the ordered flow of life, listening to the sounds of the busy community: river steamers plying up and down, workers in the orchards, the ring from three local black-smiths' anvils, traffic on the roads. In apple season the hammering of case-making and the rumble of drays carrying apples to wharves along the river resounded day and night.

His mother never complained of the loneliness or endless toil at Sunset Ranch, but Deny remarked the brief respite 'did her a world of good'. He had a deep bond with her and sensitivity for her unspoken feelings. Reticent about his own, he simply said, 'We were always such great mates.'

In 1926 the family made its first visit to Hobart. Except for a holiday at Kingston Beach with grandparents, the young Kings had never been further than Huonville, and Deny remembered the service-car driver saying, 'You'll see a lot of lights tonight, Denis.' For young people who used bark torches to go possum hunting at night, Hobart's streetlights were indeed a sight. They stayed with a family friend and, in appreciation of her hospitality, dug over her yard and planted it with potatoes.

Other friends invited them for outings—a train trip to Cadbury's chocolate factory, and a visit to the GPO clocktower to see the works in action. Best for Denis was the fire station where he spent every spare moment looking at the vehicles and equipment—the beginning of his lifelong interest in machinery.

By 1926 the outside world was steadily encroaching on the remoteness of Sunset Ranch. Apples were being carted to Hobart by truck instead of being shipped, and even out there motors could be heard on a still, foggy morning. It was a time of great excitement when a model-T Ford arrived—the first car to get so far.

Two years later Olive had begun her teaching career in Hobart but returned home for holidays, more appreciative than ever of its qualities. 'Today was a glorious day, so perfect in this lovely wilderness of ours. One felt it calling, calling, calling. Half the beauty of such a day is lost in town.'

But that wilderness was already under attack.

Logging operations came closer in 1928, bringing new machinery. Although small box mills were common on hillsides or anywhere there were trees and a road could penetrate, none had as yet been established so far out. Then in January a neighbour started the first sawmill in the Denison Valley.

By the end of 1928 a second mill had been established when Fred Bester brought in his steam plant. Deny recalled:

The boiler came on a big Haliford truck with solid rubber tyres and sprocket and chain drive. Of course it got stuck on soft patches in the road, so Charlie Woolley was engaged with his bullock team to help haul her out. The boiler was taken off the truck and hauled about a quarter of a mile. The bullocks were later used to haul logs from the bush to the mill.

'It was beautiful timber out there when we went out—a beautiful bed of timber,' Fred Bester's son Colin remembered. He recalled Denis and Charlie felling an exceptionally big tree for the mill. 'Oh, it was a tremendous big tree. Dad said, "Would you like to have a go at falling that big tree?" And the two of them felled it. It was a colossal great thing. They were there all day, falling it. Hard work.'

Bester later shifted his plant to another site nearby and put up camps with gardens for his workers and families. Although he got a truck-type International tractor for log hauling, horses and bullock teams continued in use. Denis occasionally had a few days' work at the sawmills when they were short-handed. 'One very boring job was dragging logs to the mill with a horse. The ground was dry, making the logs so much harder to move along the dusty tracks. I was always glad when it was knock-off time.'

Even at remote Sunset Ranch the onset of the depression was felt, reducing prices received for the small fruits, vegetables and other produce which involved such intensive, heavy toil for all the family. So while Denis took casual mill work, his father worked on the roads, and continued prospecting.

Charlie had always cherished the hope of finding gold, and his secretive movements were the subject of much talk in the district, where his reputation as bushman and prospector was high. He must have had some success in fossicking, because his method of payment for supplies at Judbury store was well known. The storekeeper had a gold-buyer's licence, and Guy Elliston, Denis's second cousin, remembered Charlie 'going in with his little bottle of washed gold, and paying for a year's groceries'.

In 1930, hearing of gold to the north of Port Davey, Charlie and Denis went prospecting yet again on two unproductive trips, to the South-West. Deny remembered the marathon journeys well:

> We found some good colours on the first trip and Dad put in his report to the Mines Department, because they'd given us some help. They said 'We'd like you to go again.' So we took gear for three or four weeks.
>
> The weather was atrocious and we didn't have proper wet-weather gear like you have now. It was very, very heavy work packing up a really bad graded track. We had to double pack—take one load ahead then come back for the rest. About 60 or 70 pounds we could manage in one load.
>
> We rode across the Huon, but we didn't have any rides after that! Fifty-six miles it was. We didn't have tents because they were too heavy. We just had ordinary duck for a fly. Not very waterproof.
>
> We always had a fire, even in the wet. I've never been anywhere I couldn't make a fire. The worst place is horizontal [scrub] gullies in the pouring rain. You've got a job to get one going there. But you can always scrounge something under a leaning myrtle—a few dried twigs or leaves in some little nook and even if it's been raining for days it's dry enough to light.
>
> Even in the button grass you can always lift up the leaves and find a few handfuls of dry stalks. They lie over in a big tussock like a thatch and underneath close to the main stem it's all dry stuff. When it's pouring and you're freezing cold, if you put a match to a tussock it will burn away and give you good warmth. It doesn't do them any harm. They like being burnt.

We'd been camping a lot, but that was the first long trip we'd done and the first time I'd seen the sea, except at Kingston. This was so different and quite exciting. I didn't enjoy the trip itself. It was interesting but such hard going. We were on short rations and I was starving hungry all the time. We had rice, bacon, flour, raisins, rolled oats, none of the modern dehydrated stuff. We managed to catch some fish where we camped at Long Bay. We were prospecting right on Mount Mackenzie on Bathurst Channel.

I liked the South-West straightaway—the beautiful scenery, the way the mountains slope down to the sea. And the wildness of it all.

This was the beginning of a love affair that lasted Deny's lifetime.

They found gold, but insufficient to be viable without proper equipment, which required finance they did not have. Then, in 1933, Charlie heard of a tin-mining venture on the south coast at Cox Bight. Leaving Denis to look after farm and family, he set off in November to join the Burgess Prospecting Syndicate.

The family was breaking up. Rosemary had married a local man, Ron Woolley, living at Lonnavale in the Russell Valley. Olive was teaching thirty kilometres from Hobart, living in the schoolhouse, with her mother and Win. Denis was alone at Sunset Ranch, and wrote in his memoirs of how the family coped during 1933–34:

I seemed to have an inner feeling that there was some disaster impending. These years brought sadness and disaster to us, but also the beginning of a new way of living.

Mother could see the farm would not be a success and advised Win to get employment elsewhere. When she came home to get some things, I had been alone for some time. As we said goodbye it was heart-breaking to see her walk away down the sunlit flagstone path edged with manfern fronds we had planted. She was also heartbroken at having to leave, but she put on a brave front. But I suppose it was just as well for her not to have to put in a lot more work and see it all disappear in flames.

Bushfires were always a hazard and Sunset Ranch had already been threatened in 1921, while Ollie and the children were at Clifton Grove. Spring in 1933 and early summer in 1934 had been abnormal, with very little rain and hot winds. Dry westerly winds moaned across the country. Grass matured early. Raspberries ripened in November. It was so dry that gum trees growing on the hillsides where the rock was close to the surface, died. Ollie and Olive came home for Christmas, but in January 1934 fierce fires broke out.

Deny believed they were lit to create breaks around mills, as was the practice in other years. That summer it was fatal. A mill hand who tried to extinguish a fire with what he thought was a bucket of water, in fact doused it with kerosene. It burst immediately out of control. The Bester mill, house and camp were destroyed.

Fire had threatened Sunset Ranch some days earlier. 'It started to look really serious,' Deny recalled, 'so Olive and I began getting furniture out of the house.' They worked all night to save precious possessions, including books and Charlie's Boer War souvenirs. 'We dug a hole in what was usually a waterhole with a sandy bottom. We put in the chest of drawers and other things, covered with cloth, then covered it all with sand, and before we knew it, the red dawn showed.'

The weather cooled and quietened, and as the danger seemed to have passed, Win went off to pick raspberries at Rosemary's.

On 18 January, a quiet dewy morning quickly changed when a breath of warm wind foretold another hot day. By 9 a.m. the temperature soared from 10 to 30 degrees Celsius with a rising wind. Fred Bester came in his car, evacuating Ollie and Olive to Herbert Skinner's Huonville home, before fire closed the track. Denis stayed to protect the house:

It was smoky everywhere. I had every container I could find filled with water. All these fires were smouldering round the logs and when the hot wind came, the whole lot burst into life and sprung up out of the ground. The sky grew dark and all the tree limbs caught alight. The tops of the trees showered sparks everywhere and away she went. Every little bit of inflammable material on the ground—all alight. I'd chucked the harness out. One strap lay across a little bit of wood and it got burnt in half.

I kept chucking buckets of water from the creek up on the roof, which did the job until a spark got under the shingles and started it in the ceiling. Of course I rushed inside and threw some things out—I didn't have time to do much. And that was it. The temperature was 112 [44°C]. I rescued whatever was about. There wasn't much I could do then.

But he had already performed an amazing feat which has become legendary. Single-handed he saved his mother's precious piano. How he did it reveals both the ingenuity and stamina for which he became so well known:

The piano was still inside, so I was faced with the task of getting it out. I brought the bullock dray as near to the house as possible, tipped it up with the pole in the air, then wheeled and manoeuvred the piano over the flagstone path and brought its top against the floor of the upturned dray, then heaved down on the pole so the piano lay on its back in the dray.

I brought the bullocks into position, coupled the end of the pole to the ring on the yoke, and away we went gently over the rough ground up the hill to a green spot I had been irrigating outside the garden. I unhitched and there she stayed for days until our Linnell cousins brought their truck and took it away.

You couldn't see anything much for smoke. When there was a break I could see the fire already had gone two miles across the Huon River, where it burnt out a lot of sawmills and farms, and some people perished.

I grabbed a few blankets and little things, and walked down to the neighbours at the Denison about three miles away, with trees falling down about one a minute. A lot of mill hands and wives and children were evacuated there so the house was really full.

The neighbours, the Mansfields, had moved from Hobart to the Denison in 1931. The boys, Doug and Vic, used to take the mail out to Sunset Ranch and buy eggs, potatoes and fruit. Both had learned a lot about their new environment from Denis. 'The day before the King place got burnt out,' Vic remembers, 'we kids were putting out spot fires all round the house. Then the next day the fire came boiling down into the valley. We'd all cleared out and gone down to the river. It wasn't loitering, that fire.'

They were amazed to find their house still standing, but had no idea if the King homestead had survived. 'The next thing,' Vic recalled fifty-seven years later, 'Denis comes plodding out of the smoke, cat tucked under his arm, with a stick in front of him. Completely smoke blind.'

Colin Bester, who looked on Denis as a big brother, remembers they slept on the ground that night. 'We didn't have anywhere. Didn't have a thing. Only what we stood up in. And I said to Denis, "I couldn't have much less. We'll have to start all over again."

'He said, "Oh yes, and it won't take long. It's not as bad as it looks." And I said, "Well, you can't even see!" The smoke was that thick you couldn't see fifty or sixty feet in front of you. Our eyes were terribly sore for weeks because of the smoke.'

Colin helped muster thirty survivors from the Sunset Ranch herd. Denis gave him his horse to ride ahead to be shod, while he drove the cattle on foot to the Huonville saleyards, walking over sixty-five kilometres that day. He gave the sole remaining hen of the Sunset Ranch flock to Colin, who had one hen and a rooster left. Colin remembered, 'He picked up the chook and said, "Take it home and put it with yours."' The next spring his hen produced twelve chickens.

For the Kings, the fire was indeed a tragedy. Although Denis dug the potatoes and ran stock on it when the grass grew again, Sunset Ranch was 'just a dead loss'. They had not fully paid for it so the bank reclaimed it. Within a few hours flames had wiped out the family's hopes and dreams, labours and creation of almost eighteen years.

CHAPTER 6

Bullocks, mills, motors and mines

'Denis always had that bent towards machinery.'

After the fire Denis was in shock. 'He looked like nothing on earth,' Winsome remembered. 'He had two bullocks and the dray, and his cat. He just seemed to go absolutely lost for a long time after that.'

There was little work available until the burnt-out mills were relocated, so after harvesting the potatoes at Sunset Ranch, Denis decided to go to Port Davey to explain the situation to his father.

The idea of going to sea appealed to his sense of adventure. He found a passage with Sid Dale, a fisherman who called at Cox Bight with mail and stores for the miners and took their tin to Hobart. Even though seasick in the big swell, Denis was thrilled by the challenge of ocean and weather.

They called at Recherche, the last settlement along the coast, then rounded South East and South capes under motor and sail. Fifty-six years later, Deny described his first impressions, with a precise recall of weather conditions and of the characters who made up the motley little community at Cox Bight working on the under-financed and ill-equipped claim of absentee leaseholder Jim Burgess:

> It was a beautiful clear afternoon with a south-easterly breeze. There was too much sea to off-load at Point Eric where the camps were. We went ashore in Boat Harbour and walked around with a bundle of mail and the stores we

could carry. We met Dad there and I camped with him. Behind the bush the plains stretch right across to Melaleuca and Mount Counsel to the north, where there's granite and tin-bearing gravels.

About a dozen people were working tin here and there. They were all very pleased to get their mail. Dad went back to work and I had a look around the mines. There were heaps of gravel and trenches with dirty water running away and chaps down there forking stones.

I had a yarn with each. There were three oldies. The oldest and most respected, Frank Goram, a fisherman in his seventies, had been there for years. Charlie Walker and Arthur Stubbings had been there since the 1920s. Charlie had no teeth and always had a pipe in his mouth. He couldn't read or write but was always telling stories about mining on the big west coast fields at Mount Lyell and Mount Bischoff, where he reckoned they had to smash up the boulders of tin to get them in the bags! Charlie was a steady worker, but Arthur was very flighty, always putting his peg in somewhere else. One of his favourite sayings was 'By the powers of piss'! He had a real Irish wit.

Dad and others had come down in Jim Burgess's boat. He wanted to go fishing, so he landed them at Moulter's Cove. They had to walk to Cox's carrying gear and food, making several trips packing over this very steep 1700-foot ridge. Then it was a week or more before Burgess called in with the main supplies. You couldn't rely on him.

When I'd had a look around, I got into it helping in The Big Mine. George Blegg was manager. There were five chaps. They'd had to dig a long tailrace from the mine towards the lagoons. They also had to cut another race through rock around the hillside to bring water from a creek coming off Mount Counsel. It was really hard work and they weren't paid much. So it wasn't long before they left one by one. Dad left too and the mine had to close.

Charlie and the others lived in a big hut built by the first company there in the 1890s, Freney Prospecting Company. About 15 by 4 metres, mainly galvanised iron, it was fairly dark, and the wooden floor had been removed for sluice boxes. The scrim walls were papered with pictures of the Boer War from *The Times*.

Along one side there were double-tier bunks, old bags tacked over poles, with bag mattresses stuffed with straw. Cooking was done on a big fireplace at one end. They baked bread in camp ovens and made stews in big billies. Tinned bully beef, camp pie, flour, bacon and dried peas were staples which would keep. Lunch was damper and bacon. Tinned fruit was a luxury, as were fresh vegetables, until they started their own gardens.

Each man had his own plot on the bank behind the hut. Because there were no weeds they did not require much looking after. Peas, potatoes, cabbages, carrots and rhubarb grew quite well in the sandy, granitic soil and Deny grew 'wonderful lettuces'. But sometimes white cockatoos came and dug up the potatoes when everyone was at work, and hail and wind also caused damage.

'Boat day' was a big day. Because Cox Bight was so isolated, boats were keenly awaited. When one arrived everyone downed tools to get stores ashore and tin loaded in the shortest possible time. If the miners were not there, the fishermen would not wait. Cox's was a hazardous anchorage with breaking Southern Ocean surf, and they begrudged spending half a day's good weather. Shipping tin did not pay so well as fishing and they did it only 'more or less to oblige'.

It was a difficult voyage from Hobart round the rugged, storm-swept south coast with strong winds and wild Roaring Forties seas rolling in. Therefore it could be two, three or even four months between boats. When the sea was calm and the fishing good, they would be more frequent, about every six weeks:

> The fishermen would go to the east coast from September to November because crayfish ran there first. Then we'd get a bit short of tucker, usually tinned meat and always butter. One time we ran seriously short. We didn't have good places to keep anything—just tents, no boxes or barrels—so of course rats got at the stores.
>
> After collecting tucker and mail and hearing news of the outside world, the tin had to be loaded. We'd carry it in hundredweight bags half a mile or more along the beach, through soft sand and over the rocks at Point Eric. Then it had to be taken out in the dinghy, several bags at a time. That would take half a day altogether.

A letter requiring an urgent answer meant walking along the coast to find the boat. Sometimes it brought bad news. One day *Jane Moorhead* arrived flying a black flag, and Charlie and Denis learned that Ollie was dead. On Sid Dale's next trip they went out to Hobart and returned to Huonville, where Ollie had died aged fifty-five. The hard years had taken their toll. She was buried in the Huonville Congregational cemetery.

Denis had been very close to his mother, with a deep respect and regard for her. Just before the fire he had a premonition of her death. So soon after the loss of Sunset Ranch and all it represented, it affected him deeply, and he could never talk easily about her. But her influence, the values and qualities she instilled were the foundation of his life.

Charlie returned to Cox Bight. When he had established himself on his own lease, two years after the hard-won little house had been reduced to ashes in the fierce 1934 bushfires, he sent a letter to Charlie Helm with a cheque to cover his time and work on the house extensions in 1928. At that time King had found himself financially over-extended and Helm had amicably offered to settle for board and lodging. But Charlie King had his honour and his pride.

After his mother's death in 1934 Denis went back to live at Mansfields', to work at Bester's mill up the Denison. He was more accepting of the assault on the forest than of the commercial exploitation of native animals through snaring and fur farming. Of necessity he had done plenty of scrub clearing and felling, both at home and for others, and the pattern of milling out pockets of timber never seemed to upset him.

This was selective logging, which did not destroy the whole ecosystem. The proliferation of hungry little sawmills providing material for packing cases also provided work. It was part of the frontier way of life.

Felling the trees, sawing them into lengths and splitting them to a size the horse or bullocks could pull was hard work. Sawing was done with crosscut saws, which were kept very sharp. 'The chaps who prized their axes kept them out of the riffraff's way,' Deny remembered. 'Those axes were sharp enough to shave with and were only used for falling trees or chopping a log that could not be cut with a crosscut saw.'

As well as timber for apple, pear and cherry cases, the mills cut weatherboard and scantling for houses. Mill work was seasonal, partly because of the fruit seasons, partly because in winter it was often too wet to cut and haul logs. They cut case timber from October to late February or March, then shut down, or worked intermittently.

Most of the fruit growers were very particular about case timber. Clean white wood was sought after. Millers and bushmen would go through the standing timber and pick out the most suitable stringy-barks—big for the box heads that needed wider, thicker boards, smaller trees for top, bottom and side palings.

Bullocks were important in milling operations, dragging logs from the bush to the sawmills, and it was as a bullock driver Denis found work. At Bester's mill he was in charge of the bullock pulling in the billets, logs split into sections in the bush, to be cut at the mill by a circular saw. His cousin Guy Elliston had a vivid memory of the beast. 'One of them big old brindle crossbreds. One of the biggest bullocks I've ever seen—a massive thing, colossal!'

Denis also had his own team, Barney, Canopus, Nigger, Strawberry, Lil, Aurora, Little Sookie and Lob Sang T'sering. That name, derived from his voracious reading about Tibet, was shortened by mill hands to Lobster. Snigging—dragging logs out—was quite a job:

> They would run to one side and get stuck behind stumps and roots. You had to use all the little tricks to get them out.
>
> Sometimes the tracks were so narrow you couldn't get the bullocks to pull sideways, to pull the log aside to free it. You had to use other means. One was to stand a big stout piece of wood on end with a chain over the top that the bullocks pulled on. When they started, that would lift the log up and away you'd go again—a very slow job. As you got further from the mill, the longer it took. Most were half trees, a few were in the round.
>
> The work was very hard, especially on the skids at the mill. Logs came in all dirty. The mud and bark had to be removed by scraping or hosing, projections like limb stumps removed and a layer trimmed off the side that went over the bench. Sometimes you'd have to roll them over which took all your strength. Sometimes it needed more than one man. The round ones were all right, but the half ones were terrible. You'd get them half way up and they'd come back on you. I hated those jobs.

When the timber near a mill was cut out, sometimes mill and camp moved. But Bester bought a crawler tractor which meant, as Colin explained:

We could log the mill easily. Oh, that was a great godsend. Denis was very interested and used to come and watch. He said, 'Do you know that's got a new invention? An oil-bath air cleaner to keep the dust out of the engine. That's the first engine that's come this way with one of those. It'll last a long time.' And it did. We worked it for ten years. But Denis stuck to the old bullocks.

Denis worked for three mills through the 1930s, Bester's, Mansfield's and McCullums'. Although uncongenial, it provided opportunities to further two major interests—his study of machinery and mechanics, and his passion for exploring the vast unknown areas of the Huon hinterland.

He would spend three or more days hauling logs, sufficient to keep the mill busy for several more, then go bush, exploring.

In bad weather he pursued his studies. Although an unwilling pupil for his mother and the Correspondence School, he was now keen on his chosen subject and motivated to gain a professional qualification. Never one to do things by halves, he had enrolled in the Complete Automobile Course with the Sydney International Correspondence School. His mother, always concerned about his education, was pleased, and he regretted she did not live to see him achieve his diploma.

He studied conscientiously but had trouble getting time alone. 'I'd get up real early before the others and do a bit and also try to do it after work. Archie McCullum would come along to my hut practically every night and say, "He's always reading." He didn't take into consideration it was studying I was doing.'

When Denis moved to McCullums' mill, his job was to class the timber, rack it, then load the little tram and push it to the stacks. The McCullum brothers had bought an AB four-cylinder Ford truck, adapted for bush work, and Denis was eager for hands-on experience:

> When they said I could have a go, I was so excited I couldn't
> sleep. I was keen to do it, so I let them have the bullocks and
> took on the truck driving. That excitement soon died down.
> You could have her nearly flat out and only go a bit more
> than walking pace—very good for those frightful roads.

Guy Elliston remembered the old Denison road, slabs and corduroy:

> all cut up when they were carting out the loads of timber.
> My father always reckoned Denis was the slowest driver of
> anybody. He might've been the slowest, but he always got
> there. And he kept that truck going longer than anybody
> else. That old thing went for years. He drove with feeling for
> the machine he was handling. Denis always had that bent
> towards machinery.

Denis chose not to live in the main camp, because the men 'were up half the night talking' while he tried to study. He also wanted a place for Winsome to stay if she wished to visit. She had held a series of positions as mother's help, housekeeper and shop assistant in Hobart and elsewhere. She loved to come back to the Denison, though, to be with Denis, and to be near their eldest sister Rose, living at Lonnavale in the next valley, with her growing family.

So at Ellendale Denis built a three-roomed hut from mill offcuts, and Winsome papered the interior. It overlooked the road to the Hydro-Electric Commission scheme under construction at Tarraleah. Every night Denis could see the lights of trucks carting building materials there, a sight that stimulated his ambition to become an engineer.

A disheartening experience while building the hut was a useful lesson. After a long windless period, he thought it unnecessary to put stays on the studs, walls and roof frames as he progressed. Then a storm flattened all his work, and although the other hands rallied to re-erect it, 'it didn't seem to go back into place as it was at first'.

Not one to discuss his affairs with others, Denis surprised everyone by buying a car. He used to take the McCullums' truck for service at the Huonville garage, where he had become interested in the manager's old Oakland car which he decided to buy for £30. Repairing it would help with his automobile studies and it would be useful 'to get about a bit wherever I wanted'.

It was a six-day week at the mill. On the seventh there was often maintenance to be done. If the weather had been too wet during the week for forest work, Denis would use those days to repair chains, bullock yokes, and other equipment. Colin Bester remembered:

> We had a good blacksmith's shop and he'd bring things to do in the forge. He'd be there all day, making different things. He was very, very handy. He used to teach me. It was just amazing what he knew, the answers he could come up with. If you had a problem, he'd think about it for a while, and my word, he'd sort it out. He was really good.

'Denis had the patience of Job,' Vic Mansfield added. 'He made a model steam engine and filed every cog out with a hand file. He put in hours and hours with the file and hacksaw. It took him months and months!' He also carved a model boat from Huon pine for the Mansfield boys, rigged it and fitted it with sails.

The boys were impressed too with watercolours of birds Denis had painted despite a 'knobby' finger. The permanently enlarged joint had been caused by a tiger cat, which Denis, always unwilling to inflict death on any creature, had tried to release from a snare.

His aversion to killing is further borne out by Doug Mansfield's first memory of him. 'When I was seven or eight he was ploughing for spuds and I'd follow him. A big worm turns up, so he stops the horse, puts the worm over into the last furrow, then away he goes again.'

Yet the boys remembered that it was different with snakes. 'He'd come down to the river with us. There was a log across it and one day when we were walking over, Denis was in front. There was a snake on the log and he just went choomp! with his foot, then kicked it off into the river. He broke its back. Boots and no socks, but still bang! It didn't seem to worry Denis at all.'

His sense of humour too was enjoyed by everyone who knew him. 'Denis had a wry sense of humour,' Doug Mansfield said. 'He went to Hobart one weekend and came back, announcing in his unique drawl, "I've brought something for you," producing an enormous block of chocolate. Biggest we'd ever seen! But it was one of Cadbury's wooden models!'

Another weekend the joke was on Denis, who had a strong aversion to faeces of any kind. Mrs Mansfield had baked a wallaby for Sunday dinner, filling the vent with an onion to hold the stuffing. 'Denis got the piece with the onion. He was normally quite a good eater. But he's there, going all around, picking very carefully. Mum was watching and finally said, "Oh Denis, that's only an onion."'

CHAPTER 7

Exploring

'He never took a compass with him.'

With time off, Denis loved going bush. On a day trip from the Denison mills he would walk over the hill to visit Rosemary up the Russell, or, from the Ellendale mill, to Lake Fenton in the national park, taking 'just a woolly jumper and a sandwich'. When the mill was shut he went further afield. 'You'd see Denis disappear down the river,' Vic Mansfield recalled, 'and all you could see were legs from the knees down. The rest was a bran sack up over his head and nearly down to his knees, full of provisions.'

His overcoat was a sack, with a corner pushed in for his head. Sometimes he would take it when he left for work. Vic remembered his mother asking, '"What've you got that coat for, Denis?" and his reply, "It'll rain before night." And by God, he was right. It did.'

Charlie's well-turned-out appearance was a byword, but Denis always wore short knickerbocker trousers, flannel shirt and thick-soled hobnail boots without socks. Round hobnails were very slippery on logs but good in mud, square hobnails were specifically for walking about on timber. Once going downhill in a deluge his feet were sliding in his boots, so he stuffed stringybark in as socks.

Charlie always wore a felt hat, carefully peaked in front. But although Denis disliked having a wet head, he never wore a hat. In rain he opened out his sack and wore it hoodwise, fastened with a nail under his chin. 'Other times,' Colin Bester remembered, 'he'd have it under his arm wound round with a bit of snare and he'd sit on that on a log. Oh, he had a lot of cunning little lurks. He knew all the answers.' Doug Mansfield declared, 'He never had any problem. He never took a compass with him.' 'You couldn't lose Denis on a dark night,' Guy Elliston confirmed.

Many believe that some lone bushmen who fell through horizontal were never found. But even in that dreaded scrub Denis had a charmed life. Once he and Charlie were walking on the Snowy Range in snow, when suddenly Denis disappeared. They were on top of horizontal, he trod on a weak patch and went straight through, falling to the ground below. Fortunately, Charlie, always prepared, had a rope to pull him out.

During his years at the mills Denis spent much time on the Snowy Range. According to Bester:

> No one ever went back in that part. But he walked right through. He knew all of it. He'd go away for several days, and when he came back he'd tell me all about it: the great gorges, the cracks down between the rocks hundreds of feet deep, how clear the water was, and the fish. The time he could put in back in those places and still come out just as good as he did when he went was just amazing! He was an amazing fellow!

Later, as other bushwalkers became interested, Denis was recognised as the authority, and his knowledge was sought by parties tackling the little-known range. Acknowledging his help, David Martin wrote in *The Tasmanian Tramp*, 'Between 1932 and 1939 Mr Denis King ascended many times from the Denison River Valley. It is due to his directions that our party had little difficulty in making the ascent in 1940.'

Denis mostly went alone, except when Winsome accompanied him. 'Mill hands just couldn't be bothered,' Deny said wistfully many years later. 'They'd done enough. They'd rather stay round the camps and talk. In those days you didn't talk about interesting things like nature. You'd be thought a bit funny. So there wasn't many people I could talk to. Even now when I come up with someone who likes talking about that, it's a real treat.'

He remembered once cutting a track towards the Snowy Range:

> I didn't have a compass. I just guided myself by the direction the clouds were coming from and we came out in the right place under Lake Skinner and went over the top of the mountain. That track was used for a long time.
>
> There was snow the first time. We didn't have a tent. We just made a shelter from pandanus tops with a fire in front. We had no sleeping bags in those days—just a blanket and an overcoat. The snow got too deep up higher, so we had to go back. I did more track cutting on that route later and we went there occasionally to camp by Lake Skinner.

On another two-day trip with Winsome:

> We got up towards the lakes the first night, went up over the top next day. It was a lovely fine day and we found a way through the boulders to look down over the first, most southerly, peak. You can't tell how near the edge you are, and suddenly we looked between two big high rocks—and there's the cliff about a thousand feet just in front! We dropped a big stone over and never heard it land. But we could smell the smoke when it struck other rocks going down.
>
> We found this lovely lake under Nevada Peak, with beautiful alpine grasses and richeas all different colours. No one had ever been there before. We tried to have a swim, but it was too cold although quite shallow.

Denis always gathered all available information from bushmen and prospectors. In the 1930s the unique beauty of Lake Pedder, visited by few people, was already legendary. Denis was curious to see the remote lake, formed by glacial action 300 metres above sea level in the heart of the mountains, and planned a trip.

There was no track and walkers rarely ventured into the surrounding wilderness. Denis inquired how to reach the lake and they loaded the old Oakland car and left it at Fitzgerald. He and Winsome set off walking the fifty-odd kilometres to Lake Pedder:

> We put on our sack bag packs, with dried fruit, flour, oatmeal, rice, lima beans. We used to take self-raising flour and a little frying pan. We'd make a scone mixture and cook it in the pan without fat. These rather nice pan scones'd stick to your ribs and you wouldn't get hungry, if you had a good feed. We mostly had a bit of jam and always had butter.

They followed the Port Davey track over the scrubby southern slopes of Mount Mueller, camping overnight. On Christmas Day 1935 they traversed Mount Bowes through thick rainforest to reach the Huon crossing—one log, the remains of a derelict bridge. They made their way over the open button-grass plain, camping on the southern side of the brooding bulk of Mount Solitary, waking to a beautiful sunrise, clear sky and patches of mist on the plain. The still day suited the March flies which pursued them in swarms, despite their efforts to escape by following a bushy creek across the plain. Then emerging onto a little ridge they looked right over the lake, the Frankland Range reflected in its mirror-still water, hauntingly lovely, set jewel-like in a crown of majestic mountains.

The lake was low because of dry weather, and Denis was impressed by the breadth of the long sweep of its beach of shining quartzite sand, dazzling white or delicate iridescent pink according to light. With customary interest in distances, he timed Win's crossing to the water's edge to fill a billy which took about five minutes. The water was warm and shallow, scarcely ankle-deep a hundred metres out.

After setting up camp, they walked round the lake's southern side.

Along the marshy shoreline scattered with wind-twisted melaleucas they observed swans and, to their surprise, some seagulls. They reached the Serpentine River, meandering across the swampy plains, dense with tea-tree, melaleuca and banksias, then made their way to the southern end of the many-peaked, ice-worn Frankland Range, before returning to base.

'The lovely part about visiting Lake Pedder,' Deny said over fifty years later, 'was that there was no sign of human beings having been there. There were kangaroos and wallabies, wombat tracks all along the sand, but no footprints. It was all very still and remote. It was one of the most beautiful scenes I've ever seen.'

In 1936 Denis returned to Cox Bight and spent most of the year helping his father there and also getting to know the Melaleuca site. Winter in the South-West that year was exceptionally severe:

> June was cold and frosty with very lovely clear sunny days. But the ice didn't melt, just a bit in the sun. In shady places under the hills and in the gullies it stayed for weeks and killed a lot of button grass and small trees over a foot thick. Along the beach where the water leached out of the bush it froze. Even the rock pools had ice.
>
> The New Harbour Company at Melaleuca had to boil up a tin of water to pour over their pumps to melt the ice. When I went across sometimes the mud under the button grass would be frozen. It was like walking on boards over what was normally squelching mud—quite good. They had thirty-six frosts in a row. The lagoon was frozen for weeks. It wasn't bad for working. When the sun came out it would be all right. The water was cold to start with, but it was good because everything was dry.

Denis continued his studies, putting lesson booklets into his pocket to peruse in any spare moment, sending off fees in instalments.

Anticipating working at night by kerosene lamp, he had brought down some boards from the mill. With these and driftwood he made a table still in use at Melaleuca.

Study gave him a sense of purpose. He enjoyed exercising his mind, the achievement of completing each assignment and seeing the fishing boat taking it on the first leg of its journey to Sydney, then awaiting results with the arrival of the next assignment. His marks were never below 92 per cent, a credit to his powers of concentration under far from ideal conditions. With his strong streak of self-discipline he applied himself consistently each night while Salvo George Blegg played his cornet and the other miners, weary after long hours in mud and water, sat around the hut smoking, yarning, playing cards.

When the New Harbour Tin Company ceased operations, Deny's studies received an unexpected boost. The Kings were asked to caretake, so week by week while one worked the mine at Cox's, the other would go to Melaleuca. Although when the company collapsed in 1937 they were paid nothing for their time and effort, and received nothing except a few stores, Deny had had the luxury of a hut to himself. In those weeks alone, his first stay at Melaleuca, he accomplished much. He finally gained his diploma in 1939 at the age of thirty.

At the end of 1936 Denis returned to the Ellendale sawmill. Mobile with his own car, he developed the habit of visiting the museum in Hobart in his persistent quest for information. The staff were impressed by this unusual man from the bush, with his inquiring mind and detailed, precise knowledge of his home territory. Recognising his natural talents they asked him to collect specimens of its flora and fauna. It was the first of many such requests by a number of institutions and researchers throughout his life.

Denis made his initial trip for the museum with his brother-in-law, Ron Woolley. Their packs heavy with specimen jars and bottles of preserving spirit, they walked out to the Denison and followed

Denis's old track up to Lake Skinner, east of Snowy South. They collected insects from the moss on logs and forest floor debris. At the lake they caught specimens of *Anaspides*, the tiny 'mountain shrimp' endemic to Tasmania.

Ron was unwell, so after a wretched night, with violent changeable winds, they made a beeline to the Snowy Range's northern end. With Denis leading they had to push their way through scrub, and very soon his trouser knees were worn through by the cutting-grass. It took several days' scrub-bashing to reach the source of the Russell, and they were relieved to emerge into cleared land.

The museum staff were very pleased with what he had collected, so Denis offered to go back to Lake Pedder. Heading towards Lake Judd with Win, climbing over a high spur thick with King Billy pines, Denis found a tall shrub he had not seen before, with sassafras-like serrated leaves. In the ensuing scramble through thick bush he lost the leaves he had collected and was deeply disappointed not to find another such plant. Steep terrain and horizontal scrub prevented their return to camp before darkness fell and they spent the night under a log.

After going to Lake Pedder the next day for specimens, Denis and Win decided to continue to the osmiridium site at Adamsfield, collecting on the way. 'Of course we had no map but just went by instinct. I bashed through some bush and came out into open stuff and in front of us was the southern end of the Sawback Range.' They came to 'a track of sorts' and followed it until they reached the first miner's camp. Looking round the workings, Denis's interest in mining was further whetted.

More journeys were to come. Family bonds were strong and his sisters meant a lot to Denis. While Winsome was living with him at Ellendale, in 1938 they decided to visit Olive and her husband, Jordan Fieldwick.

Jordan had an apple orchard near Triabunna on the east coast, and the four decided to travel northwards, selling apples from an old Fargo lorry. 'We didn't do real good,' Win said with dry realism. 'Things were tough. And can you imagine Den going to the door knocking?' Jordan wanted all the apple cases back and Denis hated having to ask for them.

As usual, however, for him there was a positive side: new places to see and new things to learn. In particular, Derby, an established tin-mining area, provided a seminal experience:

> We called at the Briseis tin mine. That was good. You went down a couple of hundred feet below the surface. They had big pumps to pump the tin and stuff up. They had to blow away all this basalt from over the top to get down to the alluvial tin. It was very interesting the way they were doing this on a quite big scale. Of course it put wonderful ideas into my head. Working that way instead of having to do it by hand!

After that venture Denis and Win decided in 1939 to go to Cox Bight to help their father work his mine.

CHAPTER 8

Cox Bight

'Forking stones and carry, carry, carry.'

Cox Bight is a deep bay girded by ranges, on the forbidding south coast. It is named after Captain J. H. Cox who on the brig *Mercury* sailed along the wild west coast and landed there in 1789. The eastern arm runs into the Southern Ocean at Red Point, tip of the protecting Red Point Hills, while westwards the New Harbour Range ends in rugged Cox Bluff.

Line upon line of white-capped breakers sweep in symmetry onto the wide curved beach, where brown hummocks of leathery kelp lie like lazy sea lions, and sooty oystercatchers probe the rippled silver sand, which stretches like a great stainless steel draining-board as the tide recedes. Offshore, the table of Flat Witch, the triangles and humps of the Maatsuyker Group islands and the solid mass of De Witt form a definitive horizon.

Point Eric, an outcrop of stratified rocks crowned with wind-pruned vegetation, breaks the beach halfway along, providing a landing place for boats in the lee of its eastern side. There drifts of small fawn cowries, tiny golden yellow cockles, whorled warreners and other shells gather.

Creeks brown as billy tea emerge from the dense green scrub of melaleuca and bauera to run in convoluted golden curves across shining sand, where pieces of bleached driftwood lie in surreal silver sculptures. Currawongs call in the bush, ravens and gulls scavenge along the tideline, where tracks of wombats, wallabies and lizards mingle with those of birds, and an occasional echidna makes its way.

The western curve of the beach nowadays is a favoured landing-place at low tide for light aircraft bringing bushwalkers and day-trippers. Flying in over Cox Bight reveals the panorama of the amber waters of Freney Lagoon, home of black swans, behind the thick belt of bush which grows right down to the bank of white quartzite boulders along the beach's edge. Beyond, flanked to the east by the bulk of the Bathurst Range dropping down to Bathurst Harbour in the north, stretch the broad bronze button-grass plains leading to Melaleuca.

Coast and hinterland was the country of the Needwonne people, whose huts and middens Cox noticed. Their use of fire in land management contributed to the development of button-grass moorlands, a feature of the South-West.

By 1834 the Needwonne were virtually extinct and the coast was clear for the European men who had stolen their women and introduced disease, as they exploited whale and seal populations, and stands of age-old Huon pines and other rainforest timbers. Then after whalers, sealers and piners, into the South-West came prospectors and miners.

Tin was discovered near Point Eric in 1891, the alluvial deposits ideally suited to small operations with basic equipment. But it was no job for weaklings. Although only pick and shovel were needed to wrest the tin from the gravel beds, miners also needed stamina and strength to maintain the unremitting hard work. Moreover, to survive required more than ordinary powers of endurance—facing loneliness, isolation, harsh weather and the alien environment. A man also had to plan his stores at least three months ahead with orders, making do on very basic rations, because of uncertain supplies. Charlie King had all these qualities.

Hopefuls who arrived expecting to pick up a quick packet soon left empty-handed and disillusioned. Two, arriving with a supply of sugar bags, thought all they had to do was to scoop up the tin like sand from a dune. That in itself was a joke to old hands. But the big joke was that tin is very dense and heavy, and a sugar bag would have weighed over 100 kilograms, impossible to carry. Those men didn't last long, though one found employment later as a member of parliament.

But Charlie lasted twenty-one years and Deny lived there fifty years.

In 1939 Winsome had not been to sea before and looked forward to the trip to Cox Bight. Sid Dale had agreed to take them and they had loaded their gear and stores, when Sid returned and announced he could not. His wife objected to a female passenger!

They walked, and Win earned the distinction of becoming the first woman to complete this eighty-odd kilometre trek. They repacked gear, sorting what had to go by boat, then caught a bus to Dover, and got a lift to Recherche. Sawmillers told them where the track started and they set out in rain. It was new territory to them, appealing to Denis's zest for discovery: over steep hills, down deep gullies, a glimpse of the sea near South Cape Creek, crossing New River in a leaky old boat, walking along a wild beach to ascend the inhospitable Ironbound Range in thick weather. Denis again proved a consummate 'scrounger', getting a fire going, finding 'a little nook' in scrub to put up the fly, making a track where none existed.

Their father's delight at their unexpected arrival was heartwarming reward for the six-day walk. Denis was chuffed—'We'd beat the boat.'

Charlie had moved from the crowded main hut and established his camp on a knoll covered with thick bush, nearer to his workings and wood supplies. Deny remembered, 'We settled down and enjoyed being there.' They built a frame and sides for their tent from flotsam. 'It was like being in a little house. You could stand up in it.' In front they built a fireplace with chimney of old flattened pipes nailed to a wooden frame 'which kept it lovely and warm'. Win did most of the cooking in Charlie's tent nearby, and sometimes helped at the mine.

Every morning they emerged from the sheltering bush to the track about five hundred metres from the beach, to observe sea and weather. 'Funnily enough, when the wind was sou'west and quite a big sea running, you wouldn't hear it much from the camp. You'd go out and be quite surprised. Yet when it was calm, the sea would be roaring to high heaven.'

'At Cox's you always had to carry everything—carry, carry, carry.' Ron Woolley gave Denis a pair of metal wheels and he made a cart to transport supplies from the landing. It ran well on firm beach sand, but was useless for wood-gathering in the bush. Firewood was scarce and they had to trudge several hundred metres uphill.

Denis would carry a log on his shoulders a certain distance, then return for another. A dry log twenty-five centimetres through and three metres long would weigh up to seventy-odd kilograms. He tied smaller ones together for easier carrying. When not working at the mine, Denis spent fine days getting wood, while Charlie baked bread. He used yeast grown from hops, sugar and potatoes, cooking the dough slowly in the camp oven suspended from a hook on a bar across the fireplace.

Water was fetched from a meandering brown creek east of the slope, while toilet arrangements were on the other side. The dunny is still recognisable. No makeshift job, it was built of sturdy bush struts, fallen now, and Emu Best Corrugated Iron Co. galvanised sheets all the way from Wolverhampton in Britain, the trademark emu still visible. A solid seat with a triangular hole cut in the thick timber was made for comfort.

When the Burgess syndicate collapsed, Charlie took over another claim on the eastern side of Cox's and pegged one for Denis. Charlie's new claim was shallow ground, quite good though very stony, and for a while he did fairly well. 'We got a few tons of tin out,'

Deny remembered. 'It was an interesting place. It seemed there had once been a tremendous cloudburst which had swept all the top away, leaving patches and crevices with good tin. By the outlet were all these buried logs which seemed to have been carried down.'

When that claim was worked out, Frank Goram's became available and Charlie took it over. It was hard labour, all done manually with pick and shovel, crowbar and fork, helped along with the hose and an occasional plug of gelignite:

> It was deep ground, six to eight feet, in some places up to twelve. It was just full of stones, but quite rich tin on the bottom. We got stuck into it and I helped Dad, throwing these stones all day.
>
> You'd save the big ones and make a wall to hold the rest back. You'd throw the other stuff, fork it up behind. Your walls had to be well built or they'd collapse on you. It was very disheartening to come along bright and early and find they had collapsed all over your work. You had to set to and rebuild, throw the stones back up where they came from. That was really hard work, forking these stones up above your head all day. We used to work in all weathers and walk back to camp at night about half a mile along the beach.

Even after sixty years the encroaching bush has not been able to obliterate the massive piles of stones, thrown up in the struggle to win the alluvial tin. Here and there shrubs and small plants have taken root, while lizards and snakes find ideal basking and ready shelter in the stoneworks.

A few discarded pickheads lie rusting among stones in many places almost four metres deep, above trenches over fifty metres along a moonscape gully. Like megalithic Stone Age monuments, the amazing walls, so painstakingly built, stand as testimony to the manual skills, stamina and determination of Denis and his father.

Denis stayed for twelve months, and became well versed in the toil and hazards of manual mining:

> This new mine we'd taken over was on a gravelly fan six or seven feet deep coming down off the hill and the stones were so thick you couldn't drive a pick between them. But it was very good tin on the bottom.
>
> There was a top layer of white gravel, then hard gravel with big stones, mostly quartz, going down another four feet above a layer of black granitey stained ground. Beneath that were holes with sea-worn pebbles and soft rotten iron pyrites.
>
> It was very hard to separate the pyrites from the tin. We'd drive a moil, a pointed bar about six feet long, in amongst the stones wherever we could with a ten-pound sledgehammer. It took a lot of driving to get it any depth. We'd put a couple of pickheads over the end, wedge them tight, then withdraw the bar by belting the end behind them. That would draw it out. But you had to be careful pebbles didn't get in the hole so you couldn't get the gelignite in.
>
> I made holes with an upward slope so pebbles would roll out with a bit of encouragement from a stick. You'd push the plugs in as far as they'd go, then push the one with detonator gently in behind, ram in paper or clay, light the fuse and get away until she went off.
>
> It didn't blow it up in the air much. It just loosened the ground. Our dog, old Buck, was tremendously excited when it went off. He'd tear down and start scratching and barking in spite of the smoke. But it gave us headaches, especially the raw gelignite.
>
> Then we'd turn the water race onto all this loose gravel to separate mud and stones from tin, and stay there forking

stones all day and the next. It was very exposed. The wind would sweep across with cold rain and at first we had no shelter.

When really short of food they hunted wallaby and occasionally duck with gun and dog, but did no trapping. Game was plentiful because the country was frequently burnt off, creating new feed. If the sea was smooth enough they went to a special hole for trumpeter. Fishing off the rocks meant lines tangling in the ubiquitous kelp, but this hole had a gravelly bottom. It was, however, vital to watch the sea constantly because it often swept over. A big wave coming meant scrambling to safety. Occasionally, if they found a calm place to drop in ring and net, they caught crayfish.

Denis enjoyed the opportunity to explore. He and Charlie walked towards South West Cape as far as Mount Karamu, bashing back through deep gullies over and under treacherous blankets of bauera, discovering a series of waterfalls and an unusual shrub he had never seen anywhere before. He and Win loved camping walkabouts to Mount Counsel, or into the mountains behind Cox's.

The elusive thylacine was still about, and they had close encounters. Charlie, veteran bushman who was familiar with tiger tracks up the Weld and knew all the creatures of the unpeopled fastnesses of the South-West, sighted one in bush near Melaleuca. They even visited the Cox's campsite. Deny recalled several episodes:

> I'd caught a wallaby for dog food and buried part, putting logs over so tiger cats couldn't get at it. Dad came back from Melaleuca at night and heard this terrible screaming howl outside the camp. It seems he'd disturbed a thylacine unburying the meat. It had rolled these big logs away and taken it. You can tell when a tiger has eaten a carcass. It just takes everything out, eats bones and all, and leaves the skin clean.

Not long before I'd nearly reached Melaleuca and suddenly the dog's hackles stood on end from his head right to his tail. He growled and went sniffing around, apparently where this animal had been—the only one he'd ever do that with.

Next time Father was coming back from Melaleuca, Buck was with him not far from where the house is now. The dog disappeared into the bush and was barking. Dad followed and saw Buck had this tiger bailed up. The tiger would sit down and open its mouth at the dog. Dad said it looked all mouth. Then it made its chance to jump up and run, and it was too quick for Buck in the scrub.

Allan Walker, who worked for Charlie in 1940, remembered other close encounters:

There were plenty of tiger tracks about on the beaches and plains. Once I carefully made a loop and next morning found they'd followed my scent round overnight. They have an unmistakable track. I knew that. Denis knew that. When they're hunting they make a noise a bit like a dog. And they have a high-pitched squealing whistle, a bit like a very young foal.

At Cox's the meat safe had to be hung up to blazes or she'd go. They could pull down something at eight or nine feet without trouble. You could hear them chasing kangaroos sometimes when the water was up with a tide or a storm on the plains across Moth Creek. You could hear the kangaroo running—chop, chop, chop, chop. The only thing that could have frightened them would be a tiger. They're not frightened of anything else. A tiger can run one down with that strong steady gait of his.

Denis was still working at Cox Bight when war was declared in September 1939. He remembered the momentous news coming through and its effects in this isolated outpost of empire:

> Dad had a little radio. We used to listen on shortwave to the BBC. We were listening very attentively after we heard that Mr Chamberlain was going to make an announcement. We tuned in to hear him say, 'We are at war with Germany.' I had imagined that when war broke out everyone would drop everything and run to arms. But the Prime Minister said, 'Stick to your jobs and you'll be told what to do.' So I kept on at the mine.

Five months later he was offered the position he had so long wanted with the Hydro-Electric Commission, on the Tarraleah power station construction site. Here he had another seminal experience. For the first time he saw a bulldozer. Fascinated by its power and how easily it moved stumps and stones, he recognised its potential for mining.

After Cox Bight's daily challenges, he found the job as an electrician's offsider dull. Even when he volunteered to help fitters and plumbers too, there was insufficient work. 'I didn't like trying to pretend I was working when I wasn't. I thought there were other things I could do better.'

Three months later he resigned and enlisted in the Army Engineers.

CHAPTER 9

Tough yet tender

'Old Man King.'

After Deny left in 1940, Charlie took on Allan Walker, aged seventeen. Walker, later a mining consultant, remembered vividly his first job and experience of the isolation and harsh weather of the South-West. With respect and wry affection he recalled his first employer as a hard taskmaster and dogmatic. This was perhaps aggravated by sixty-three-year-old Charlie's growing deafness, which made discussions or asking questions difficult.

Yet he was a good miner, a fine bushman and a splendid cook, keen to impart his considerable knowledge and skills. He was resourceful too. When Allan cut his foot Charlie sewed it up with darning needle and linen thread.

> Old Man King taught me a lot. He taught me how to use a prospecting dish, one of the great arts. He stood over me. 'I let you take that time off while I'm paying you. But you should know how to do it.' And he's dead right. Because of that skill, I was always able to get a job.
>
> Old King wouldn't work the ground unless he got good results. Heavy, a bag of tin. I can tell you who had to carry it too. He wasn't going to waste bags either. We always filled them to the limit. Denis used to carry two, according to the Old Man. Up that little ladder out of those works at Cox Bight, across the plain, down that steep hill, across the little flat and along the beach. That beach was bad walking when

it was soft. Murder! And at the other end it was just raw stone—hell to walk along.

The Old Man would forever lecture a boy, which doubtless did me a great deal of good. Because he was right. He insisted on setting a fire when the camp was left for a day or two. Once he carefully set it, after the old one had been raked out and cooled. He said, 'This stick here, this stick there, and this stick should be just so.' Then without thinking, he reached for the matches and lit it! He didn't swear, just pulled it to pieces hurriedly and made me reset it.

Charlie had made his camp very practical. Two tents were sleeping quarters, and after Denis and Win left, the third became a kitchen–living area. With typical ingenuity he contrived storage space in his 'bedroom' with shelves of driftwood stacked with big square biscuit tins. In these he kept precious possessions, including a 'multitude of books' and his good clothes, 'of which he had quite a few', according to Walker.

Still working the Cox's mine, Charlie was also moving camp to the New Harbour Company's Melaleuca site. Walker was expected to do his share:

> She was a hard eight miles, carrying stuff across that blasted plain, day after day in midwinter. In thigh boots, wind and mud. Endless books and tins of jam—you name it—and the telescope. Load up, come back. Raining like hell. At high tide it backs up on those plains, so up to your thighs in water. Putting your feet in holes you couldn't see. Those little creeks—about a foot wide and who knows how deep. A bit of a battle.

> But Old Man King was a tough cookie. He was immensely strong and he never stopped. I can still see him ploughing like blazes through scrub up to his chest. Then

down he went! All that was left for a few seconds was his big hat on the water!

Melaleuca was not then an inviting site. 'It was absolutely bare, just raw button grass. Nothing. Just a patch of scrub, and little brushy stuff along the creek. There were six huts and only two had roofs. That was it.'

After Walker left, Charlie employed three men in succession, but each was called up. Frustrated by the difficulty of obtaining labour, he wrote to the Department of Mines to request his son's release from military service to help in the mine, but without success.

Other hardships and war shortages were felt even in remote Port Davey and these difficulties were compounded by adjoining lease-holders misappropriating his equipment. Charlie sat many a night in his Cox Bight tent, and later in his hut at Melaleuca, penning letters by lamplight in his strong clear hand to the department about his frustrations. He was even unable to send out his tin through lack of bags.

Not least of his problems was communication, depending solely on Sid Dale and other co-operative fishermen, whose movements were dictated by weather. Yet, despite all difficulties, there was no question of giving up. On the contrary, Charlie was always consid-ering ways and means of increasing production, as tin was needed for the war effort. His yearly output was over three and a half tonnes of concentrate, equivalent to more than two and a half tonnes of metallic tin. Mining manually, this represented enormous effort. A consignment weighing approximately nine hundredweight (450 kilograms) was bringing £115 after freight and cartage had been paid, and before miner's rights and survey fees, and rents on occupa-tion licences, water licences and dam sites had been met.

In August 1944 Charlie described plans to 'spend a considerable sum of money' carrying out Deny's scheme to bring water from the head of Melaleuca Creek over three kilometres to a catchment dam.

A reliable water supply, necessary for sluicing, had never been available, and would justify expenditure on new plant. Deny was to bring a theodolite, when he came home on leave, to check the levels Charlie had estimated, before implementing the plan. Cutting the race would be 'a rough job, with spurs and bush to contend with in parts, and open button grass in others, and some sections have to be shot out of rock'.

Deny's application for discharge on compassionate grounds was refused. His letters, however, must have been a comfort to his father. He shared his thoughts about the mine's future and ideas for equipment they could install to make it easier to work. He also discussed Win's plans to return, advising his father, 'Not too much stuff cluttering the joint up is all you would need do to please her.' He promised action to rid the garden of slugs, and concluded, 'Take care of yourself. Don't get working too hard. It's time you took things a bit easier.'

Charlie aimed to be self-sufficient where possible and the garden was important for fresh food and also recreation. A natural gardener, he and Deny always took care when bringing plants in, not to introduce pests or weeds. When he saw a white cabbage butterfly he did not rest until he had destroyed it.

Charlie also had a tender side. He loved his family dearly and missed them very much. Their wellbeing was his continuing concern even at such a difficult distance, and his yearning is glimpsed in his letters. He took care too to keep his affairs in order, in case of illness or accident. Increasing deafness accentuated his isolation, tingeing solitude with loneliness, forcing him more and more into his own world. A thoughtful reader, he wrote away for books. The companionship of his dogs, Buck, an intelligent cross-bred border collie, and pure-bred Trixie, both trained by Charlie, also meant much to him.

He took solace too in wild creatures and had a deep rapport with birds, which had learned to trust this quiet, measured man. At Melaleuca he kept a tin of jam inside the hut, especially for the yellow-throated honeyeaters. They flew in and out freely, even brushing past if he were in the doorway. They came to meet him as he walked home from work, alighting on his shoulder. When he was on the lagoon they flew right out and perched on the boat.

A shy rare Lewin's rail befriended him, coming often to pick up crumbs around his feet. A brush bronzewing pigeon became so tame it sat on his knee, fed from his hand, and lay in the sun beside Buck. Blue wrens, dusky robins, olive whistlers, New Holland honeyeaters, striated fieldwrens, scrubwrens and emu-wrens also frequented the camp and were a continual source of pleasure. Charlie had an affinity too with the swans which flew over and sometimes fed in Melaleuca Lagoon. He talked with them and had the rare ability to call them.

He had done some collecting for the Australian Museum in 1939, sending specimens of two dusky pouched mice and two swamp rats. A handsome green and coppery tree frog with brass-coloured eyes was also sent but not examined until years later when a frog of the same species was described and named after another collector.

Charlie's skills and services as a bushman were still in demand. In 1941 and in 1946 the Department of Lands asked him to walk a route along the coast, reporting on its suitability for a road into Port Davey. His well-considered descriptions contained practical details of grades, location of bridges required, and sources of building materials.

During the five years Charlie awaited Denis's return from the war his pride in him was quietly apparent in his letters to others. Charlie's values and choice of lifestyle were a strong influence on all his children, especially on his son. From his father Denis learned the courage and developed the inner resources to choose also to live apart from his fellows, where nature was still supreme.

CHAPTER 10

TX2261

'A very versatile and fit sapper. He'd tackle anything.'

The army changed life for Denis, now almost thirty-one, with new opportunities, pointing him in new directions. The first change was his name. His mates called him Deny and it stuck.

He was turned down by the air force, and the navy recruiting office was closed when he tried. The army was his least preferred choice, yet when he inquired at the barracks he was told, 'Yes, you're the sort they want.' He remarked wryly, 'I don't suppose they cared whether I was the right sort or wrong.'

From boyhood he had dreaded the thought of going to war, but felt impelled because his father and uncles had. He feared being terribly frightened, but knew he had no option. 'My conscience began to prick,' he wrote. 'I could not rest, knowing my time had come.' On 6 June 1940 in Hobart he joined No 1 Section, 2/9 Field Company, Royal Australian Engineers in the Second AIF.

Having enlisted he enjoyed the challenge of the training, the camaraderie, new experiences and sense of adventure. His desire to travel had been aroused by books. Now the world was opening up.

All his life Deny's strength and physique were the subject of comment. Stocky, nuggety, deep-chested with powerful shoulders, strong as a bullock, were descriptions applied to him. Army records show he was 5 feet 5 inches (165 centimetres) tall, of fair complexion, with brown hair and blue eyes; even the scar inflicted by the tiger cat was noted.

Although service personnel were not permitted to keep diaries, Deny's habit was too firmly established to discontinue. He became a closet chronicler using Australian Comforts Fund notepads on his first tour of duty, in the Middle East, and a tiny notebook during New Guinea service. Although intermittent, these diaries, together with his memoirs and reminiscences of companions, provide a lively picture of those formative years.

Army life was a dramatic change. Deny had to forfeit his accustomed independence and solitude, and conform to strict discipline, sleeping in a hut with some twenty men, whose noise and drinking habits revolted him:

> Arriving at camp after leave with a heart of lead, one felt like a mortal about to descend to the realm of King Pluto, pausing for a last look at the bright sunlit earth. I would awaken in the morning with a feeling akin to horror, to the dreadful thought that I was in the army; that free life had vanished and I had left behind the lovely bush. But when the very Empire was in grave danger, one's petty feeling could not be considered.

He spent six months at Brighton Army Camp north of Hobart, training as a sapper, as privates in the Engineers were known. He received specialist pay as Engineer Artificer. When there was no mechanical work, he wielded shovel or axe, or did whatever was necessary. Road- and bridge-building were two important functions of a field company.

The original lieutenant in charge, Gordon Colebatch, remembered his men as 'a fine bunch. Deny King proved to be one of the finest because of his great practical ability and skill as an engine hand and electrician, and because he was outstanding in physical ability, and quite unflappable under stress. He was the ideal sapper, very versatile and fit. He'd tackle anything.'

Deny's first paid work was as a teamster. He had his own eight bullock team. Between 1934 and 1939 he worked at three timber mills in the Huon hinterland.

Win, Charlie and Deny outside the Nissen-style timber and iron house that Deny built in 1946–47 on Melaleuca's open plain.

TX2261 Sapper King was respected and liked by both his commanding officers and army mates. They called him Deny.

Charlie King, experienced bushman and miner, prospecting in a stream near Melaleuca in the 1950s.

Cox Bight from the air. Freney Lagoon is in the foreground, Point Eric, centre. The 1930s King mine and camp were beyond.

Havelock Bluff at the end of the Ironbounds. In 1949 Deny traversed this daunting range in record time to meet Margaret.

The house on Moth Creek, 1947. Weather station at right, New Harbour Company huts at left and Smoke Signal Hill on the horizon.

Margaret with Nufty. She used to tie messages round his neck and send him to find his master Charlie in the garden

Deny in pensive mood, pondering one of the innumerable maintenance problems at Melaleuca.

Although older than most of the sixty-three men in his section, Deny had no ambition to become a sergeant. Captain Arthur Tilly, his commander in New Guinea said, 'He was muscly strong from digging tin and throwing bags of it around. But he didn't throw his weight around. You couldn't take offence at anything he did.' Even the cooks had a soft spot for Deny, 'a good tooth man', and always put seconds aside for him.

The army had only one problem with Deny. Used to bushwalking and rough terrains, he had a unique stride and tempo and had difficulty marching. Colebatch wanted his section to be judged best on every parade, so the sergeant always placed Deny right in the middle where he was not readily noticed. His mate Keith Heeney remembered:

> Everybody got out of step except Deny! So we made a ladder for the regulation step and he marched along it, backwards and forwards until he fell into our step.
>
> He was slow talking and people didn't realise what a great bushman he was and what an asset he was to the unit, with his knowledge and ideas. He could improvise, and was very good with explosives and ropes. By the time we'd finished training, everybody in the 2/9th Field Company knew who Deny King was.
>
> He'd never complain about the sand, heat, rain, mud, mossies. Under all bad conditions he'd say, 'You've got to put up with those sorts of things.' That inspired others to do the same if they could.

While training, Deny made his second trip up the east coast. With full equipment it was a very different journey from the previous year's with his sisters. Colebatch remembered how, after a day's exercise in a downpour, which frayed everyone's temper but Deny's, he stopped a fight developing in a bar. 'Quietly moving between a corporal and a transport driver, both broad-shouldered and six feet tall, he said in his unique drawl, "Look, you fellers, we'll soon have a real war to fight, so why not cut it out?" They were so surprised that the argument ended immediately.'

Off duty Deny continued drawing and painting, and he persevered with studies. Responsible for censoring platoon mail, Tilly remembered Deny's correspondence courses, including one on diesel engines, which he passed very well. Tilly could see, however, he was struggling with the tertiary standard maths in a hydro-electric engineering course and tried to help. When he found Deny had done no secondary maths, he advised dropping that course for another. Deny followed his advice. 'Fortunately I couldn't get through my algebra. Otherwise I might have been polishing a chair somewhere in the Hydro buildings.'

Deny left Tasmania for the first time in January 1941 when his section was transferred to Victoria. While there, before his overseas embarkation, he took the opportunity to catch up with Win, then working in the Maribyrnong munitions factory, and together they saw Melbourne's sights.

In February the company boarded *Mauretania*, bound for the Middle East via Bombay. India's crowded squalor was shocking after the Tasmanian bush. 'Everything seemed so dirty you could hardly bear to eat—beggars sitting in the dust, spitting betel nut on the pavements. The smell reminded me of brush possums. It was with you all the time.'

There the soldiers left *Mauretania*'s comparative comfort, trans-shipping to an old freighter infested with 'whacking great cockroaches, and refrigeration gone bung'. After disembarking at Port Tewfik in Egypt, crossing the Suez Canal by ferry they experienced their first air raid .

In Palestine they camped at Hill 69, a World War I site, where they made roads, with a camel team carting dirt to cover the sand. For Deny it was a contrast to handling a bullock team hauling logs in the forest, with very different commands. 'We had to go "Sss, sss, sss," to make them sit down, and "Hoit, hoit, hoit," to make them get up.' On route marches picking oranges was a new experience too for someone who grew up in a region famous for apples.

Major Dick Drummond remembered his first encounter with Deny, as well he might. Inspecting a road culvert with Colebatch, the major remarked on several birds which flew out. Birds were scarce, and these were the first that seemed familiar: '"Look at the swallows," I said to Colebatch. A quiet drawl came from over my shoulder. "They're not swallows, sir. They're swifts."'

The company moved north into Lebanon, preparing for the Syrian campaign. It was stationed beside a British Royal Engineers unit, which had been told to build two bridges. But having no Bailey bridging, they were unable to perform the task. No. 1 Section was then asked how long the Australians would take. The sergeant, a carpenter, estimated that by using some good Indian timber on site, they could build the longer bridge in two days, the shorter in one.

They were the same type they had built on training exercises in Tasmania, but timber here was in logs. Deny came into his own. He and another sapper, Ross Walker, expert axemen and adzemen, squared the round timber into baulks, to the amazement of the Royal Engineers, while other sappers assembled the piles and decking and built the approaches.

Both bridges were completed on time.

When the company moved into Syria on the opening day of the campaign against the Vichy French, the war suddenly became very real. 'We saw our first dead people—war casualties just laying about. Nobody seemed to be worrying about gathering them up.' A mate remembered Deny saying, 'They get fair dinkum here. They shoot at you.'

No. 1 Section was given the task of making an airstrip, and the sappers were pleased with their achievement when RAF Tomahawk fighters were able to land late in the same day. It was another seminal experience for Deny.

The company was then based outside Aleppo, with small detachments constructing defence works along the Turkish border. Deny enjoyed opportunities to explore country so different from South-West Tasmania and looked forward to going to Greece, but following Japan's entry into the war, they were withdrawn from Syria and embarked at Port Tewfik.

They disembarked in Adelaide in March 1942, and moved into the hills, where their expertise was put to good use on local projects, and Deny was delighted to see and hear kookaburras for the first time.

Visiting his father in May he became involved in a poignant episode in the saga of the South-West. Called upon by police because of his local knowledge and skills as a bushman, Deny was granted special leave to assist a party searching for missing Melbourne man, Critchley Parker.

Parker, an experienced hiker, but unfit for military service, had gone to Port Davey seeking a site for his impractical plan to resettle Jewish refugees. Charlie, whom Parker described as 'an honest man with whom I had a pleasant stay', rowed him across Bathurst Channel in late March. With ten days' supplies, Parker planned to walk to Fitzgerald.

The party left Hobart in early May to cover the ninety-odd kilometres through rough country to Port Davey but, despite prolonged efforts, failed to find Parker. After the search was abandoned, Deny rejoined his unit. He was distressed months later to hear that the missing hiker's body had been found only a few kilometres beyond the endpoint of the search. Parker had died before it had even begun. The coronial inquest established cause of death as starvation and exposure.

The army had taken over Northern Territory road maintenance and Deny's company was responsible for resurfacing a section of the

Stuart Highway. Now instead of camels they had modern road plant. Seven months maintaining earthmoving equipment and driving a bulldozer was invaluable experience for Deny. He realised even more clearly the potential for machinery at Melaleuca. He began considering how to mechanise the mine and talked of this to his father when home on leave in February 1943.

He also turned his mind to improving grenades and inventing a new instrument, a dial sawbench gauge. He sent submissions to the Army Inventions Directorate. Although none was adopted, he received a letter of commendation on his ingenious ideas.

The company spent three months retraining and bridge-building on the Queensland Atherton Tableland. Then in May 1943 they sailed for New Guinea.

In Port Moresby three days later the sight of a vessel sunk in an air raid, and the many American aircraft, including one on fire crashing into the sea, were sharp reminders of the proximity of the fighting. Several night raids and accompanying anti-aircraft displays heightened this realisation.

After weeks building hospital wards, laying water mains and sewer pipes, the company moved west along the coast and up the shallow, tortuous Lakekamu River to Bulldog, an old mining site at the foot of the highlands.

Deny was in his element, observing and recording every unknown plant, bird, insect and animal species in this tropical environment, comparing each with what he already knew. Going upriver he noted turtle tracks, a crocodile, fifteen bird species, and vivid blue Ulysses butterflies. Clearing a campsite at jungle's edge, they found millipedes 'as thick as broom handles', centipedes as large, and a very big death adder. At dusk streams of flying foxes flew past upriver for hours, and if Deny was camped near a fig tree with ripening fruit, their squabbling kept him awake.

The company's project was to assist building a road north over the mighty Owen Stanley Range to Edie Creek, to join the existing road to Wau and Bulolo. Tilly appreciated Deny's bushcraft and knowledge:

> If timber was required for a bridge, Deny was the man to locate suitable trees. I'd send him out for a certain length and diameter girder, and he'd find it in half an hour. Send the others out and they'd be gone half the morning, and instead of coming back with a ten or twelve inch, they'd have eight.

The road was to be corduroyed, by laying logs together transversely to form the surface. Deny and others split trees for cords and had to discover which trees were suitable. Because there were so many species they had to look closely. Some were tough, while most of the free-grained timbers had soft white wood. They worked with the locals, who assisted getting timber and carrying it out.

Deny was keenly interested in the people and their way of life. He studied how outrigger canoes were built and how they functioned. Along the river's lower reaches he noticed how the villagers spread sago palm pith to dry on leaf mats. In the mountains he commented on their fires and gardens, noting they traded fruit and vegetables for paper and salt. 'They suck salt like we do sweets.'

In 'wickedly steep' country work was hard and unremitting in the heat. Labouring seven days a week, nine to ten hours each day, the men were often intensely discouraged when the results of their toil were washed out by heavy rain and flooding.

The mosquitoes were ferocious. Men fell ill with malaria, and some, including Deny, contracted dengue fever. 'It is rotten! Makes one very irritable' was his only diary entry for over a fortnight in February 1944. But when an order came to wear long sleeves and gaiters to reduce exposure to mosquitoes, Deny and many others developed dermatitis from dye in their jungle greens.

As the Japanese withdrew, the company was ordered to move on foot north to Edie Creek, at 2200 metres, a formidable march Deny took in his stride. Edie Creek was the site of a rich goldfield discovered in 1926, and the Bulolo Valley interested him, with its miles of gravel river flats, the abandoned dredges visible from the road. Everyone wanted to try gold panning, with little success until Deny showed them.

He was enthralled with the rich diversity of new plants and birds. On rest days he borrowed Tilly's or Drummond's field glasses and went walkabout, observing birds and sketching them in coloured pencil. Years later Deny wrote nostalgically of this time:

> At dawn we woke to the melodious whistle of the butcher-bird and the happy, engaging chatter of the shy friarbird, followed by the musical note of the drongos. The air is soon filled with calls of all descriptions, a great relief, breaking the incessant shrills of the cicadas and crickets day and night, which make the jungle seem more sinister than ever, and the still, warm night with the phosphorous glow from the fungi in rotting vegetation more ghostly.
>
> The distant ranges stand out clear and blue, with a small cloud or two clinging about the peaks or lazing languidly in a gorge. As the day advances it soon becomes hot.
>
> Birdsongs dwindle as the birds are mainly at rest during the heat. Heavy clouds from beyond the mountains obscure the peaks and gradually extend over the whole sky, from which heavy rain or thunder showers fall in the afternoon.

From Edie Creek they went by road transport to Zenag, a large plateau in a mountain gap. The unit's task was to construct a jeep road from Zenag to the Markham River over a saddle and down along the Wampit River. Initially there was no equipment and again all the work had to be manual. It was steep, rugged terrain, subject to spectacular landslides.

In time D2 Caterpillar tractors as well as D4 and D6 bulldozers arrived, and Deny was responsible for maintaining them. The D2's capabilities impressed him and he was already considering its potential at Melaleuca. He also became keenly aware of the potential of aircraft in isolated situations.

Off duty others found new diversions, making rings from gold they had panned, and constructing model aircraft. Deny preferred butterfly collecting and birdwatching, but paid close attention to what was involved in ring-making.

In April 1944 a storm swept away five bridges, so once again Deny was out in the forest searching for timber. His section completed a replacement of the last thirty-five-metre span in four days and despite all setbacks, the road was finished in the allocated six weeks. The irony was that the war zone had moved, so the road no longer served a prime military purpose.

At the end of May 1944 the company embarked in Lae for Australia. On reaching Brisbane, one of Deny's first calls was the museum to identify birds he had seen. To his delight and the staff's surprise, some were unknown species.

Deny boarded the train south for well-deserved leave, four years to the day after he had enlisted. Posted to the Atherton Tableland for further training in January 1945, Deny was injured. The accident occurred during a demonstration for reporters and brass hats, to show how quickly they could bridge a gully. For speed, panels were stacked along the job but, according to Deny, it was incorrectly done.

'It took at least six blokes to carry one of these panels. A cobber and I were walking past with another heavy bit of equipment, when the whole stack came down across my legs and broke one. It hurt like fury. They got me out and put me in hospital.'

For Deny it proved a most fortuitous accident. It ended his war days. And, because of it, he met the woman who would become the most important person in his life.

CHAPTER 11

Margaret

'When I first saw her I thought she looked pretty good.'

After treatment at Mareeba, Deny was sent to the Toowoomba army hospital. There an attractive dark-haired Red Cross officer caught his attention. 'When I first saw her I thought she looked pretty good.'

The officer, Margaret Cadell, three years younger than Deny, was intrigued by this quiet, slow-speaking man with keen blue eyes and boyish good looks. He was so different from most soldiers: while they played poker, he was engrossed in painting birds. She was an occupational therapist, but Deny was not interested in the crafts she taught. His birds were all-absorbing.

After two months, 'just when things were getting interesting', Margaret was sent to Darwin. Deny had fallen in love. For Margaret, though, he was just one of many men needing her compassion and kindness.

Margaret Ann Cadell's background and upbringing were very different from Deny's. She came from a well-established family with a station of over 10,000 hectares at Deepwater, near Tenterfield in northern New South Wales. Born on 2 March 1912, she was the first child and only daughter of Donald and Fanny Cadell, whose families were extended yet close-knit.

Donald was station manager. Governesses and ponies were part of Margaret's childhood. Fanny, who was assertive, did not get on with her mother-in-law. Perhaps family friction exacerbated the depression Donald felt because of poor seasons and bad prices. Ten years after his marriage, a combination of reasons brought forty-seven-year-old Donald Cadell to breaking point. There appears little doubt he took his own life, a tragedy for Margaret aged nine.

From the time Margaret was twelve, a wealthy aunt paid her fees at Abbotsleigh, an exclusive Sydney girls' school. She found boarding quite an ordeal and had an undistinguished school career. Overshadowed by her mother, she was shy. But she made a lifelong friend in Nan Holmes, whose father gave Margaret her start.

After finishing school, Margaret wanted to attend art classes, so her mother moved to Sydney. They settled in a North Shore suburb in a house with a court, for tennis was Margaret's favourite game. Mr Holmes encouraged Margaret to use her artistic talent designing textiles and, through introductions he arranged, she began receiving commissions. When her mother developed cancer, Margaret cared for her. At the outbreak of war she went to work for the Postmaster General's Department drafting plans for an underground telephone network for Sydney.

Margaret's brother John, an RAAF pilot, was posted missing, presumed dead, in the Middle East in 1942. After her grieving mother died, Margaret decided to become involved in helping other servicemen. She joined the Red Cross and was sent to Greenslopes Army Hospital in Brisbane in 1943.

She was moved to Toowoomba, where, among patients in the orthopaedic ward she came across TX2261, a Tasmanian sapper from 2/9 Field Company, painting birds while waiting for his fractured tibia to mend. Just before she was transferred to Darwin, TX2261 made his way to the Red Cross hut and, daringly optimistic, asked her to correspond. Then on her final visit to his ward, he gave her a self-addressed envelope.

The sweet-faced Red Cross officer with the shy smile had been asked by other soldiers for her address, and saw responding to their letters as an extension of her professional caring.

For Deny, however, it was more serious. Isolated for so much of his life, he had few opportunities to meet a possible partner. He had begun to doubt he would ever find a wife and enjoy the sort of family life his parents had created. Margaret Cadell was the woman of his dreams. He determined to win her interest, and began his long and persistent courtship.

In early June, almost five years since enlisting, he was transferred to Tasmania, and after a bout of mumps, was demobilised at Brighton Camp on 15 October 1945. He had served 1958 days, including 794 overseas; and his Savings Bank account was credited with his gratuity of £281/2/11.

Months in hospital gave Deny time to consider the future. Having seen something of cities and various parts of Australia and the world, he had firmly resolved that the lifestyle he already knew at Port Davey was what he wanted. There was challenge day by day—problems to engage his mind and to solve; and purposeful outdoor physical work to which he had always been accustomed. He would make his own decisions, choose his own times, work to his own pace, step out with his own stride. With knowledge gained and experience acquired in the army, he would change the ways of working the mine. He would reduce the manual labour, make it more efficient with the aid of machinery.

He would watch the weather, the clouds and the stars; listen to the winds and the frogs; tend his garden and observe his beloved birds, marvelling still at their migrations. He would await the seasons and look on the wildflowers in all their richness of varieties and colours throughout the year, especially rejoicing in spring's beauty; and he would burn off the bush and button grass as the Aborigines had done for centuries, to ensure regeneration of smaller, rarer species.

He would build a home to withstand the onslaught of the wildest storms, a home where he could bring his bride, which one day would know the sound of children. But first he had to persuade her to come to this Eden. So with war and all that he had learnt from it behind him, Deny took up his pen and paintbrush in a new campaign—to woo Margaret Cadell.

Winsome also returned to Melaleuca. Fortunately for Deny, Clyde Clayton was interested in this independent and spirited woman, so different from town girls. Since boyhood Clyde had come to Port Davey with his stepfather Sid Dale. So the Kings' camp on Moth Creek at Melaleuca Lagoon became a port of call.

Deny entrusted Clyde with the letters he wrote so assiduously to Margaret, describing life in the South-West in engaging detail, in his attempt to arouse her interest. Clyde and his boat *Arlie D* carried her longed-for and treasured replies.

Deny was delighted to receive his self-addressed envelope, more than nine months after he had last seen Margaret. It had followed him from Toowoomba to Tasmania, from hospital to Brighton Camp, and finally to Port Davey. It was only a single sheet of Red Cross paper, dated 6 October 1945, with no salutation:

> As I promised, this is the note in your envelope! I expect it will take weeks to catch up with you, but anyway, I've sent it along. My best wishes for happiness in the new kind of life—and hope your leg is quite all right by now—Margaret A. Cadell.

In the same mail in another envelope came six more pages, acknowledging letters he had already sent, thus feeding Deny's hopes:

> Dear Mr King—
> I was so glad to receive your letters—it was good of you to write as I had promised to write first and tell all about my impressions of this strange North—and also about the birds here. It's good to know that your discharge is on the way—you will notice that I began this letter with your

civilian title instead of 'Sapper'—as I guess you will be out of the old army now.

Deny was pleased she took the trouble to fill one page describing birds she had seen. His opinion soared higher on reading, 'I have been offered lots of parrots by patients, but always refuse, as I hate birds in cages, would so much rather watch them flying about in the world.' Her comment 'I used to always look up birds in that bird book', also pleased him.

He watched eagerly for the smoke signal announcing a boat at Cox's, or the sight of a mast above the bush along Melaleuca Inlet, before her next letter, written almost seven months later, arrived. Again it was friendly but formal. He was amused that Margaret was boarding in Sydney with a Mrs Wren. He adorned all his letters, even the envelopes, with little pen and ink bird drawings and often drew wrens, frequent visitors to Melaleuca garden and house.

> Thank you very much for your letter written in February— it chased me down from the Territory thro' parts of Queensland finally to Sydney. I received it three weeks ago and have been waiting for my Easter holidays to answer. Thank you, too, for your letter and Christmas card you painted, and the photo you enclosed in your last letter. You must live in a very beautiful place. It must be so peaceful and tranquil, and for this I envy you greatly. Sydney is the exact reverse. It is crowded and hot and dirty.

Margaret had begun a two-year university course and said 'with luck, and a lot of hard work' she hoped to get a diploma in social science.

She used the orchids Deny had sent as bookmarks, remarking encouragingly, 'I don't wonder you feel you want to spend hours painting them, they are very lovely. I do hope you paint birds sometimes, because you do them very well.'

It was no whirlwind courtship, depending as it did on the erratic visits of boats, in turn dependent on the vagaries of fishing seasons and the notorious South-West weather. The platonic correspondence continued, spasmodically on Margaret's part, far more enthusiastically on Deny's. Deny lived for her letters. Margaret's life, however, was already full with study and friends, so replying to letters was often neglected.

Deny often described music and other wireless programs, as well as the weather, the mine and his plans for it, Win and his father, the garden and of course, his constant joy, the birds. Letter by letter he tried to build a picture of the place he loved above all others, and his chosen lifestyle. With considerable self-control, he refrained from mentioning his cherished hope that one day she would share it.

Margaret's third letter, more than five months later, started promisingly:

> Dear Denison,
> Thank you for your letter. As you see, I use your Christian name, as you do not like Mr. You are quite right in saying all this trouble and strife in the cities is so depressing. Sydney is such a horrible place now. I hate reading papers and listening to the news. The war does not seem over, does it?

When he read, 'Shall look forward to seeing your photos. You are really so lucky to live right away from the turmoil of the cities. Don't ever be persuaded to leave it for the "civilization" of the city. I am sure you would hate it.' Deny dared to hope the seeds he was carefully sowing were beginning to sprout.

Although she still signed off, 'Sincerely, Margaret A. Cadell', Deny took up pen, paintbrush and camera with fresh-kindled anticipation, for his next subtle assault on her heart and mind. She seemed responsive to his landscape and its remoteness apparently appealed.

A year and a day since her first letter, her fourth, again from Sydney where she still studied, brought smiles to Deny. The arrival of his second batch of photos coincided with her chance reading of *Walkabout*'s January 1945 issue. It featured an article about South-West Tasmania, mentioning Charlie King, and was illustrated with photos, which she compared closely with Deny's. Her interest in things Tasmanian was growing, as she mentioned noticing the division of Denison in election results, wondering if his name was connected.

There was even more encouragement. Deny had asked if she had considered visiting Tasmania. Margaret replied that a cousin had suggested she do her practical course work in Hobart over the summer holidays. She had already applied and was waiting for acceptance from the hospital or Red Cross.

She sent Deny her cousin Elsie Campbell's Hobart address, and wrote:

> Perhaps if you or your sister should happen to make the trip to Hobart between 10th Dec. to the end of Feb. you might like to look me up. We could drink a cup of tea together and I could hear about your Port Davey, instead of just reading about it.

She also included 'rather an awful snap of myself'. But it was the postscript, crowded into the bottom-right corner, that lifted Deny's spirit even more. 'P.S. As I use your Christian name—won't you use mine?'

CHAPTER 12

A protracted courtship

'Too wet. Don't come.'

Deny was elated when Margaret's postcard arrived wishing him season's greetings and success for 1947, because she confirmed her Hobart dates and gave her address. He immediately sent a hasty note on the returning *Arlie D*, with a painting of the yellow-throated honeyeater, regular visitor to his sugar bowl.

Margaret replied in mid-January thanking him for the painting, and mentioned an article about him she had found in *The Tasmanian Tramp*. She had enjoyed exploring parts of Tasmania and Deny's heart lifted when she declared, 'I hate the thought of returning to city life.' Although the Red Cross position had not eventuated, she was helping Elsie with National Fitness Council children's camps and said she had found out how to return to Hobart if Deny came while she was away.

By the time he received this promising letter Deny assumed she had already left for Sydney as planned and was intensely disappointed to read another letter written two months later saying she had stayed on, because Red Cross had finally offered six weeks' work needed for her course. But by then the opportunity to meet was long past.

Margaret did not know whether she even wanted to meet her unusual correspondent. Friends with whom Elsie stayed, Elaine and Dorothy Pearce, who also became Margaret's friends, remembered her uncertainty:

One day she said, 'Do you know of Deny King at Port Davey?' And we said, 'Oh yes, everyone knows of Deny King. But we haven't met him. How do you know him?' So she told us how they had met. We thought this was very romantic and said, 'Oh, you must see him. You must let him know you're here.' And she said, 'Oh no, no, I can't even remember which one he was. There were so many of those soldier boys and several still keep in touch.' We pushed her, but she didn't.

Deny, frustrated at missing her, decided to go to Sydney. Margaret panicked when he announced his intention. She sent a telegram: 'Too wet. Don't come.' It was a ludicrous excuse to try to deter a man living in one of the wettest parts of Australia! However, Deny took the hint, bided his time, and continued courting from afar.

Margaret's relief was obvious. 'I am glad you did not come to Sydney because you would have hated it. Things are far too expensive here.' She added illogically, 'Wait for a few years and I am sure you would find all sorts of interesting things.'

Deny persevered so diligently trying to hold her interest, that she wrote two months later, 'Have at least six letters from you waiting to be answered.' He smiled at her discomfited admission:

> Deny, I was so surprised to learn you are not the youngster I had supposed. I think I may often have written in an 'elderly aunt' strain, as I imagined you to be at least ten years my junior, and I find you are older than I am!

While on a trip to Hobart with tin, Deny called on Elsie, in search of news. She spoke of this meeting:

> To my shame, I was not impressed. He rolled in, in this funny way he had of walking, and talked with an Australian drawl. Marg was attractive, she always dressed very carefully, she was a real artist, keen on music and theatre. And

> I didn't think they'd have a thing in common! How wrong
> I was!

Deny pursued his scheme to induce Margaret to visit, by sending boxes of wildflowers. They were dead by the time she arrived back from a Christmas visit to relatives in Brisbane. Her acknowledgment, however, sparked hope again. 'I was disappointed but perhaps I shall see them growing some day.' Margaret described helping a friend with her new baby, and hinted she liked children, preferring domesticity to sitting in hot noisy offices. Hope grew when he read her declaration: 'Some day I shall be sensible, and go bush and stay there.'

Her next letter in March 1948 announced that, with her studies finished, she was going to Brisbane for a year as a Red Cross social worker. The comment that she looked forward to working with ex-servicemen disquieted Deny. His only comfort was that she gave him the society's address. He began at once to plan a visit.

He waited six months before hearing from her again. It was the end of June before she wrote, and Deny did not receive the letter until September. Referring to 'that holiday on the mainland you sometimes mention', she commented discouragingly, 'Brisbane is so far, isn't it?' Then finally she admitted, 'I don't really remember what you look like. We may not recognise one another.'

Several letters followed in quick succession, alternately raising and lowering Deny's hopes. In July Margaret wrote about the tent she had just bought for camping weekends with friends, admitting she was inexpert at pitching it, but reiterating how she loved outdoor life. The following page dealt the dreaded blow. She had booked her passage to England for February, and planned to stay away at least three years.

Two weeks later a fortuitous meeting with an old friend rekindled her interest in Tasmania, and again refuelled Deny's hopes. This friend mentioned she had been to Tasmania and visited Port Davey, where she met the King family. Her enthusiasm for the scenery, birds and Deny's house caught Margaret's imagination.

Describing another camping trip, she remarked, 'You say you may be coming to the mainland later. If you get as far as Brisbane, perhaps you would like to join one of our expeditions. It is so good to light a fire, boil a billy and yarn.'

Deny's planning went into top gear.

On his next trip to Hobart, he went to see Elsie as usual for news of Margaret. Over two years Elsie had revised her first hasty impression and each time she met Deny she realised 'there was a great deal more character to this man than first suspected'. He told her that, not wishing to be put off with another last-minute telegram, he planned to arrive unannounced in Brisbane.

He booked his flight for December, but then could not refrain from telling Margaret. This time she did not prevaricate but sent a list of bed and breakfast accommodation, inviting him to take evening meals at her flat. Deny set off from Port Davey with high hopes.

A camping trip to Bribie Island, with Margaret's tent pitched expertly for once, snug in the bush behind the beach, gave Deny the opportunity he had waited for so patiently for three years. As they sat in the dunes overlooking the moonlit ocean, Deny asked Margaret to marry him.

Margaret was undecided. At the age of thirty-six, marriage was no longer an expectation nor a particular desire. She had many friends and interests. Her plans to travel were made. Also, after two solid years of study, she was keen to develop her chosen career, and to acquire almoner qualifications in Britain, where she had arranged to work in a major hospital.

She wavered.

Deny, in his wisdom, did not push for an immediate answer. Instead, he suggested coming to Port Davey for 'a holiday'. He was concerned she was so 'run down' from her 'melancholy' work in a poky, stuffy, windowless office. If she came to stay for a few weeks, she could see what it was like, and find out if she wanted to accept his proposal.

Margaret agreed. Deny was ecstatic. He flew to Tasmania, busily planning the long-hoped-for visit early in 1949. They had agreed that *if* she decided to marry him, Margaret should still go abroad, but only for three months' sightseeing before returning for their wedding.

In his first letter after returning he made a comment which appeared regularly thereafter: 'The heart aches are pretty bad.' In his second, written aboard *Arlie D*, Deny described arrangements for her to stay in Hobart with family friends, who had a cakeshop where Win had once worked, giving their address, phone number, tram route, stop number and '4 penny ticket'.

He was envisaging every step of her way. His detailed description of what she would see as she stepped off the tram, opened the small wire gate and walked up the path with handrail, is typical of his observant memory and sense of topography. But with delicious anticipation, he teased that when she reached the glass door and knocked, 'I will leave the rest to you.'

A comment, 'Stop rolling, *Arlie D*' followed, before he described a concert by the Hobart Highland Pipe Band he and Win attended. Keen to find every scrap of information about his beloved's family background, he had also found a book on Scottish clans in the state library. Margaret could hardly have failed to be touched by her suitor's eagerness and initiative, and his declaration, 'Dearest I feel I could never be happy without you now.'

His assurance that 'Win will be aboard *Arlie D* to look after you' came from the heart. As ever he relied on his sister's co-operation. Win, however, always Deny's closest companion and confidante, was probably dismayed when he set his heart on this woman from such a different background. She might secretly have disapproved of his choice of someone without living skills for an isolated environment, and may well have resented the prospect of being supplanted in the house she had helped build and the home she had helped create for her father and brother.

As Deny's pursuit of Margaret continued so resolutely, Win had realised it was time to move out and married Clyde in November 1948. After trying unsuccessfully to buy land at Recherche, they decided to live on *Arlie D*, until they could build at Port Davey.

Clyde had the mail contract, and joked he was the only man paid to carry his own. 'We'd get five shillings a trip. Oh, big fee, them days!' Clyde collected Deny's mailbag from Bellerive Post Office, and loaded supplies which had been delivered to the wharf.

Every page of Deny's third post-Brisbane letter, written the day after Christmas, was decorated with pen sketches of the coastline, and details of Melaleuca, including a plate of strawberries with the endearing note, 'for your dinner, don't delay'.

In the past Margaret had chided him if he dared write anything not 'sensible'. Now that his love was revealed and he was free to declare it, he unburdened his heart:

> The holiday has done such a lot of good that I really don't feel the same bloke that went away, when everything was a trouble. Now there does seem to be something worthwhile to live and work for and look to the future, instead of just emptiness. That blankness is now filled with some very dear lassy.

Gently teasing, he added, 'Suppose you will not class that bit as sensible writing.'

> Win and Clyde are as happy as can be. Clyde says he does not know why he was single so long. Win told me today she would not miss this happiness for anything. It is good to see

people happy. It is catching and makes everyone else very glad…I hope you don't mind my appearing overconfident that you are coming this way instead of going that way.

Love Love Love XXX Yours ever Deny

Describing a trip to Settlement Point and Kelly Basin in Port Davey, he told of an extraordinary experience camping near middens and an ancient cave. Waking as dawn began to light the sky, he saw a most unusual dark cloud, 'like a heavy man holding a shield before him. I thought it must be a ghost of an Aboriginal who had lived in the shelter of the cave. This seems to have been a very popular place for the blacks in bygone days.' It made a deep impression, and his shaded pencil drawing occupied the centre of the page.

Margaret's responses, however, were still restrained. In her first she mentioned cleaning her flat and finding reminders of him: a pair of boots, a piece of paper on which he had sketched her nose, and photos. As to his careful directions she simply said, 'Perhaps I will follow them one day.'

Her second was even more non-committal. She hoped to know within a week her sailing date for England. Inquiring about Clyde's schedule, she declared evasively, 'You probably know my aversion to making definite plans. So the trip to Port Davey is just a suggestion in case we don't leave until mid-March.' But she did add, 'It would be good to see you again.'

Deny's patience and optimism were sorely tested by Margaret's vacillation. After a last round of parties and visits to friends, theatre and the races, she left her Brisbane job and returned to Sydney for more lunches at her club and smart restaurants. She went to see the Archibald and Wynne exhibitions, the bank and her lawyer to make a new will. She shopped for her trip, buying materials for 'frocks for voyage and evening blouses', which entailed visits to the dressmaker; and finalised travel arrangements.

Win had loyally played her part offering a passage on *Arlie D.* So after receiving another letter from Deny early in February Margaret booked her Hobart flight at last. She even had sprigs put on her old army boots for the walk from New Harbour to Melaleuca. Yet she remained unsettled. 'Deny, I'm not at all sure *what* I want to do this year. And for me that is very unusual—so see what you have done!' She suggested he should have some mending for her to do 'in case it's wet and blizzardy or I am a complete dud at the mine'. In closing she confessed, 'Have been thinking about you such a lot—far too much for my peace of mind. I do hope old Fate is a sport and lets us see each other soon.'

This letter, like others, was impossibly slow reaching Melaleuca, and without definite knowledge of Margaret's plans, Deny left nothing to chance. He was determined to be in Hobart if and when she arrived. *Arlie D* was not due to return for some weeks. Without hesitation Deny took the only option—to walk out.

The day he was leaving Melaleuca, Margaret was shopping, lunching, dining and going to the theatre in Sydney. Deny put his suit in his pack, filled a homemade billy can with beans and bacon, slung it around his neck, and set off for Cockle Creek at 7 a.m. in the cold, wind and rain. In an epic feat which became another Deny King legend, he covered the distance in two and a half days, walking some eighty kilometres in thirty hours. It was a marathon journey; a good walker now sometimes does it on the track in four days— usually it requires five.

With every step driven by his longing for Margaret, he strode across swampy button-grass expanses, along wild deserted beaches, bashed through thick bush with bauera tangling his feet, cutting-grass scratching his face and hands, branches tearing at his clothes. He brushed off leeches, swatted March flies, squashed mosquitoes. The first night he camped on the Louisa Plains, before tackling the gruelling Ironbound Range.

The weather had closed in, so in swirling mist and dank cloud he scrambled up the formidably steep ridges, and dropped down through forested gullies onto the next scrub-bound plain. He lunched at Lousy Bay, waded Deadman's Creek and others, coming at last to the New River.

This was no wading matter. He had to swim. Leaving his pack, he crossed with two milk tin 'life rafts', containing matches, kerosene and other emergency supplies. He rowed back in the dinghy kept on the other side and collected the pack. Then, as there was no moon, he camped briefly in the bush at windswept Prion Bay, to wait out the blowing raining darkness.

Setting off again at first light, eating beans as he walked, he headed across the South Cape Range, up through the rainforest slopes and down through the deep tangled gullies, watching from the ridges for *Arlie D* and the weather, to try to foretell her movements. Arriving at last at Recherche he saw her in the bay, preparing to leave. Deny warned Clyde of the high seas, so they returned to Dover, where Deny caught the bus to Hobart.

Margaret recorded in her diary on Thursday 10 February, 'Phone call from Denis to say that he had walked through. Surprising!' Obviously there was much more to her suitor from the South-West than she had even begun to realise, or could at this stage understand. On Friday she collected her ticket. On Saturday she had a fitting for her evening blouses, then packed for Port Davey with very different clothes, writing, 'Turned in about 11 p.m., wondering what the next few days would bring.'

Deny was waiting for her on Sunday. Her first impression was his transparent joy as he greeted her and, in the intensity of the embrace he had so long yearned to give her, she felt the strength of the man who held her. At last she was entering his world.

Deny took her to friends, and the following day they caught three buses to reach Recherche, where *Arlie D* waited. There Margaret met Win and Clyde, who had played such a vital part in Deny's courtship. It was a meeting of opposites: Red Cross officer with her university diploma, and munitions worker; daughter of the squattocracy, and fisherman who had been at sea since boyhood. But Win and Clyde could only be genuine in their hospitality. Their open-hearted, unaffected kindness touched Margaret.

Margaret began to see Deny in a new light, as she observed him managing the dinghy, lifting heavy stores and stowing them, taking *Arlie D*'s helm, discussing weather and conditions so knowledgeably. Her introduction to the South-West was inauspicious. She had never been on such a boat and she was seasick. Adding to her discomfort she was too inhibited to ask about toilet arrangements, and perhaps Win was too embarrassed to explain it was a bucket below deck.

Waiting out the weather at Dover, the tempo was completely different from the hectic rush of Brisbane and Sydney, and the chill in sharp contrast to the enervating heat. Then, six days after Margaret had left Sydney, *Arlie D* sailed again. Sitting aft with Deny, Margaret watched the unknown coastline, felt the cold wind and sea spray stinging her face, and perhaps shivered within, wondering what was ahead and how she would cope.

A dawn start from Recherche with 'a fairly big swell' presented no problems as they stood out from jagged rocky South East Cape, along the rugged coastline past the dramatic perpendicular cliffs of South Cape, the lonely wind-shriven islands of the Maatsuyker Group and the solid bulk of Cox Bluff, so familiar to Deny. Pointing out Smoke Signal Hill, he was teased about how he always kept it under hopeful surveillance. Now, for once in almost four years, when Clyde handed over the mailbag it would fail to thrill Deny with anticipation.

As *Arlie D* rounded the stegosaurus spine of South West Cape, where winds come down the coast and a big swell rolls in from the west or south-west, Margaret again succumbed to the ignominy of seasickness and felt its full misery. So the prospect of the nauseous return journey cast a shadow over the romantic possibilities of her stay. Indeed, it predisposed her unfavourably towards living in such isolation, dependent on boats for contact with the outside world.

Yet, when *Arlie D* reached the aptly named Breaksea Islands and entered the sheltered waters of Port Davey, the discomfort of the voyage paled into insignificance. Margaret began to respond to the majesty of the great waterway and its encircling mountains bathed in the calm light of a wondrous sun-bright afternoon.

Deny silently rejoiced at Margaret's amazement as she looked on the unspoiled beauty of his remote kingdom. He followed her gaze as *Arlie D* entered Bathurst Channel and her eyes scanned the steep bush-clad shorelines, the Cézanne-green veins of dense scrub flowing down the gullies, spilling out over the sheltered sides of the hills and mountains. On windward inclines, bare slopes gleamed richly with button grass, and white quartzite shone like snow on rocky ridges.

As the clouds clustered and tumbled, *Arlie D* passed through the dark eddies of the Bathurst Narrows, flanked by the lofty pyramid of Mount Rugby to the north and the more homely Mount Beattie to the south. Margaret was enveloped in a silence which sang to her soul. She felt she had come to the end of the world.

As Bathurst Harbour opened before her, Deny thrilled as Margaret's eyes swept over the mysterious sheen of the great cloth of Matisse-blue waters, as they skimmed the pristine crescent beaches nestling biscuit-gold in bush-green coves. He watched as she marvelled at range on Heysen-purple range melting into lilac on the horizon. He knew then what he had always dared to hope. The spell of his chosen country was falling over his beloved.

Arlie D turned into a wide secluded bay, studded with a string of islands crowned with rainforest, the Celery Tops, and headed towards the winding bush-bordered Melaleuca Inlet. The rapid wingbeats of a brace of black duck, the rich flash of a chestnut teal, the arrowhead ripple of an invisible water rat, the bone-white roots of melaleuca twisted like ancient serpentine skeletons through the peaty-black mudbanks, the swift swoop of swallows skimming the tannin-stained water—the artist in Margaret absorbed every detail so prodigally offered by nature to all her senses.

Reaching a point where the creek was no longer navigable, Clyde moored *Arlie D* deftly to a couple of gum trees. Deny loaded the dinghy for the last stage of the journey, across the brown waters of reed-rimmed Melaleuca Lagoon where black swans floated and fed. Fifteen minutes of rowing to another arcane inlet where meandering Moth Creek slipped quietly into the lagoon and Deny said, 'We're nearly home.'

Home?

When Margaret caught her first glimpse of the house designed and built by Deny, incongruous on the bank like a discarded tin can on the edge of the empty expanse of fired plain, she *knew* she had come to the end of the world. But she had not travelled so far to be daunted. Besides, there was something about Deny here in his own surroundings which stirred her in a new way.

On his own territory, at ease in his environment, at one with its creatures, in harmony with its grand silences and its great storms, Deny was quite unlike any other man she had ever met. His gentle calm and his quiet humour, his sturdy good looks and inner self-sufficiency combined to create an aura, an attraction which she was not the first, or last, woman to feel. But Deny had not even noticed the others.

The strange little house was spartan but not primitive; modest but imaginative; basic but with unmistakable ambience. It *was* home. Home to two remarkable men, who were at home only in remote and challenging places. Melaleuca was both. After years living in tents and huts buffeted by the unleashed elements of the

Roaring Forties, Deny had devised this house to withstand gales and disperse deluges, and had begun building it in November 1945. He had adapted the idea of the Nissen hut, basic accommodation during army years, recognising its virtues and its capacity to survive the fiercest weather.

In 1946 sheets of corrugated iron were acquired for the outer cladding, rolled to the required curve at a Hobart metal-shop and transported by Clyde. Glass and cement were also brought in, as was sawn timber, given Deny by the McCullum brothers at Ellendale. Much of the timber Deny sought in the bush around Bathurst Harbour, cut and brought back to Melaleuca, and then hewed by hand into the required dimensions.

Transporting local timber was possible because Charlie had bought a boat and barge. *Ark Royal*, taken over from the New Harbour Company, was solidly constructed from oregon. It was towed by rowing a clinker-built dinghy, *Nifty*, which Charlie acquired secondhand for £8 in Hobart.

Alternating work on the house, at the mine, in the garden, wood-getting and all the other tasks necessary for his self-reliant lifestyle, Deny had put many months of thought, effort and meticulous attention into building the snug dwelling. Over three and a half metres high, six metres wide and nine metres in length, it consisted of living room, kitchen and pantry, bathroom and three single bedrooms. One of the most southerly houses in Tasmania, it was surely the most unusual.

Margaret, stiff and salty from the long journey, and utterly exhausted by the turmoil of her emotions, was delighted to find the luxury of a hot bath in soft, pure rainwater. As she relaxed, she had no idea what labour and love it involved. Deny had to carry the water inside and heat it in kerosene tins over the fire—a fire for which every single piece of wood had to be cut and rowed eleven kilometres by dinghy.

On retiring to her sleeping-bag, Margaret discovered more obvious evidence of Deny's thoughtfulness. He had warmed it with a hot brick carefully wrapped in newspaper. The cosy bed signalled his welcome.

CHAPTER 13

Patience rewarded

"Spect so.'

On Monday 21 February 1949, when Charlie's collie Nufty came in to greet her, Margaret awoke to a new world. Lying in the small room, formerly Win's, she looked around in confusion. Its wooden walls only reached the curtained doorway, and above, the lofty plywood ceiling with its graceful trussed beams of sawn eucalypt reinforced with hand-split celery-top pine followed the curved roofline. The window overlooked the bank where the house perched above Moth Creek, glittering in the morning sun.

She smelled the distinctive scent of peat, which had kept the fire in overnight, heard the kettle purring and the cheerful clatter of teapot, mugs and spoons in the adjoining kitchen. Deny entered, carrying in his big work-worn hands a mug of tea made just how she liked it, and smiled at her in a way that had already penetrated her defences more than she would admit.

Always quick to notice other people's feelings, Deny sensed her uncertainty, her need for comfort and reassurance. Golden light flowed into the living room across the front of the house, and he seated her at the table where a patch of sun would warm her while he served porridge.

Margaret's eyes roved everywhere, absorbing details she had been too tired to notice the previous night: the thoughtfully sited chimney in the centre of the living area, with the sitting-room open fireplace backing onto the kitchen cooking range with its big black kettle; the mantelpiece of hand-hewn celery-top pine, varnished bark still intact; the handsome kerosene ceiling lamp; a low shelf piled with books beside an armchair crafted from bush timber.

Everything was functional, practical. Everything spoke of thought and care. Even though ill at ease, tense with her own unknowing, Margaret began to feel a little at ease with the creator of this place, this man who had pursued her so persistently for years against such odds. This man who had persuaded her, almost in spite of herself, to come to this wild remoteness. This man so different from every other she knew.

Her designer's eye delighted in all the ingenious utensils and implements Deny had fashioned: spoons and stirrers carved and whittled from wood; dustpans cut from kerosene tins, with well-worn wooden handles; pokers, toasting forks, doorstops, bookends, brackets; shelves and niches contrived in challenging curves; and furniture perfectly proportioned to the space. In the corner was a solid all-purpose table, richly stained with a brew of celery-top pine bark, flanked by built-in bench and rectangular stools.

Stepping outside the cocoon of this dwelling she was struck by the immensity of the landscape she had glimpsed through the windows—the tea-brown waters of brush-fringed Moth Creek curving away into the scrubby plain and foothills at the base of massive Mount Counsel, which dominated the south-eastern horizon.

Space and distance, weather and sky, mountains, horizons were beyond anything she had ever experienced, even in her country childhood. Empty of anyone except Deny and his father, Win and Clyde who came and went on *Arlie D*, and Norwegian mine helper Freddie Edvardsen. Empty of people, but not of opportunity.

Deny was offering a unique opportunity to create a new life in this awesome space. His genuine devotion and intense love were hers. Could she return them? Did she have the courage to accept the challenge of making her home, raising a family, so far from all the amenities and facilities she had always taken for granted? In this world where weather and tide counted more than clock and calendar? Margaret, already stirred more deeply than she realised by Deny and his kingdom, was plunged into a maelstrom of emotions.

Her first venture into the landscape was to see the Southern Cross engines, Deny's pride and joy. Margaret, however, was more interested in the profusion of flowers on the way: graceful nodding heads of button grass, delicate pink and white bauera, fairy aprons of purple bladderwort floating on wiry stems above boggy puddles. At the mine she was touched to see pansies, carefully planted so that their smiling yellow and black faces would cheer the eyes and thoughts of whoever was standing hour on weary hour, working the big nozzle sluicing tin. Clearly this was no ordinary miner. Clearly he was no ordinary man.

When Deny described how he had obtained the four-cylinder Southern Cross, how it had reached Melaleuca and been installed, Margaret gained yet another insight into the determination of this unusual man. After his discharge Deny had hunted for a suitable engine with which to start fulfilling his dream of mechanising the mine. He found it at a Hobart shipyard, and it gave its name to Southern Cross Bay in The Narrows, where Clyde anchored the last night of the delivery voyage.

Unloading the tonne-and-a-half engine had needed all Deny's and Clyde's ingenuity. They tied *Arlie D* to the bank, then erected a pair of sturdy bush timber shearlegs, leaning out over the boat. These were supported by wire rope from a powerful hand-operated forest devil winch attached to a dead man anchor, a log fixed horizontally in the ground. An endless chain suspended from the head of the shearlegs lifted the engine, and *Arlie D* was manoeuvred from under it, 'pretty quick in case it fell'.

The sturdy *Ark Royal* was brought in and the engine gently lowered. Charlie's latest acquisition, the five metre, one horsepower

Blue Boat towed her across the lagoon and up Moth Creek to the canal abutting the mine. Here shearlegs were used again to lift the engine, which was then levered and skidded along planks to a concrete bed. The engine drove a pump supplying high pressure water for sluicing, and a sawmill.

A month later Deny bought a one-tonne two-cylinder engine. Transported, unloaded and manoeuvred into position by the same process, it drove the gravel pump.

Margaret spent two cold windy days indoors with Win. Then she watched with some misgivings as Clyde seized the chance of a break in the weather and *Arlie D* left on its primary business, crayfishing. Charlie, kind and courtly even in his deafness, entertained her while Deny was at work, showing her his gardens.

He made them in any suitable patches of soil and took pride in his produce. As well as staple potatoes, swedes and cabbages, Charlie grew excellent lettuces, celery, carrots, beans and peas. He had also planted an orchard with apples, pears, plums, cherries, a quince and an apricot. He grew small fruits too, red and black currants, raspberries, loganberries, youngberries, strawberries and gooseberries, and a flourishing rhubarb patch.

On the fifth day Margaret recorded her 'first walk on button grass in boots' to Kings Knob, a solitary hillock in the flat vastness beyond the mine. There she gained a view of the route of the thirteen-kilometre walk to Cox Bight which they took next day. She enjoyed her expedition, but found it difficult, with bog and big tussocks to stride over. They camped at Point Eric, where she slept in a tent Freddie lent her. Morning broke clear and bright, and towering turquoise rollers swept in foam-frosted bands across the wide bay.

Deny wanted to show her the old mine. For Margaret it was rough going through burnt-off bush and button grass, jumping creeks which snaked secretly through thick tangled bauera, coral fern and melaleuca. The amazing excavations and rock ramparts, dramatic proof of Deny's skills and stamina, were another revelation for Margaret and when she saw the old campsite the house at Melaleuca suddenly seemed a palace.

Her first experience of the difficulties of crayfishing off the jagged rocks, and her first encounter with crayfish, 'huge fierce things', opened her eyes more respectfully towards Win and Clyde. It helped her recognise their adroitness and toughness, in handling not only a boat, but also these creatures she had only before seen on plates in chic restaurants.

Traversing the ridge past the workings, they climbed the low hill above Point Eric, so she could enjoy the commanding view of the bay with its silhouette of islands. Margaret, pausing to catch breath, sensed, like Deny, the presence of Aboriginal inhabitants and their spirit ancestors, as she rested by majestic grey granite tors. Some intact, some fantastically frost-split, they stood like Stonehenge sarsens, guardians of the great plain spreading to the north. A pair of white-breasted sea eagles patrolled, floating high over the sharp peak of Foley's Pimple, and down on the rippled waters of rushy Freney Lagoon swans were feeding.

As they skirted the base of Mount Counsel, the insistent sound of the sea receded, and the quiet and sense of solitude, so precious to Deny, enveloped them. The vast silence was broken by the swishing of button grass against legs and the gurgling of glutinous peaty black mud in boggy patches along the narrow foot pad. Deny pointed out the distinctive tracks of wallabies, wombats, quolls and ground parrots, and carefully avoided neat piles of distinctive wombat droppings on prominent tussocks and clods.

Up on the right, the scar of the water race so laboriously built by Charlie and others wound along the foothills. To the left button grass after a summer burn-off stretched black as peat, or sprang green with regrowth. Deny told Margaret how burning off had been part of Aboriginal land management to encourage new feed for game. Explorers and prospectors continued the practice to facilitate travel, as did fishermen wanting easy game for bait.

Nothing was too small or insignificant for Deny to show Margaret. A tiny white helichrysum daisy, favoured by his precious 'grass parrots', a starry bush of white baeckea, a small green grasshopper flashing red and yellow underparts, or a tiny gold and green moth fluttering among the stunted tea-tree were all worthy of his closest observation and consideration. He watched for solitary bright-green ground parrots flushed by the thud of footfall on peat, or a diminutive emu-wren perched on a tussock. He scanned the sky, reading the clouds, admiring the slow flight of black cockatoos or the silhouettes of ravens. He breathed the scent of boronia and the honeyed fragrance of the tea-tree's bridal blossom.

Thick scrub surged in green waves up the gullies and folds along Mount Counsel's bulk, and the cheerful calling of crescent honey-eaters and echoing cries of currawongs accompanied Deny and Margaret. Margaret was grateful for pauses to watch a cruising hawk or a pipit rising, and glad when they stopped at little creeks tumbling down from the slopes, to drink the golden water which rippled over the white sand through ferns. As she rested, Deny swatted March flies and dropped them on the surface for the galaxiids, tiny fish known as native trout.

Half Woody Hill, a curious conical mount thickly wooded to the south and starkly bare to the north, came into view, and beyond it the little pyramid of Pandora's Hill nestling against the slopes of the Bathurst Range. To the west Mount Brock's peak stood out from the Melaleuca Range, bronze or deep purple according to light. To the north Mount Rugby's dramatic peak and the jagged outline of the Western Arthurs rose misty blue on the horizon.

To encourage Margaret for the last creek crossing and the final stretch, Deny cheered her with the promise of a hot bath, and told her how the bath had got there. When the New Harbour Company had left, he had carried it on his head and shoulders from their camp at Melaleuca to Cox's, joking that it was a good way of keeping off the rain! Then, when he was building the house at Melaleuca, it was carried all the way back.

Several days later they went off together in *Nifty*. Rowing down Melaleuca Inlet with steady purposeful strokes, Deny turned into a small creek which looped its shining way along the foot of little knolls and hillocks. No lover could have wished for a more secluded, romantic place, overhung with ferns and flowers and bush a-twitter with tiny birds. Margaret's cryptic diary entry, 'Quite memorable enough without writing of it here!' indicates Deny's strategies were succeeding.

The next day, 2 March, her thirty-seventh birthday, saw them all setting off 'for a jaunt in *Blue Boat*'. They camped near Swan Island on the far side of Bathurst Harbour, on 'a lovely gravelly beach'. It was a birthday like no other for Margaret. She was being seduced, slowly but surely, by the wilderness and the breed of man it produced. That night through Deny's telescope they looked at the stars, so bright and near in the clear sky she longed to reach up and pluck a handful.

A wonderful dawn followed with reflections of the Arthurs and the Norolds on glassy waters, until the swans took off, running and flapping to gain their lift, their white wing beats mirrored in unison, as, necks outstretched, they headed to another cove. Then a gale sprang up. The wild South-West was showing another face.

Back at Melaleuca Margaret did some difficult thinking. There was absolutely no doubt of the integrity of Deny's love and his passion for her. However, it was not only a matter of her own feelings for him, but all the implications of life in this isolation.

She questioned her own inner resources, looking deep within

herself for self-reliance, endurance and courage. She wondered whether her own sense of identity was sufficient to allow her not only to survive but also to grow in the immensity of this unpopulated place. The size and scale of the landscape evoked a profound sense of wonder, but also induced keen awareness of the insignificance of the individual.

The description of Port Davey in the south-west corner of Tasmania had conveyed almost a sense of cosiness. Nothing was further from the reality. An eternity of ocean, an infinity of mountains, many still unnamed, endless swathes of impenetrable bush intersected by a multitude of rivers mostly also unnamed, lay between Melaleuca and the rest of the world. It *was* the end of the world.

On a day of sparkling blue skies and bright sunlight it was an artist's palette of colours, bewitchingly beautiful. But when the gales swept in from the south-west, driving the pregnant rain clouds before them, that world was reduced to gathered greys. Waves and water sulked, like tarnished silver. Mighty mountains became stark silhouettes, slopes shrouded with sheets of rain or streaked with showers. Grey upon gloomy grey, layer upon lowering layer, a world which had lost its light.

The timeless, impersonal aloofness was almost annihilating. Margaret felt threatened by the overpowering presence of this landscape. Overwhelmed, oppressed, and deeply apprehensive.

Did she dare?

On 9 March, she walked with Deny to see a lightning strike on a hill along the eastern side of Melaleuca Inlet. They sat on a nearby slope looking across the olive-green plain latticed with brown creeks which brawled down the steep gullies of the Fulton Range. They watched the wind rippling the pewter surface of Bathurst Harbour. They gazed on the wide sky's ever-changing cloudscape, wreathing and shadowing the guardians of The Narrows, majestic Mount

Rugby, and its humbler partner, Mount Beattie. When he proposed to Margaret again, Deny hoped that the power of this land, allied with his love, would bring a positive response.

But again disappointment awaited in her hesitant reply to his question, 'Will you marry me?'

Her half-hearted answer contrasted with his ardour. ''Spect so,' she said.

Deny led her to a picturesque gravelly beach where wavelets ran up in lacy frills on the gleaming white sand, and myriad tiny yellow, red and green tea-tree leaves lay like confetti. Margaret told him she would go to England as planned, before returning in October to marry him. She wrote in her diary, 'Afraid he was gravely hurt but was wonderful about it.'

Her acceptance left its mark on the landscape. From then that little hill bore her reply as its name. In King's lingo it was always 'Speckso Hill'.

CHAPTER 14

At last!

*'It does give one a strange feeling to write or say
"I am being married in November"!!'*

Deny had hoped that Margaret would feel as strongly as he did and that marriage would take precedence over any other commitment. However, although deeply disappointed at her conditional acceptance, he did not attempt to persuade her to change her plans. Instead, he encouraged them.

Margaret was rather uncomfortable. His understanding, generosity of spirit and acceptance of her decision reinforced her realisation of his unselfish love. While engendering more confusion, it also helped her incipient love.

She had another problem too, legacies from her mother and brother. She confided to Elsie, 'I don't know how on earth I'm ever going to tell him. I don't think he has money. But I feel the man should be head of the household.' The extreme isolation of Melaleuca and dependence on others for communication seriously concerned her, and here she saw a use for her money. She discussed with Deny the idea of buying their own boat, and a radio transmitter/receiver.

Meanwhile Deny continued introducing her to facets of Port Davey life. As well as explaining some of the mysteries of the mine, he initiated her into routines of Melaleuca living and household management. The practical bachelor habit of washing clothes in the bathwater did not impress her, until she realised how hard-won the firewood was for heating water. But Deny's and Charlie's skills at making bread, scones and jam gained her immediate approval.

Deny taught her the art of setting a good fire, both in hearth and stove, and how to regulate oven temperatures by the judicious use of appropriate wood. She learned to use the light, yellow wood Deny called dogwood, finely split and prized as 'morning sticks' for kindling only. The chunky short cross-sections of dense-grained manuka, in an infinite variety of amoebic shapes, were best for a hot stove.

Margaret soon realised how much time and effort went into maintaining the wood supply. The day after proposing, Deny, wishing to show more of the serene and beautiful scenery which would be hers to enjoy, took her, with Charlie, wood-getting in *Blue Boat*.

Down Melaleuca Inlet they cruised, out into the wide waters of Bathurst Harbour, to the clustered Celery Top Islands, densely wooded, rocky cliffs interspersed with slivers of beach, smooth green sedgy 'wallaby lawns', and rock pools rimmed with bubbles of golden brown foam and festooned with strings of beads of amber sea-grapes.

Deny always chose standing dead trees inland, so as not to destroy the shoreline. Margaret watched the accomplished bushmen fell selected trees with axe and saw, and carry the timber on their shoulders through tangled bush to the boat. The pleasures of a picnic on a gravelly beach could not disguise the hard work and skill necessary to replenish the wood pile.

Two days later Deny organised another excursion, through The Narrows as far as the sentinel Breaksea Islands to fish in Port Davey. It was the anniversary of her brother John's death. Deny, observant of every nuance of Margaret's moods, 'noticed and wanted to know' about her sadness and, comforted by his care, she became ever more aware of all his love could mean.

Deny derived immense pleasure too in sharing the tiny delights of nature which illuminated each day: the furry crook of an unfolding fern, the sheen of a fallen feather, a shred of silvery paperbark silken to the touch, raindrops sparkling on delicate melaleuca foliage, a kerchief of cloud, a promise of rainbow, the jewel brilliance of a damsel fly, the shimmer of gnats dancing over a pond, even the sleek coil of a sleeping tiger snake, replete with hapless frog.

He rejoiced in showing her 'birdies' he loved: tiny bobbing blue wrens, busy brown scrubwrens, inquisitive dusky robins and melodious olive whistlers, friendly yellow-throated honeyeaters, crescent honeyeaters with their chinking call, furtive, speckled ground thrushes, and favourite of all, the bright-eyed, companionable grey shrike thrushes with their rich conversational whistle.

One morning he woke her to watch the apricot sun rise over Mount Counsel, and later walked her up the bank to see it set in a gleam of gold behind the western ranges. He walked her in the enfolding dark to listen to ground parrots proclaiming their territories across the plain, and to the croaking chorus of frogs round the mine.

Almost subconsciously, as Deny gently wooed her, the truths which he had always known started becoming real to Margaret in this remote place, at once both incredibly challenging and unbelievably liberating. She became even more aware also, how the elements dominated life at Port Davey, as Win and Clyde watched the weather, awaiting their opportunity to go fishing.

Late in March, 'ready to leave', she began watching for Win and Clyde's signal. It was another week before 'the smoke went up'. After a quiet morning when Deny 'cut hair all round, excepting me', there was suddenly 'a short panic and we were on our way' to New Harbour and *Arlie D*. The ten-kilometre walk took Margaret three hours and by halfway she was very tired, although Deny carried her gear. After staying aboard overnight he took his sad farewell, heading resolutely back to work.

Arlie D put out to sea twice, but because of rough conditions turned back to sheltered New Harbour. Margaret was wretchedly seasick. On the third attempt, although 'the seas were just huge and the coastline fearsome-looking', the swell was long and Margaret did not feel ill. Bright sun and plenty to watch kept her mind off her troubles. She proudly took the helm while Win and Clyde bagged crayfish, recording 'the stink was truly awful. Win is very wonderful, all she does aboard.'

In a heart-to-heart talk, Win vouched for Deny's knowledge of the coastline and his ability as a skipper. So Margaret wrote to Deny suggesting she could put £500 or £700 towards 'our boat', tactfully saying:

> I feel you will regard marriage as a partnership and not be hurt by this suggestion.
>
> A wonderful feeling, isn't it, taking the helm to feel her turn to port or starboard at one's turn of the wheel? Sitting there, the thought of you—us—having a ship did not seem so awful. It seemed quite possible and sensible and safe. I saw her in my mind's eye—a nice strong boat, smaller than *Arlie D*, but trim and not smelly, the cabin snug and tidy.

During four busy days in Hobart Margaret broke the news of her engagement and shopped, preparing parcels to send by *Arlie D*. She booked her Sydney flight, began wedding plans, and visited the Mines Department for information about ring-making. In Sydney she revelled in breaking 'this startling news of mine', showing photos and maps, and reporting back to Deny, 'Everyone has been awfully nice about it.'

Elsie told the family she judged Deny 'to be a sterling person, absolutely sound and dependable'. When she later asked, 'What gave you the courage to marry a person like that, in the wilderness?' Margaret replied, 'I was so tired and fed-up with the superficial way that men mostly treated you. I somehow knew this was different. He was genuine.'

Two friends teased her. One said she wondered if it was the PLACE, not the man she was marrying. The other declared the MAN would be most important in such a place. Margaret replied, 'probably the place, plus the way of life, had largely made the man as nice as he is, and so different from the ordinary, mundane menfolk that frequent cities'.

Margaret was beginning to agree with Deny's favourite adage. Absence was making her heart grow fonder. She had fallen in love and signed off an April letter with more feeling than ever before, 'Wish I could curl down comfortably with my head on your left shoulder—I love you very much.'

Busy with endless shopping, visits to hairdresser, dressmaker, milliner, doctor, dentist, meals with friends, and evenings at the theatre, she tried to cram all the habits of her old lifestyle into these final weeks. She visited the Royal Show to inspect radio equipment, and became interested in the Vacola display of preserving outfits, suggesting to an aunt that one would make the perfect wedding gift.

She pursued the matter of technology for ring-making, visiting bullion merchants, suppliers of assay requisites and scientific apparatus, sending Deny information and materials: a salamander pot, crucible, tongs, chamois leather, as requested, plus mercury, copper and sal ammoniac. Exasperated, she wrote, 'If making a ring is quarter as hard as finding out how—then don't attempt it!' At most places she was greeted with raised eyebrows and the remark, 'But you don't make wedding rings, you buy them.'

She knitted him a second jumper, advised him of airmail rates to England, sent aerogrammes to use, and declared, 'Am feeling so happy and contented. Even though I have only been 7 weeks with you and those brief times in Brisbane, I feel awfully sure that all will be well. This amazes me—I mean the shortness of the time—but even so, I feel sure we'll be happy together.'

At Melaleuca Deny had taken up his pen again to pour out his heartaches and hopes to Margaret Darling. So lovelorn was he that he painstakingly examined broom, brushes and even nailbrush for Margaret's 'tresses', carefully extracting every hair for 'a nice harvest of what is more to me than the golden fleece'. He confided, 'It was so cold in beddy last night in spite of having a brick. Didn't I long for something soft and warm to cuddle up to?'

The spasmodic mail service was now even more frustrating because of Margaret's travel schedule. Deny's imagination worked overtime, trying to picture his beloved every waking hour, wherever she might be. Before she had even sailed he was counting the days until her return, writing resignedly, ''Spects by the time I get an answer you will be thinking of coming back.'

That indeed happened. Deny, wearing a jumper Margaret had knitted at Melaleuca, wrote in diary form. But opportunities to dispatch letters were rare. When Margaret left on the *Melbourne Star*, she was disappointed she had received only one letter and none awaited on board. On reaching London she was elated to find eight, addressed in his careful printing. Two more never arrived.

Acknowledging them, she wrote, 'I think of you so often and feel already I am sharing my life with you.' Admitting to several mild attacks of 'cold feet', she declared they soon went, on looking at his photo and thinking of their plans. 'As you say, it *does* give one a strange feeling to write or say, "I am being married in Nov"!!'

It was almost two months before Deny received Margaret's first letter. He was pleased to read, 'Looking for news from you for the last 4 weeks, and not having any word at all makes me realize it will be well worth the £180 for the radio transmitter, to be able to send a message or telegram. Do so hope you approve of my letter, applying for licence, £1 pa. I did so wish for your help and advice.'

He was impressed to read that 'his lassy' had begun to learn Morse Code with help from the ship's radio officer. Meanwhile Margaret sometimes wrote to Win or wired, in an effort to maintain contact.

A few days later he calculated the position of the *Melbourne Star*. He wished he knew the ship's wavelength to try to pick it up, admitting he couldn't 'help getting down in the dumps occasionally'. But in his next letter he chided himself: 'I feel so selfish to ever feel heartaches when I should be rejoicing at your going on such a tour. I should never have a melancholy moment when I know you are happy and that you will have me and that we will spend most of our lives at heart together.'

'You have taught me quite a few things', he averred. 'I don't seem to mind washing so much now, don't haggle with myself—will I or won't I wash that shirt or singlet or will it do till next time.' He took Margaret's advice to eat more meat. 'Got a couple of roos yesterday. Poor things. I feel so ashamed to hurt them and wish we could get fresh meat from other sources. Have increased my meat ration nearly 50 per cent and feel much better with much more available working power.'

He had discussed getting their own boat with Win and gave considerable thought to its details:

> A nice little wheelhouse, plenty of windows, plenty of fresh air and warmed by pipes connected with the engine. A bucket kept handy for those desirous of being seasick so they would not have to be out in the cold hanging over the rail, a thermos of coffee, hardish green cushions where you could take a nap and even change a nappy too.

The task of making Margaret's wedding ring preoccupied him, retrieving the gold from tin washing and making the mould, remembering what 'the boys in NG' had done. Building their bed happily engaged his thoughts too. 'Drew up a plan and need your advice. Thought we could have high sides with hinges to let down when making up beddy of a morning and to sit on edge. I like high sides of a cold night to keep out draughts and make it seem more cosy.'

A further source of pleasure were the books Margaret had sent. Ernestine Hill's novel about Matthew Flinders, *My Love Must Wait*, particularly appealed. 'A very touching story. I had a little sob several times. Weakling you will think me. Maybe I would have thought so too a few years ago. But now I know what love is and how their hearts must have ached through those long years and here is me thinking six months is a long time.'

'Going hard at the mine where the tin was showing black', Deny aimed to get at least two tonnes by the end of September. In May he and Charlie had stripped another big paddock, working a fortnight without a day lost. He also refurbished one of the New Harbour Company huts, papering it to make it snug and comfortable, if Win and Clyde wanted to stay ashore.

They appreciated his work when they moved in for some months during winter, while Clyde, with Win's and Deny's help, reconditioned *Arlie D*. Deny helped get the timber and build the slip, then pull the boat 'up on the skids' in Melaleuca Inlet. He also assisted in the awkward task of punching out old iron nails and fastenings. 'The knuckles come in for a good dusting. But it is so nice to be able to do something that is really helping and making others happy.' He was particularly proud a twelve-metre plank they used was Huon pine from a log he found in Bathurst Harbour. 'So *Arlie* is the first boat to have timber cut by the first mechanised mill in Port Davey.'

Despite 'bad heart aches', his evenings were happily spent, constructing his wedding gift for Margaret—a beautiful work box, of musk, Huon pine, gum and tea-tree. 'I am trying to put my best into it, but it is a poor best and I am a slow worker.' The work, however, was facilitated by the loan of Clyde's 'lighting set up', providing electric light in kitchen and bathroom, which prompted Deny to think about installing their own.

When Deny expected Margaret's return in seventy days, he did not know she had extended her stay by several weeks and now planned to reach Sydney late October. Weeks were already passing too slowly for Deny. He tried diverting his thoughts by reading stories of great people, but they only beset him with tormenting doubts which diminished his sense of self-worth. 'They make me feel I have wasted and fooled my life away without enough in me to have got anywhere or done anything worthwhile. The only thing I consider I have done that's of any consequence is that I have won your love. And now I don't know how I am going to be worthy of it.'

Vulnerable to Margaret's mention of cold feet, he wrote, 'It strikes fear in my heart. Do hope you don't get too many.' Touchingly affirming his love, he declared, 'I give you my word, dear, that my love for you is everlasting and will not die out like a sea breeze on a summer night. Will always do all in my power to help you and make you happy. Have thought of all the wildest places I would go if you never came back.'

Deny learned of Margaret's revised plans from Win, and looked up the *Strathaird* in Clyde's shipping books. By sailing date he was counting in hours, delighting she was coming hundreds of miles closer each day. He wrote, 'While making our new beddy, I wonder what stories you will have to tell me as we lie awake in the moonlight too happy to sleep.'

Margaret packed her London time with theatre, cinema, visiting famous art galleries, Kew Gardens and Hampton Court. She had teas, lunches, dinners and suppers at smart restaurants. At a reception at the Dorchester she was introduced to Anthony Eden. Port Davey seemed more than a world away.

She went to see where John had been stationed and travelled to Scotland, where she collected pebbles and a piece of granite. 'Den would love it. Light on the mountains as at Port Davey.' In Switzerland she and Elsie climbed peaks near Montreux, collecting a piece of slate from the highest for Deny.

On Deny's birthday she finally received his letters. 'I had almost given up hope of hearing again before Aust. ports. I can hardly wait to get back. Would never have believed that I'd feel this way. Not long now. Feet haven't been very cold.' Margaret was one of the first aboard *Strathaird* and found her thoughts 'flying ahead so very often' as she worked on her trousseau, making a silk nightdress and knitting socks to wear in her gumboots.

At Melbourne she dispatched two trunks to *Arlie D* in Hobart. In Sydney it was another whirl of greetings, meetings and farewells, and meticulously arranged business appointments.

On 26 October after spending the morning at AWA, learning how to assemble the 'lovely toy', their radio, Margaret wrote her last letter to Deny. Eight hours after signing off, 'Feet fairly warm—how are yours?' she had a phone call at 11 p.m. Deny had arrived in Hobart with hewardias for her wedding bouquet.

Feet colder than she would admit, Margaret had hedged about her Hobart arrival, with the excuse that planes would be booked out because of the Melbourne Cup. Four days after hearing his voice, however, Margaret flew to Hobart and Deny, overjoyed, met her. They visited the two-way outpost radio base VIH to meet the operators and receive their call sign, 8ZS. And there they listened together to the Melbourne Cup!

Then after more than four and a half years, the day for which Deny had longed arrived at last.

On Saturday 5 November 1949, Deny and Margaret were married in the Nixon Chapel of beautiful St David's Cathedral. Deny placed on Margaret's finger the ring of Port Davey gold he had so carefully won, the ring into whose making they had both put so much time and effort, and that so truly represented Deny's love.

Elsie's mother gave a small reception at elegant Hadley's Hotel, meeting place of the Hobart establishment. Then, leaving the world to which Margaret was accustomed and in which she moved so

Outside the Charles King Memorial Hut in 1960: Sir Edmund Hillary centre, with Deny, Margaret, dorts and walker Max Moore.

Far left: Deny's favourite wildflower, the striking hewardia (*Isophysis tasmanica*). He took some to Hobart for Margaret's wedding bouquet.

Cone of the extinct *Banksia kingii*, named after Deny, who discovered it in his mine and brought it to palaeobotanists' attention.

Janet and Mary in jumpers and shorts made by Margaret beside the lavender hedge in the flourishing garden at Melaleuca.

Right: Deny by the tailings race at the mine in 1975. White quartzite gravel contrasts with Mount Rugby in the background.

The path from the waterfront to the house through rhododendrons, myrtles, tree ferns and foxgloves planted by Deny and Margaret.

The Melaleuca living room with the historic piano, windowseat and convoluted tea-tree root, a favourite perch for visiting birds.

Deny's birdies, clockwise from above. Male superb fairy-wren, the 'bluebird of happiness' Deny often wrote about. Beautiful firetail, a finch which flocked to Deny's bird-feeding tables. The yellow-throated honeyeater that frequented the sugar bowl in the house. A crescent honeyeater. The grey shrike-thrush, Deny's favourite feathered companion. Because of their melodious voices he called all thrushes 'Richard', after singer Richard Tauber. Male orange-bellied parrot. Deny's concern for its dwindling numbers led to the establishment of a recovery program.

easily, Deny and Margaret crossed by ferry to Bellerive to board the fishing boat which would take them to a completely different world.

That evening they set off on *Arlie D* with Win and Clyde for Port Davey, to begin their married life at Melaleuca.

CHAPTER 15

Parenthood

'Mary very sweet, Deny so proud of her!'

Three days after the wedding *Arlie D* tied up to the gum trees in Melaleuca Inlet. With sunset bright on the mountains, Deny rowed his bride across the lagoon, his heart glowing too. Helping her from the dinghy at the waterfront, he said with pride and joy, 'We're home!' Hearing Margaret's heartfelt echo 'Home!', his world was complete.

After seeing *Arlie D* off next day, they began the pleasant task of unpacking wedding presents, belongings and treasures Margaret had accumulated, and their 'new toy'. On a calm sunny morning, they went to Bathurst Harbour, to cut spars for aerial masts. Deny and Freddie spent two days erecting them, then tried operating the radio. To their great disappointment only the receiver functioned and they had to wait four weeks to send the transmitter out for servicing.

In the meantime Deny pressed ahead with house improvements, while Margaret, a natural homemaker, made curtains and began bathroom refurbishing; and both worked in the garden. On wet days they painted Christmas cards depicting local wildflowers, one of Deny's traditions Margaret gladly adopted.

Mr King, as she still called her father-in-law, lined the porch with gum boughs, and Margaret decorated the house with bunches of blandfordias, cheerful red and yellow Christmas bells. She baked a cake, and made a pudding in their new pressure cooker, and Deny cooked a 'roo', his term for wallaby, in the camp oven. But it didn't feel like Christmas for Margaret, and Freddie Edvardsen's departure on Boxing Day increased her feeling of loneliness.

The South-West was, however, becoming the chosen destination for hardy bushwalkers and yachties, drawn by its unspoilt grandeur. Two days after Christmas the summer influx started with eight Hobart Walking Club members and a boat with four crew. Margaret unexpectedly found herself hostess, providing for twelve extra.

Toby Cheverton, a frequent visitor in his yacht *Lallaby*, and his party were especially welcome, bringing mail and the transmitter. After another abortive attempt, there was great excitement when Margaret got a message through, while Deny was in the bath! Now her fear of Melaleuca's isolation was at least partially allayed.

Suddenly the King world was busy with other people and their affairs. Deny was a natural host and although houseproud Margaret was dismayed by hobnails on her polished floor, she always enjoyed the diversity of guests and found evenings by the fire yarning a real pleasure. Walkers came in each evening, grateful for supper. 'Made ovaltine for 11.' Deny extended hospitality even further, baking bread for their homeward trip, one of his many kindly customs.

On New Year's Eve Margaret was introduced to a service increasingly requested of Deny and Charlie and always given freely—assisting walkers by transporting them and stores in *Blue Boat* to Bathurst Harbour, ferrying them across the channel, or the harbour to Old River. Deny always took advantage of extra hands for wood-getting en route, while Charlie used the opportunity to care for Critchley Parker's grave. Margaret, hearing that sad story, felt a renewed sense of human puniness in this wild, untamed land, and respected the sense of responsibility the Kings showed towards those venturing into it.

Her feeling of loneliness diminished as her confidence with the radio increased, and she had the satisfaction of sending, and comfort of receiving, her first telegrams. Walkers and boaties quickly took advantage of the opportunity to communicate with the outside world, so as Deny and Margaret found themselves receiving messages and sending telegrams on others' behalf, Margaret instituted a message book to deal with this unexpected development.

With Charlie producing prodigious crops of vegetables and small fruits, there was plenty to occupy her also in garden and kitchen. Her first day's effort bottling nine jars of currants and making seven kilograms of strawberry jam began the marathons of jam-making and preserving which became the Melaleuca summer tradition. Using her new preserving outfit, Margaret learned to bottle meat, mutton-birds and crayfish, as well as vegetables and fruit, even bananas.

'Mr K' and Deny helped prepare berry fruits, and after delighting walkers with 'huge plates of strawberries', they still picked another nine kilograms within days and resolved 'not to have so many strawb. plants next year!' For Deny and Charlie, who had always appreciated Win's housekeeping, it was 'a treat', coming back from the mine again to fresh hot meals in a clean, polished home gay with flowers. But Margaret's attempt to introduce a daily routine, with 'a new rule—dinner at 6.30 p.m.' was not appreciated by men who needed every daylight hour.

Margaret had always been prone to tiredness, headaches and off-colour bouts, so when she was feeling unwell in the early weeks at Melaleuca she just thought it was 'a pest'. But on New Year's Day 1950 she started to wonder. She had begun calling Deny 'Bear', because of his hairy chest, shoulders and back, and now she realised 'little bear' might be on the way. By 11 January she wrote, 'Have no doubts now!' Rejoicing that their hopes for starting a family had been so swiftly realised, by consulting *Black's Medical Dictionary* she and Deny estimated the date of 'small bear's arrival'. Margaret 'felt awfully sick' and wrote to a Hobart doctor, glad she could send the letter with another walking party.

Led by Charlie's old Huon acquaintance, Lance Geeves, this group also received a warm welcome and hot meal, and departed with fresh bread. For Lance's teenage son Bob it was the beginning of a lifelong friendship with Deny.

Apart from her morning sickness, and many days she variously described as cold, bleak, blowy, miserable, showery, stormy, rainy or windy, it was a halcyon summer for Deny and Margaret. Deny was very flexible in his activities and always used the weather to best advantage. Besides working at the mine, entertaining, gardening, and house improvements, he was rebuilding *Nifty*. On fine days they often went 'ta-tas', Deny's term for a picnic or camping trip in search of food and firewood, when he also collected kelp for garden mulch and oyster shells to burn and crush for lime.

They would pack tucker box and camping gear 'plus telescope and Mr K plus binoculars' and go off down Bathurst Harbour and Port Davey, fishing for trumpeter and cod, crayfishing and wood-gathering, Deny always on the lookout for Huon pine logs. He told Margaret of the piners' settlements up Spring River and at the Davey River mouth a century earlier, and she was aghast at the truly pioneering conditions those women endured raising their families.

In the gullies where the leatherwoods were snowy with blossom, Deny and Charlie looked for bee trees. On their 'First Bee Day' Margaret was impressed by their bushcraft. 'D set to work and felled the second big tree. Grand to watch him.' That night it was bread and honey for tea. Next day 'everything was sticky and honeycomb everywhere', as they strained and bottled the beautiful clear honey, setting aside some to give away.

Margaret was initiated into mutton-birding too. On a clear March day they left for the Breaksea Islands, green-capped with wind-shorn vegetation. The steep leeside was riven with a blowhole gulch which roared and spumed, and often made landing impossible, although Deny and Charlie were experienced at scrambling ashore in the heaving swell. This time the sea was smooth. Clambering up rocky slopes to scorched brown earth pocked with burrows among the tussocks, they took 'about 20 fluffy downy birdies', and Margaret thought of 'future small sleeping bags!'

Lunch was usually fresh-caught fish cooked over the campfire. This day, though, their net, set three times, had been tangled and torn successively by a gummy shark, a groper and a 'tiger shark'. Margaret mended it next day, and baked mutton-birds, which the menfolk had plucked by the light of a pressure lantern.

While Margaret continued house furbishing, Deny finished *Nifty*. 'D has done a long and patient job to patch her up so well,' she wrote. 'She looks very nice—cream inside, blue gunwale, name on stern in blue.' At night Deny was still painstakingly sandpapering 'dear box', while Margaret began making baby clothes, and they enjoyed 'great talk and discussion about boys' names'. She also made shirts for Deny and knitted him worksocks from homespun wool.

Deny, always solicitous, lifted the heavy tins of water from the fire to tubs on the porch where Margaret did the laundry, and he carried and hung out the washing. On cold wet days he built up the fire for her comfort while she knitted, read or wrote letters, and on fine days he carried a chair outside so she could sit in the sun to sew. She helped Deny with outdoor jobs, oiling house timbers, painting doors, window frames, even engines. On one wood-getting expedition she even helped fell a large celery-top pine. Deny was proud of her.

He was also concerned for her condition. With winter's onset there would be few boats, so opportunities to reach Hobart would be limited. In April, therefore, they decided she should go out on *Arlie D*'s next trip. Their idyll was over. For the next four weeks Margaret lived in a state of uncertainty, watching for a smoke signal.

Almost six months pregnant, she found the walk across to New Harbour long and difficult, but 'D helped and encouraged all the way'. She felt very sad leaving Deny, and was seasick four times before Recherche. *Arlie D* reached Hobart next afternoon and despite 'an awful room' at the boarding house, Margaret was glad to be back in her own world. After a good report from the doctor set her mind at rest, she bought wool and began knitting for 'Small'. Two weeks later she flew to Sydney, where she arranged her affairs to enable purchase of a boat, before returning to Hobart to await 'Small's' arrival.

Once more it was a long lonely winter for Deny. The day after Margaret left, he again began keeping a diary, a habit he continued with few breaks for over forty years. He started with brief entries but soon they recorded progress on the project he had commenced before Margaret's departure—the much-needed extension. Their small bedroom was almost filled with 'beddy' and soon space would be needed for a cot. So the six-metre rear extension, with north- and west-facing windows, would be spacious enough for both, and would include sewing corner, a dividing wall of cupboards, storeroom and laundry. Outside, the drying area would be improved.

Deny had begun excavating the bank while Margaret was still home. Watching him wheeling innumerable barrowloads of gravel preparing the foundations and path to the clothesline, she described it as 'a long and tedious job'. Deny, however, was used to pacing himself to long-term goals.

Whenever Melaleuca mine water supplies froze, Deny went to Bond Bay to help Win and Clyde build their house. By the end of July he noted the first signs of spring and had found a duck nest with nine eggs. With favourable weather in August, mine work speeded up, bringing good yields. Radio conditions also improved and he received several messages from Margaret. In wet weather he worked on the extensions, counting the days until his beloved returned.

On Sunday 27 August 1950, a day of squalls, showers, hail and thunder, Deny recorded reception as good when at 9 a.m.—'got word that we'd had a daughter'. His constant companion, the grey thrush, celebrated with him. 'Richard Tauber came and whistled at the door so long and joyfully.' Deny sent a message to Margaret, then typically spent the day on carpentry, washing and cooking.

September and spring cheered Deny: the first cuckoo call, first sightings of snipe and swallows, and finding more well-filled duck nests. He manured the strawberries, planted spuds, and started the spring burn-off. Early in October he killed the season's first snake with his 'whanging stick', and out in the valley hewardias starred the slopes with beautiful deep purple flowers.

Longer daylight meant better working conditions, and Deny, determined to achieve a good tin yield, took advantage of every hour. In fine weather he carried tin, each bag weighing fifty kilograms, one at a time on his shoulder, from the mine across the button grass 125 metres or more to the dinghy and then to be transhipped to *Arlie D*. Later he measured the area worked that year, 750 square metres, with a yield averaging just over one kilogram per square metre.

Gardening was now the order of the day, planting vegetable and flower seeds as the ground warmed. Deny and Charlie were keen to have a flourishing garden when Margaret returned. Despite good conditions there were no messages from her, and Deny made two rare references to his feelings—'worried', and 'still worried'. November also brought transmission troubles, and Deny got only one message through, by relaying it to Robbins Island, a last resort.

Just over a year since their wedding and six months since Margaret had left, Deny sailed for Hobart. *Arlie D* docked at 4 a.m. and Deny lost no time reaching Margaret. At last he could enfold her in his embrace again and at the age of forty-one, he held his first-born in his arms. He and Margaret gloated over their precious Mary Winsome.

There were more major changes in the King family's life. Margaret bought a three-bedroomed house in Norfolk Crescent, Sandy Bay, for a Hobart base. It overlooked the Derwent, so she could watch for Deny's comings and goings. She had already made inquiries about possible boats. They chose *Colleen II*, a thirteen-metre, eighteen-tonne celery-top pine ketch, a proven blue-water yacht with canoe stern and two-metre draught, which they inspected four days after Deny's arrival. A fishing boat would have better suited their needs, but Margaret probably aspired to something with more style, more in keeping with her previous way of life.

The day after Deny saw the boat, they interviewed the owner, and three days later had an hour's trial in a stiff northerly. On 28 November she was slipped for underwater inspection, then the purchase was made and her name was changed to *Melaleuca*.

Deny decided also to install a forty horsepower diesel Thornycroft instead of her Cadillac petrol engine. He ordered a new three-blade propeller, and spent the next month refitting and installing new electrical equipment.

On 2 January 1951 at noon, with Mary's bassinette wedged between table and bunk, *Melaleuca* got under way. The first day of her voyage to her new home port was perfect in warm sunshine with a light sea breeze, greeting Sydney–Hobart race yachts and others from the Huon regatta. The first night aboard, anchored at Partridge Island, they were lulled to sleep by waves lapping on the rocky shore, wind soughing in the casuarinas, and the scent of blue gums.

The honeymoon was short. Next morning the stove did not function and Deny had to row ashore to boil the billy. Then it took time rigging the gear to hoist the dinghy aboard. At South West Cape they met a nor'wester with big seas and backwash off The Pyramids.

After much tacking among the succession of islands serried sharp as sharks' teeth, they were 'glad to get inside the heads at 8 p.m.' But their troubles were not over. Heavy rain fell as they ran for shelter in Schooner Cove, Margaret was seasick as she tended Mary below and the cabin roof began to leak.

The last leg of the journey took longer because on Bathurst Harbour they saw *Blue Boat*. Charlie was taking a walking party to Mount Mackenzie, so Deny, eager to show the new boat, turned and towed them. When they finally reached Melaleuca Inlet the tide was low. Deny, unaccustomed to *Melaleuca*'s draught, ran her aground. It was an inauspicious ending to his first voyage as skipper, tired from long weeks working on the boat, and anxious for his precious passengers.

In anticlimax they went home in *Blue Boat*, arriving at dusk with a fretful hungry baby. Deny had to return to get *Melaleuca* off the mud at high tide. He brought her into the bank single-handed, something he was to do many times, and began the long heavy process of unloading into *Blue Boat*, transporting everything across the lagoon, up Moth Creek, unloading again at the little landing, to carry stores up to the house and equipment to the mine.

Over the next days, hot and blowfly-ridden, in between unpacking and tidying, Margaret rubbed preservative on thirty-nine dozen eggs, coped with a fractious baby, and the first twelve summer visitors, who appeared while she was baking bread. So she served lunch in two relays. The following day she was back to making jam and cooking mutton-birds.

Deny, meantime, eager to try *Melaleuca* further, had set off on a pleasure trip exploring the great waterways at their doorstep. With diesel engine, living accommodation and space for camping gear, not to mention firewood, *Melaleuca* offered unlimited range and the opportunity to socialise, which Deny was quick to use.

After unloading stores, he, Charlie, Doug Watkins and Max

Cutcliffe, walkers befriended the previous year, went to Bramble Cove, a sheltered anchorage on the northern side of Port Davey. Popular with boaties, the cove had been a busy whaling station for some decades from the 1850s. Deny always enjoyed investigating such places, working out how people had lived and died, as he penetrated the bush behind the beach to visit a little cemetery. Three other boats were overnighting at Bramble and Deny enjoyed showing their crews *Melaleuca*, which was to become so well-known in these waters.

Heading out early next morning they passed the rocky needle-points off northern Breaksea, sailing through North Passage into the open waters of Port Davey, twin-breasted Kathleen Island with its deep cleavage on the starboard. It was the height of the sailing season and they saw two more boats near Whalers Point, where the great groves of bull kelp swirled and writhed like prehistoric sea monsters.

They entered more sheltered waters again in Payne Bay, then crossed Bond Bay, studded with inconspicuous reefs where low schist points ran out from the silver beach. On reaching the narrow entrance to Kelly Basin, Deny was challenged by the suddenly shallow water. Very conscious of *Melaleuca*'s draught, he stopped well out in Bond Bay, where four boats were already at anchor.

Deny took the opportunity to revisit the rich Aboriginal middens at Kelly Basin, and observe the birdlife—white-faced herons stalking through the shallows, pied and sooty cormorants perched like ptero-dactyls on dead branches drying their wings, a cruising sea eagle, and a flock of sulphur-crested cockatoos feeding on the banksias.

Three weeks later, after re-aligning the engine and shaft, Deny planned another trip, taking Margaret and Mary. They spent an afternoon stowing gear, and Margaret wrote, 'Have quite an affec-tion for *Melaleuca* already, tho' find it hard to believe she is ours.'

This trip proved to be of short duration. Because of a rapidly falling tide, *Melaleuca* grounded again at the markers in Melaleuca

Inlet, so Deny seized the opportunity to replace them. When they finally reached Bathurst Harbour they met a boat with their mailbag, and Margaret enjoyed socialising with the women, especially as 'Mary much admired and nursed by all'. Then, after a hot night on deck, they awoke to smoke and ash everywhere from big fires north of Mount Rugby, so they turned for home. It was a hot dry summer, and many fires were lit by careless visitors.

The next trip was more successful. Lasting four days, it combined fishing for the first time off the Shanks Islands in the South Passage of Port Davey and at beautiful Spain Bay, with wood-getting along the channel. Deny had made a cauf or 'water box' for storing fish alive, in typical King's lingo named 'Royal Ridiculus'. It served well, providing many meals of fresh trumpeter.

By now Deny was wary of tide conditions in Melaleuca Inlet, and learning the hard way about difficulties mooring in strong winds. He discovered more reefs and rocks in the waterways than were ever apparent in *Nifty* or *Blue Boat*, and was realising there was always work to be done on the boat.

Sometimes Margaret went across the lagoon with him, feeding Mary as they went, settling her on a canvas sheet, while she and Deny worked on *Melaleuca*. It was precious time alone together. Margaret now called Charlie 'Grandfather', and sometimes entrusted Mary to him while she went to the mine. She described returning and finding 'M looked sweet being sung to by G'father'. But she did find his constant presence a trial.

His deafness helped to ensure some privacy in conversations in the house with its thin partitions. But when they had visitors, which Charlie also enjoyed, she became irritated, because 'they bellowed at G'father' or 'G'father [was] particularly annoying—would not stop talking'. However, she continued many little kindnesses, always making his favourite cake and cutting crusts off sandwiches for his prospecting trips. In return he brought her hewardias.

Mary was a placid, cheerful baby, and watching her progress was a source of never-ending wonder, and sometimes concern. Every new phase caused excitement and Margaret loved dressing her up to visit Win and Clyde, now living at Bond Bay when not at sea.

Hearing items which they transmitted to the ABC—about boats, record rainfall, snow and floods—was another excitement. It was a surprise too on election day to hear on the news that the 'King family marooned in South-West Tasmania could not vote, so were exempt as well as those on Macquarie Island'. The radio also provided evening relaxation, 'Amateur Hour' and 'Clive Amadio's Quintet' being favourite programs. But if there were no visitors, Margaret went early to bed, because she still often fed Mary in the night.

At the end of March she realised she was pregnant again.

Margaret began weaning Mary, Deny took over night feeds, and had pleasure building her cot. On Mother's Day he brought Mary and bottle to Margaret in bed, with 'a wee bunch of white wild flowers arranged in a cream tin in the pie funnel!' But despite all he did to make life easier, Margaret 'looked forward very much to going to Hobart'. Morning sick again, her anxiety at having no medical help resurfaced.

Deny worked hard for a good tin load and in late May when he had twenty bags, Margaret made a celebration cake, icing it '1 TON'. He worked hard too preparing *Melaleuca* for her first fully-loaded trip and enlarged the hatch to facilitate loading tin, firewood and household trunks.

Two attempts to leave in early June were thwarted by weather. On the second they returned so Margaret could wash nappies and bake more bread. And Mary's first tooth came through. On the third, using both sail and motor they reached Hobart in three and a half days, the peat stove Deny had installed proving a boon in the wintry conditions.

While Deny was unloading the tin, then loading a new stove and gear for the return voyage, Margaret had the reassurance of taking Mary to the clinic and visiting her doctor. Although the tenants had not yet moved out, Margaret began unpacking and invited Win and Clyde to tea.

It was a very gratifying evening. 'M very sweet, D so proud of her.'

CHAPTER 16

The family at Melaleuca

'We didn't feel at all deprived.'

When Deny sailed in July 1951, waving as he passed Norfolk Crescent, he did not realise what a long separation lay ahead. Sad at leaving Margaret alone a second time for her last months of pregnancy, he kept in touch by telegram and when possible by letter.

Although the barometer was falling, Deny, determined to arrive before the birth, hoisted the mainsail at 4 a.m. on 22 November. With bad weather reports, Margaret had given up hope of his coming. She was thrilled when he phoned from Recherche, and next day *Melaleuca*, with pennant she had made flying from the masthead, came into the mooring she had arranged below Norfolk Crescent. Then after jobs aboard, Deny was home to a hot meal and bed, 'dog weary'. But he was not destined to sleep long. Margaret woke him to take her to hospital, where their second daughter was born on 25 November.

Janet Margaret was 'a well and lusty babe who takes her tucker beautifully'. But Margaret had longed to give Deny a son, and a second daughter would never match their delight and pride in their firstborn.

Two days after Margaret and baby came home, walkers started calling to arrange their Port Davey visits. Deny was busy on *Melaleuca*, though not too busy to play with Mary, who beguiled him with her latest word, 'dada'. Then only three weeks after arriving, he sailed again.

Deny hardly had time to be lonely. Boats were arriving and walkers were coming through almost every day. Aircraft were also landing at Cox's with visitors, so walking the twenty-five kilometres return, he took the opportunity to get letters and strawberries out to Margaret.

Beach landings depended on tide and weather, so pilots were searching for a location for an alternative strip. From the air button grass looks deceptively smooth and level, but the tussocks and the boggy peat between are quite hazardous.

In 1947, Neil Gaston, a pilot from Brown and Dureau's aerial survey, had arranged for Deny to remove the tussocks on an area behind the house as an emergency strip. He had also asked Clyde to prepare a space at Bond Bay, but Clyde judged the terrain unsuitable and, when Gaston flew over, waved him away. Gaston circled and dropped a note saying he would attempt to land on Deny's tract.

He succeeded in bringing 'Auntie', his de Havilland Dragon Rapide, a twin-engined wood and fabric biplane, down on the rough flat. Before leaving he took the precaution of draining fuel to lighten the aircraft and had his photographer walk to Cox's for pick-up. Yet despite his care, on attempting take-off, Auntie, almost at flying speed, hit soft ground and nosed over. The propellers dug into the mud, sprayed clods and broke. The toolbox narrowly missed Gaston's head, shattered the windscreen, and hurtled onwards, disgorging tools which Deny was still finding for weeks.

On their return from taking Gaston to Hobart, Deny, Charlie and Clyde built a corduroy strip, which took three weeks' hard work. Clyde recalled, 'We never stopped for rain. Deny did the most, of course. Win kept up the tucker.' The improvised runway consisted of two parallel strips, 160 metres long and two and a half metres wide. Deny estimated that 3000 poles were used. Mainly tea-tree, they had to be cut and rowed upriver in *Ark Royal* towed by *Nifty*. They were laid straight on the ground and wired crisscross together. Then gravel dug from the bank was spread to make the surface smooth and firm.

The aircraft was grounded for almost six weeks, so before take-off Deny, realising that water had entered, bored a drainage hole, and it poured out. Alan Hume, chief engineer for the Aero Club of Southern Tasmania, landed his Tiger Moth at Cox Bight with new propellers, which had to be carried to Melaleuca. The repaired Dragon was dragged up to the strip awaiting a strong wind to assist take off, which went smoothly.

Gaston deeply appreciated Deny's and Clyde's help and voluntary work, and as a memento gave Deny a broken propeller. Deny had a barometer inserted and mounted it on the chimney breast.

In February 1952, Hume flew into Cox Bight again to pursue the search for an airstrip site and enlisted Deny's help, exploring on *Melaleuca* around Port Davey with Clyde. Hume had great regard for Deny. 'A most delightful chap. Just a natural gentleman without any affectation, and a person you trust. If he gave his word on something, that was it. I couldn't speak more highly of anyone than I can of Deny.' The respect was mutual, and Hume enjoyed the Kings' friendship for many years.

The next pilot, however, aroused Deny's lasting ire. He also broke the propeller landing on the button grass near Melaleuca in April 1952, when Deny and Charlie had gone to Hobart with a load of tin. Instead of occupying one of the miners' huts, always available for visitors, pilot and companion settled in the house for a month. They broke the lock on the main bedroom, slept in 'dear beddy', wore Deny's clothes, including special thick woollen socks kept for mine work, helped themselves to stores, and used Deny's gun to shoot native ducks he had tamed. The final insult was their radio message that they were toughing it out 'in a hut' in most difficult conditions.

Deny, the soul of hospitality, was incensed by their abuse.

The message, broadcast as news, caused alarm in Hobart and considerable consternation to Deny and Margaret. Deny sent a counter-message to the radio station, disclaiming the exaggerations, listing the amenities 'of our moderately comfortable home' including radio transmitter, electric light, inner spring mattress and many books. He concluded, 'To those who have walked overland to Port Davey their story seems ridiculous.'

Deny's outrage was further fuelled on return to Melaleuca, finding that sawn timber boards reserved for streaming boxes at the mine had been used for a makeshift airstrip. He then had to retrieve them, because they were too valuable to abandon. A week later the offending pilot, perhaps attempting to make amends, dropped a note from Margaret and a parcel of meat.

A fortnight's prospecting in May 1952 with Clyde and Win, Charlie and Bill Denne on *Arlie D*, was a venture after Deny's heart. Sailing north of Port Davey past Low Rocky Point, they entered Lewis River. It was a rocky entry, so in 'quite enough sea' Deny and Bill went ahead in the dinghy to pilot *Arlie D* through the channel. Win recalled, 'The last we saw of them was the dinghy standing on end in the big swell. We were very relieved to see them again when we entered the river.'

Walking and camping in new country, finding eighteen minerals and varied geological formations, was deeply satisfying and stimulating for Deny. The rocks smelled of cats, said by old prospectors to indicate the presence of minerals, and they discovered traces of copper mining, as well as good seams of galena already investigated to a yard's depth. Panning in nearby creeks yielded rutile and flaky gold. They also came across some Aboriginal occupation and burial sites, which gave Deny plenty to ponder.

In readiness for his family's return Deny, who could turn his hand to anything, began making more furniture—a chair and bed for Mary, a meat safe, window frames for the extension and a new heater for the boat. A good run yielded twenty-one bags of tin in thirty-six working days, so in August he began preparing for his next trip. To distribute the weight as evenly as possible he always spread the bags under the cabin floor as well as over it, and in the engine room too, which hardly made for comfort. He also took firewood for Margaret.

In August, receiving his message advising hoped-for departure and arrival dates, Margaret anxiously began weather-watching again. A blustery nor'wester caused considerable worry, so she ceased looking for *Melaleuca*'s mast appearing around Sandy Bay Point. Four evenings later, however, 'in they walked'.

Margaret had planned to return in April, but 'had such an attack of cold feet. Really felt we were MAD to think of taking two lovely little babies down there in this weather. It would be AWFUL to have to put in a week at Recherche with napkins for two!' She was concerned too that the extension had made little progress, but consoled Deny, 'You are only one human being, not six, altho' you try to do the work of 6, sometimes.'

So although she was missing him, there was still no question of returning to Melaleuca's isolation and inconvenience, giving up the security of closeness to clinic and doctor, the comforts and convenience of her new home, city amenities, and companionship of other women, especially mothers with whom she could talk babies.

When Deny sailed on his birthday, against Margaret's wish as the barometer was falling, *Melaleuca*, the once proud yacht, had become a regular workboat:

> The cabin was so full it was difficult to get below—8 bundles of plywood on the floor, 3 bags of spuds, 2 sugar, hot water system, many cases of tinned food stowed under seats. Down aft is five bags of cement, half blood and bone, one super, some sulphate ammonia, four fuel oil, one kerosene, one shellite, one 44 gallon drum on deck besides a case of glass and 4 lengths of pipe.

At Melaleuca, Deny set to work on the extension, cementing foundations for the hot water system and future washtubs, digging drains, building frames, studs and battens for the structure, and erecting scaffolding. By early November, when the blandfordia, bottlebrush and tea-tree were flowering and the sandflies had begun to make their tiresome presence felt, Deny had the roofing on and the end wall built of vertical boards, and was tackling the flooring. He made and installed the windows, commenced fitting the plywood lining and making the doors. By early December the extension was livable. Deny cleaned it, moved in beddy, and tidied the house in keen anticipation of Margaret's homecoming.

After more repairs to *Melaleuca*, burning off, and finishing his Christmas cards, Deny made his third trip to Hobart for the year. Longing for his family, Deny set a record, leaving Kelly Basin 'at crack of dawn' to arrive at Sandy Bay the same evening. He had pangs of sadness seeing how his daughters had grown, realising how much he had missed. Now at last they would all be together.

Janet's immunisations were done, and with the house extension completed, Margaret had no reason to postpone returning to Melaleuca. After 'huge days shopping' for basin, sink, floor coverings and many household items she began packing, and interviewing potential tenants.

When *Melaleuca* was slipped, Doug Watkins and members of the Hobart Walking Club who appreciated Deny's transport at Port Davey, helped paint her hull, establishing a custom of reciprocal assistance. Deny worked on engine repairs and started the marathon of loading drums of fuel, stores and a kerosene refrigerator, before a lorry of household goods and a crate of fowls arrived.

A walking party at Melaleuca helped unload and transport to the house. Margaret was very pleased with the new room, 'so big and bare and clean,' but less happy with the house. Despite Deny's efforts, it looked 'AWFUL', cluttered with all the boxes and bundles to be unpacked—into cupboards not yet built.

Deny, though weary, was full of joy. This was the beginning of the happiest ten years of his life. For Mary and Janet it was the beginning of an idyllic childhood. Because Deny had such a rich family life growing up at Sunset Ranch, he wanted a similar experience at Melaleuca for his children. He loved playing with them, telling stories and reading to them, and gave them a lot of freedom.

Deny's 1953 new year wish to Margaret was 'Not so many napkins and potkins!' But while coping with seventy-seven visitors and the summer fruit, for months Margaret had to endure further building upheaval. Deny even soldered water tanks on the living-room floor.

He cleared his old bedroom for Grandfather, and after relocating partitions, they finally had an enlarged, remodelled kitchen complete with refrigerator, sink, cupboards, bench and shelves, and a new, bigger bathroom. Greatest boon of all, Deny plumbed in water and a hot water system. Margaret headed her 31 March diary entry 'TAPS RUNNING', describing the moment as 'WONDERFUL'.

Another boon was the more frequent advent of Aero Club aircraft, dropping mailbags and supplies by arrangement with chief pilot Lloyd Jones. With mail more often Margaret felt much less isolated, and she really appreciated the fresh food. 'Auster flew over at 1 p.m. and dropped our half sheep.' Even bananas, plums and tomatoes survived the drop.

Deny and Charlie had always grown flowers as well as vegetables, and with Deny's help Margaret extended the flower gardens. A lavender hedge for bees, perfume, and colour was a feature, as were her favourite blue flowers—borders of lobelias, drifts of forget-me-nots, and clumps of stately delphiniums.

To mark the Queen's coronation they planted a grove of banksias and lemon-scented boronias, and a melaleuca hedge. Clipped annually by Deny, it became a glorious ribbon of blended mauve and purple in spring and summer, providing a windbreak for tender plants. They also planted four celery-top pines and Deny hung a blue tablecloth 'flag' from the aerial, ceremonially lowering it at sunset, before listening to the coronation broadcast from London.

However, bleak dark days and miserable weather, when the children had to be kept indoors and the voluminous washing couldn't be hung out, began to depress Margaret. She confided to her diary her longing to return to town. Deny, devoted to Margaret and adoring his daughters, often stayed home to mind them and did a big share of domestic jobs, baking bread and cooking. Recording his help one weatherbound day Margaret wrote 'so my morale was not as low as the VILE weather would otherwise have made it'.

Margaret had always been careful to ensure 'the babes' spent plenty of time outdoors. Although she took great pride in making their clothes and having them nicely dressed, she did not mind letting them play in dirt, mud and puddles. They helped Deny stacking peat and gardening. Deny and Margaret took them for picnics at the little beach on the lagoon. They often took lunch to the mine and while Margaret helped Deny cut peat or pick up tin, the children splashed in the water. When the family went 'ta-tas', they played in *Melaleuca*'s cockpit and revelled in the delights of many gravelly and sandy beaches.

With only fifteen months between them, and no other playmates, Mary and Janet were close companions, developing their own vocabulary. 'We didn't feel at all deprived,' Janet recalled. 'We didn't want other kids. It was quite fine just having us.'

Margaret always encouraged creative play. She read to the children every night by the fire, and many games were inspired by stories they heard. 'Our games were like chapter story books and we'd each have particular characters.' She also fostered her daughters' artistic talents. 'Drawing was a game and we drew virtually every day. We'd just draw imaginative things and get them into some sort of story frame.' They invented words and many names for each other. Deny was never Dad or Daddy. After a series of names finally he became Nung-Nung or Nungy. Margaret was sometimes Moosie and Mary was always Pet to her parents.

As well as unbounded imagination in their play there was a practical side. Deny made them swings, horizontal bars and wheelbarrows and they took great interest in all his doings. Mary remembered:

> We used to go and help sometimes and had our own little mine. Dad showed us how to sluice the pay dirt and stream it by hand in a race, the old-fashioned way. We had our own tin bags with M&JK on them, because Dad's were always branded CDK. He used to brand the seconds separately, and sometimes gave us these. Our bags were sent out with the others, so we had our own income, which was kept till we were a bit older and knew what money was.

Deny dug a paddling pool near the house. But when they learned to swim, Moth Creek and the lagoon became their favourite playground. Deny had also bought another small dinghy, *Scamp*, as *Melaleuca*'s tender. So the girls would row off for picnics, swimming excursions and adventures.

Deny paid little attention to birthdays, but Margaret made much of them. 'Because Mary and I were down here in isolation and couldn't have parties with lots of children, Mummy made them a big thing.' Still cherished is a wooden horse big enough to ride, made by Deny for Janet's seventh birthday. Another year her parents gave Janet a journal. On its cover Margaret lettered her name in beautiful calligraphy and Deny painted the yellow-throated honeyeater sitting on the sugar bowl.

Margaret also made much of Christmas. She had to plan ahead with orders from David Jones. Once the weather was so bad the aircraft couldn't fly over and the carefully chosen presents did not arrive. So on Christmas Eve Margaret made little toys to fill the stockings; the children were never disappointed. Margaret's family and friends always sent birthday and Christmas gifts too, and because of her delight in opening parcels Deny nicknamed her Pandora.

Although visitors were coming in ever-increasing numbers, Margaret was concerned to develop the children's social skills and experiences further. So in June 1953, after only six months at Melaleuca, when Deny took the tin to Hobart, she and the girls also went so the children could go to playschool, and visit family and friends in Sydney and Coolangatta.

It had been a disappointing year for Deny, with tin yields not commensurate with his efforts. Although the Melaleuca ground was much easier to work than the Cox's lease, it still demanded immense energy and stamina. After digging and testing a series of holes, Deny and Charlie would decide where to mine, marking out a 'paddock', a rectangle of about half a hectare.

Deny would then commence stripping, removing the peat overburden of button grass and low scrub with pick and mattock to expose the tin-bearing gravel on the bedrock beneath the mud. This pay dirt then had to be shovelled into barrows and wheeled to a heap for nozzling. Stripping was best done in fine weather when the ground was relatively dry. But nozzling and sluicing required much water, so depended on rain having filled storage ponds, previous excavations dammed with peat sods and connected by ditches or races.

Working the sluice box involved constant shovelling, raking and forking to assist the water, which was controlled by a gate. A powerful jet from a large nozzle squirted the pay dirt down a nine-metre timber box to wash the mullock along a race to the tailings heap.

Deny made shovel-like implements with large blades of coarse metal mesh fixed to long tea-tree pole handles. These were used for stirring up the wash in the sluice box, to separate sand, silt, gravel, clods and stones from the heavier tin-bearing material, cassiterite.

Cassiterite, SnO_2, is a very high density material, three times heavier than other common minerals. The winnowing allowed the tin to sink to the bottom. Even hoes and an extra hose might be used against the flow to stir up the lighter sediments and stop the sand from setting hard. Then with a pitchfork Deny would toss out the stones. After sluicing, the tin would be 'picked up' by hand from the bottom of the race, often gravel or jagged bedrock. So 'picking up' was not as easy as the name implied, hard both on shovel and wielder.

When enough tin had been sluiced, it was streamed in the wooden sluice box, cleaned with more running water. The tin would then be carried or barrowed to a wooden box built further down the race for its final cleaning, which required judgment and skill. It flowed over a shallow wire tray into a wooden streaming box some forty-five centimetres wide.

Corduroy material was nailed in the bottom to catch any gold particles, while tin and sand would be washed further down a fifteen-centimetre fall. There Deny, back braced, would stand in the water with his square-mouthed shovel, working solids slowly and rhythmically against the water to keep the sand flowing out and the tin up the box. The rate of water flow was critical, requiring constant monitoring. It was governed by the sluice gate at the dam, and by valves and riffles or wooden bars across the base of the sluice box at intervals.

The lighter particles would be carried away leaving the cassiterite residue, shiny black grains, to be scooped out with a shovel into storage drums to dry before bagging.

Streaming required great care to ensure the best price, as tin with impurities incurred penalty rates, and Deny took a pride in the purity of his product. Mines Department inspector David Jennings regarded Deny as a very skilful operator.

The tin at Melaleuca was 'clean', that is, it did not contain much spinel or pyrites. Deny was usually dealing with fairly coarse material, some consisting of composite grains, two-thirds tin and one-third quartz. This was often streamed again, when the tin might be dislodged from the quartz. Any remaining composite grains were seconds.

The tin was placed in two hessian bags—an inner hundred-weight bag, weighing some fifty kilograms, tied, and then an outer one. It was another heavy job to be done with great skill and care, feeding in the cleaned tin through a big funnel. The top of the outer bag was rolled over, with the corners left as ears, and then sewn with a large carpet-type needle and string, which tied them off to make little handles. Charlie usually helped with that task.

The plump little bags were barrowed or moved by 'forky sled', a forked eucalypt branch with plank platform. A few days before Deny hoped to leave for Hobart, *Ark Royal* was towed up the canal. The bags were then loaded by hand and transported down the canal, along Moth Creek, across the lagoon to *Melaleuca*, to be hoisted aboard by a derrick attached to her mast.

Now it was time to introduce change. Deny started planning to proceed with his dream of mechanising the mine. His wartime experience convinced him that the D2 Caterpillar tractor, versatile and easy to handle, was ideal for stripping overburden and excavating and moving pay dirt. Considering the difficulties of transport and landing, its relatively small size made it a better proposition than a bigger machine. Its reliability and Deny's familiarity with it were also in its favour, as he would have to maintain it, without easy access to expert assistance or spare parts. In November 1953 he visited his Hobart bank manager 're our new plunge the D2—quite a successful interview'. At a cost of over £2000, it was a debt Deny did not lightly incur.

In December they were home again for their first family Christmas at Melaleuca. Margaret's best present was a copper and two washtubs which Deny installed. A bout of rubella was her finale to a hectic year. Then they welcomed 1954 with a glass of sherry, while Deny planned for the arrival of the new tractor.

CHAPTER 17

Building the airstrip

'A colossal task.'

The eagerly awaited tractor, complete with bulldozer blade, was the first of its model in Tasmania. Early in January 1954 Deny was reconnoitring Melaleuca Inlet for the best place to bring the D2 ashore. He found a spot with deep water near the bank, then planned a route to the mine, making fords at the creeks.

The D2 was to come from Hobart on the fishing boat *Toorah*, so for weeks Deny watched the weather anxiously. It was delayed at Recherche, then after a fruitless trip to Bathurst Harbour, Deny saw a smoke signal downriver. The salesman and mechanic flew to Cox Bight and walked across to join Deny in *Blue Boat* heading to *Toorah*. They fitted the dozer blade and started building the bridge from boat to shore with heavy timber brought for the purpose.

It took another morning's work getting the tractor ashore and unloading drums of fuel onto *Melaleuca*. Then they set off taking the D2 to its new home. Deny had chosen the route carefully across button grass where the mud was least deep and walked ahead indicating the way. But the salesman ignored Deny, put it into high gear and rushed on. The result was inevitable. The D2 bogged.

They spent another day extricating it. Then, watched by Margaret and daughters, 'Tracla' crossed the last creek and reached the mine. The following day there were lessons on working it for Deny, Clyde and Win, while Charlie looked on approvingly.

Before their first house guests arrived in January Margaret was nervous. Old family friend Kathleen Walker and Brisbane camping companion, entomologist Dr Patricia Marks fitted in well, however, and appreciated all Margaret and Deny did to make their visit interesting. It was the perfect time of the year for mosquitoes, and Marks, a University of Queensland expert on mosquitoes and midges, enjoyed Deny's story of west coast mosquitoes so large that fishermen had to cover their boat hatches with nets to keep them out.

Deny, as keen in his quest for knowledge as any scientist, helped further her research and Marks was delighted by the insects and invertebrates he showed her. She recorded eight, possibly nine, species of larvae in prospecting holes around the mine, and in rock pools around Bathurst Harbour and Port Davey. Six adult species were recorded 'biting, resting in house, flying and resting round prospecting holes, flying in tent, biting by night on boat, biting on beach and on island'. One species was sent to Melbourne University for further identification.

Sandflies, sent to another expert, were also thought to be undescribed and known only in Victoria. March flies were of great interest to a third entomologist safe from their stings in his mainland laboratory, so Deny continued collecting these unpopular insects.

South-West Tasmania was becoming important to scientists seeking new species. Melbourne botanist Mervyn Davis and friend also arrived in January. Again Deny spent time taking them on collecting trips and Margaret helped by writing on mounted specimens. Davis's list for Port Davey at the Tasmanian Herbarium includes fifty-one specimens of over forty species. Charlie and Deny had already assisted collector Consett Davis, who published his article, 'Preliminary Survey of the Vegetation near New Harbour, South-West Tasmania' in the 1941 *Papers and Proceedings of the Royal Society of Tasmania*. Later in 1954 Deny received word from Hope Macpherson, curator of molluscs at the National Museum of Victoria, requesting him to collect limpets and barnacles.

The tractor personnel were the next to stay. Because of the bogging fiasco and departure delayed by weather, the atmosphere could have been strained. Despite the trouble their carelessness caused, Deny held no grudge, and Margaret was disarmed because they admired the children and helped in the house.

Dirk Tober and girlfriend Margot were among others who enjoyed the Kings' hospitality, staying several months on their yacht *Onrust* in Bathurst Harbour, exploring the wild landscape and deserted waterways so different from their native Holland. They especially appreciated the Kings' bath and laundry, and Margaret's haircutting services.

In May the Kings acquired neighbours. *Toorah* brought a Mines Department inspection party, leaving Polish geologist Marion Stefanski and his assistant. They erected several prefabricated buildings five kilometres downstream, and frequently came to borrow tools and to interrupt Margaret's day, getting her to send or receive radio messages.

Helping the Mines men also caused a recurring back problem for Deny. Working on their faulty engine, he managed to get it running, but in the process slipped a disc. Margaret tried to twist it back, but failed and 'hurt him dreadfully'. She had to get Freddie and *Onrust*'s crew to help her, then 'had a very bad time getting him into bed'. Although incapacitated for a week, Deny, unable to remain idle long, 'pottered about, cut a little wood'.

The D2 had already proved itself, stripping a paddock far more quickly than could have been done manually, allowing more time for sluicing pay dirt and streaming tin. Margaret, visiting the mine after twelve housebound days, 'for a turn on Our Tractor' was 'amazed at the amount of pay dirt ready to put through. D cleaned end of race, *on* went the water, *in* went the pay dirt—very exciting.'

The sound of a plane always caused excitement, raising hopes of mail. The first to hear it shouted 'Aircraft!' and then Margaret and children would race up to the old strip, where the pilot flew low for a drop. Sometimes, disappointingly, there was none. Other times a bonanza of parcels, library books and letters would arrive in a big canvas mailbag. Once the bag came undone. Many letters fell into Melaleuca Creek and for days the children hunted for others among the button grass. Another time meat parcel contents were scattered into the tussocks, and one day a carton of detergent came adrift, snowing its contents, to Janet's delight.

Supplies of fresh food, especially meat, were always welcome to vary the staple diet of trumpeter, crayfish, wallaby and mutton-bird. Except for one occasion. When the menfolk returned from mutton-birding with about two hundred, Margaret spent the next two days bottling and baking them, and the house reeked with their distinctive smell. They had just finished dinner the following day when, to their surprise, they heard an aircraft. To Margaret's horror, meat came as well as mail. She then bottled nine jars of steak and confided to her diary she 'felt very weary and tired of food in the mass'.

With Mary's fourth birthday approaching, Margaret's concern for her social development resurfaced. She wanted Mary to have a party, and to attend kindergarten. So in July 1954 with twenty-two bags of tin aboard, the whole family, including Grandfather and Nufty, went to Hobart. With Freddie and two unwelcome passengers from the Mines Department, Melaleuca had '8 souls aboard—the largest passenger list so far!—for a really dreadful trip'. But for Grandfather there was relief when Clyde sailed by and passed over his false teeth, repaired in Hobart.

It was Charlie's last trip. His deteriorating health was an increasing concern, especially for Margaret. On medical advice the anguishing decision was made to put him into a nursing home. For Charlie it was heartbreaking to leave the place he loved, where he had lived so independently for over twenty years; realising he might never again see the mine he had established, the gardens he had created, and little of the grand-daughters on whom he doted.

For Deny, it was almost the end of a long, deeply valued association with the man he respected above all others, who had instilled in him all his values and taught him so much in a place they both had made their own.

A week later Deny left for Melaleuca alone. The house seemed unbearably lonely, echoing with voices and memories. He worked long hours on a very good paddock averaging a bag of tin a day, and after sewing up nineteen he ran out of bags. He derived great satisfaction from the D2's performance, and took care to maintain it regularly as the ever-present quartzite grit played havoc with machinery, causing wear to its tracks, running gear and control linkages.

As August days lengthened, daffodils and anemones he and Margaret had planted burst into cheerful flower, and Deny spent more time in the garden. Thinking of his father as he planted the vegetables, he pondered similarities in his parents' life with his own. More than ever he realised how often they had been separated by the demands of finding work, and recognised the fortitude that separation had demanded of them.

Deny made several trips with Mines Department men. In *Blue Boat* they crossed Bathurst Harbour to North River for the four-hour walk across the button-grass Rowitta Plains and the climb of almost one thousand metres to Mount Norold's summit, a long day. It was only two months since he had left Hobart, but he longed for his family.

They had missed him too. When fisherman Rupert Denne's wife Joyce told Margaret she could pick up Deny's messages to VIH on her radio, Margaret lost no time buying a receiver. Interviewed for an ABC program about the South-West, Margaret 'tried hard to put over the case for including historical side'. Although media interviews always highlighted the King family's isolation, Deny had made her very aware they were by no means the first residents since Aboriginal occupation. He always acknowledged the long line before them who had wrested their living from the wild South-West waters and lands.

In October Deny visited his father, and made a family trip to see Olive. They went by train to give the children a new experience, and thoroughly enjoyed their short break. A holiday was a rare event for Deny, and he described the stay on the Pipers River farm as a 'lovely loafing time'. A trip to Bell Bay aluminium smelters, a visit to Low Head lighthouse, and to the Launceston tin assayer to see crushing, smelting and assaying stimulated Deny's inquiring mind. Back in Hobart a visit to the Correspondence School for a lesson on teaching held a surprise. Deny met his own old teacher!

To Margaret's relief, the return voyage to Melaleuca was smooth. The decks, even more cluttered than usual, fortunately stayed dry, as the cargo included the new wind generator parts with four cases of large batteries, and a new washing machine. The only casualties were one chook which Margaret promptly cooked, and Deny, who was hit by the boom in the dark and later had a black eye.

Deny worked hard assembling and erecting the wind generator. After a week they finally switched on for 'glorious LIGHT at night'. Next day Deny installed the washing machine and Margaret had the immense satisfaction of using it. It was a great advance five years on, from heating water in kerosene tins over the fire and washing by hand in a tin tub on the porch. Just as Deny was gradually modernising the mine, she looked back with a sense of achievement on the many household improvements she had initiated.

Margaret's anxiety without easy access to medical help increased when Deny had back trouble again, and a bout of illness kept her in bed for a week, 'a wretched way to end the old year'. At the beginning of 1955, therefore, Deny suggested a herculean task he had been contemplating for some time.

It was to build an airstrip.

His favoured site was on thirty-odd hectares halfway between house and mine. After Mines Department geologist Stefanski tested it and found no tin, the leaseholder gave permission for the strip, and when the lease lapsed Deny acquired it. Margaret 'felt it was a colossal job for D to tackle' and watching him turn the first sod fifteen days later she confessed to feeling 'hopeless at the task'.

Once again Deny was equal to an undertaking that would have daunted most men. Building the airstrip involved removing all the button grass and other vegetation and stripping the peat down to the underlying gravel, which then had to be levelled and smoothed, an area of about a hectare. With the tractor it was possible, although still enormously labour-intensive.

Yet the circumstances of Charlie's last visit confirmed the advantages an airstrip would provide. They had arranged that he should fly in to Kelly Basin, where pilots sometimes landed on the sand spit. Deny made the trip to Port Davey, only to find the flight had been abandoned. In January the whole family went again to collect Grandfather. But Charlie was not well, and Deny sometimes stayed home caring for him.

After five weeks Charlie left unwillingly from Kelly's. It was Deny's last sight of his father. Charlie went to stay with Olive, where he became ill again and was hospitalised. Olive sent a message, 'Come soon', but the hospital countermanded it. Four weeks later another message advised that Charlie was dangerously ill. Deny, heavy-hearted, walked to New Harbour and left for Hobart with Clyde and Win.

He was too late. Charlie died on 6 June while Deny was still at Melaleuca, but Deny did not get that message until next day off De Witt Island. He and Win went to Launceston for the funeral. The *Mercury* of 10 June 1955 paid tribute to the fine old bushman, carrying a headline: 'UNCROWNED KING OF THE SOUTH-WEST' DIES. It was the end of an era, but not of a dynasty.

Deny returned to Melaleuca by an aircraft which landed at Cox Bight. It was his first flight to the South-West.

A month later he was preparing *Melaleuca* for another trip with forty-seven bags of tin. Each year Margaret wanted to escape the worst weather at Melaleuca, so enrolled the children in kindergarten in winter. Margaret and girls returned with Deny for Christmas, bringing a second dog, 'Mrs Nufty, a very aristocratic twelve guineas worth', a vacuum cleaner and a record player. The trip took eight days because of bad weather, and on reaching Melaleuca Inlet at last, the boat stuck on a mudbank.

They arrived home in time for Janet's fourth birthday, 'Parents had to have several cups of strong coffee to waken them up—both so weary.' When the bees swarmed ten days later, Margaret remarked, 'No one even blinked an eyelid—let alone banged a tin!! I sadly thought—alas, old age has set in.'

With Margaret tutoring, Mary and Janet took to Correspondence School lessons with alacrity, and she was proud of their progress. Occasionally Deny also organised their studies. But remembering his own childhood preference for being outside, he was more inclined to be lenient. He often took them to the mine and on expeditions in *Blue Boat*, when they absorbed much of his knowledge and love of nature.

Deny could work on the airstrip only when the ground was relatively dry, and for three successive Februaries, when there was no water for sluicing, he devoted himself to the task. When he recommenced in February 1956, Margaret was again overwhelmed, depressed at the enormity of the job yet to be tackled. Deny's continued back trouble and an abdominal hernia caused further concern.

But Deny pressed on, squaring up and cleaning off loose dirt with the dozer blade angled, smoothing the surface, often working more than eight hours a day. The D2, designed as a tracked tractor, was difficult to use to produce a level surface. Because it had such short tracks and the blade made it front heavy, any unevenness caused the machine to pitch. This created 'a beautiful set of rolling waves', as Deny said, hardly ideal for an airstrip.

In early March Deny asked Lloyd Jones to inspect the strip, some 400 yards (360-odd metres) long. Deny did not mention the disappointment which followed, but Margaret recorded her devastation to the reply: 'Regret cannot use it until legal length, 500 yards. Poor D. I felt so sad for him—all his slavery to get the strip useable for this week was for nothing.'

In February 1957 'D began the awful strip [again]—a monster task', and the tractor stuck on the second blade-load of tough rooty peat. It bogged the next day also but Deny persevered, driven on because Margaret was ill once more. He picked up stones, placing them in the drains he built, filled holes with gravel and painstakingly levelled bumps. He then towed a big beam over the whole surface to smooth it, working day after day in cold, heat and rain squalls till dark. Finally he applied a thin layer of slurry over the whole area and dragged the beam over yet again. When Margaret recovered she had a ride beside him on the tractor commenting, 'Strip looks huge. We speculated about first landing,' stating with every justification, 'very proud of his effort'.

Although Deny redoubled his labours to finish the strip when Margaret's doctor recommended her going to Hobart, she left with Clyde and Win on their new boat, *Stormalong*. After two weeks of exhaustive tests and inconclusive X-rays, Margaret returned. It was her first flight to Port Davey and Deny, who resolutely continued working on the strip in her absence, was very disappointed the pilot landed her at Cox Bight and she had to walk home.

It was Deny himself who was the first to land on the airstrip. In November 1957 his hernia required urgent attention. Margaret had 'forcibly to stop him taking six library books', but nevertheless his pack was 'huge' as he walked in thick drizzle to Cox's for a flight.

Two weeks later, after a successful operation, he returned in a Cessna 182 to land on the strip, greeted with great excitement by his family.

It was a blessing he did not have to walk from Cox's, as he had developed pneumonia. The next day he had a dangerously high temperature and Margaret was distraught, thinking it a recurrence of malaria. She contacted VIH requesting advice, and medication was dispatched immediately in an air drop. The following day, to her amazement and delight, another aircraft landed, bringing a doctor friend. Margaret wrote, 'House just utter chaos, but didn't care—a wonderful thing to have a Dr to visit D.' Deny's only regret was that he was in bed and 'couldn't see all the fun'. But the value of the strip was well and truly proved and fittingly Deny was first to benefit from his heroic labours.

The Mines Department made a contribution of £500 towards the airstrip, an important facility for them too, and £45 for boat hire. Deny lent them *Nifty* when their boat was unserviceable, often helped repair equipment, and transported personnel on field trips. When they were away he even made the ten-kilometre round-trip to feed their fowls. Margaret was always generous with hospitality and they often stayed for meals and even the night.

Another historic event took place earlier that year. In March 1957 Clyde brought round the piano Deny had saved from the Sunset Ranch fire. The family went to Bond Bay, so Deny could help unload, with Freddie and crew from another boat. Margaret found it was 'a terrifying operation', and when it was safely installed in Win's room, they had a celebratory drink. But Clyde's pride was rather dented, because Win had taken out a thirty-shilling insurance policy for its journey!

The year 1957 was also the first whole year Margaret and the girls spent at Melaleuca. Deny always had a project under way. He built a greenhouse, sheds for wood, peat and tracla. And after extending the house waterfront and creating a bathing beach, he built a large workshop beside the house.

But before the walls were even up, the 'children strewed many toys all over the floor. D felt it would only be half his in the future.' So he set up swings in a corner for his beloved 'dorts', and it was called 'the playroom'. In the house he also rebuilt the chimney and fireplace to install the new Rayburn stove and hot water service.

Apart from Margaret's and Deny's enforced trips out for health reasons, the family made only one trip to Hobart, when they lived aboard *Melaleuca* at the Royal Yacht Club wharf. The return trip was memorable. A freshening wind and big slop forced Deny to moor in New Harbour overnight. When the wind increased to a gale, Deny decided to wait it out.

So Margaret and the girls set off on a 'wretched walk' back to Melaleuca in sleet and strong wind. Deny accompanied them halfway, to Margaret's relief. It was a tough ten-kilometre walk for a five- and a seven-year-old and Margaret feared they would not make it by dark. But they had inherited their father's stamina and took it in their stride.

The day after they left Deny was ashore stretching his legs when sudden violent squalls swept in, forcing him to wait until they abated before he could return to *Melaleuca*. Miner Trevor Burrell walked across to help. But they were weatherbound for another twenty-four hours.

On the third day Deny decided 'to have a go' and headed out into 'a very big and jumbly sea'. Heavy hail showers flattened the sea, until the gale strengthened again, causing an even bigger slop and a south-west swell. *Stormalong* was a welcome sight outside Breaksea Islands, when 'Trev put on kettle and we had coffee'. Hoisting the staysail they made good time into Port Davey. *Stormalong* accompanied them, and they finally arrived, to Margaret's joy, after an eleven-hour trip.

While in Hobart, Margaret had arranged for Mary and Janet to attend school. In February 1958 they made their first flight from the Melaleuca airstrip. Watching them take off, Deny, who was to sail around, was as dismayed as his daughters at the thought of another separation.

CHAPTER 18

All in a day's work

'Gardening before breakfast, helped with school, sewed up tin, prepared new sledge but it tipped over twice in 20 yards, brought tin (12 bags) down to shed, took up two loads of fuel oil, docked wood.'

Deny arrived in Hobart the night before school started and Margaret was glad of his moral support. The tenants had left the house dirty, so Deny, although exhausted from his voyage, tackled the kitchen. Then as well as escorting the children each day, and entertaining Margaret's Aunt Edith at home and on *Melaleuca* on Regatta Day, Deny, despite a bad back, worked on the boat on the slip. He removed eighteen pieces of ballast from under the floorboards, hosed it out, sanded, painted, installed new fuel and water tanks, repaired generator and voltage regulator, fitted a new fuel pump and had the radio checked. A terse log-book entry for two days records 'refitted pipe and sinks and floor not without trouble'.

Deny repainted the flagpole for the Queen Mother's visit and stayed for Margaret's birthday in early March. After reloading ballast and loading Mines Department gear, fuel, coke, stores and water, he sailed, just missing the governor landing on his airstrip the day before he arrived.

Deny's next visitors were artist Leonard Long with veteran Tasmanian bushwalker Jack Thwaites and Harold C. Reynolds, a University of California scientist. Long was painting for an exhibition. Reynolds, the Kings' first American house guest, wanted to collect pygmy possums for research and was 'extremely grateful' for Deny's help.

Deny took them all for a trip around Bathurst Harbour, 'Len very busy sketching all the way', then on to Kelly Basin, where Reynolds stayed ashore overnight, collecting. Deny and his nephew Dennis Fieldwick, Olive's son, who was helping at the mine, set nets and pots at Kathleen Island, caught mutton-birds and collected wood.

At Melaleuca, Deny overhauled his equipment and started a new paddock. Long, who stayed nine more days, described his host as a 'great man of the bush'. It was an influential experience for Deny too. Long's paintings interested him and he recorded each new scene in his diary. Seeing Long at work, expressing his response to and appreciation of his beloved wilderness, Deny remembered how much he had enjoyed doing small watercolour scenes in New Guinea. It gave him the idea of tackling landscape painting himself.

Deny continued with tasks Margaret had pencilled into his diary, including planting over 100 daffodil bulbs. When Dennis left after Easter, he returned to town for a month. The family stayed again with Olive and Jordan, and Deny, always keen to learn, visited a vegetable processing works and a butter factory. In Hobart he made important purchases—a Lister pumping set for the mine, a Stewart Turner eight horsepower engine for *Blue Boat*, and desks and chairs for the girls, who were to continue Correspondence School lessons at Melaleuca.

They were delighted to be back. They loved their desks, but were less keen on schoolwork and worked well only if Deny took charge. It was an exceptionally cold winter with heavy frosts making it a white world. Deny took them in *Nifty* on the lagoon, smashing the ice as he rowed. There was little wind, so they had to revert to lamps for a month and ration power, curtailing washing machine use and other conveniences. To make matters worse, the house water-pump froze, cracking the casing, and repair proved difficult.

To Deny's distress the cold was too much for Nufty and on radio instructions from a vet they dosed him with sulphur. The children were also sick, and Deny's back trouble recurred. Then on a rare fine day, although Margaret was unwell, they took Nufty on a wood-getting trip, hoping it might do him good. The wood was sodden and the rocky shore difficult, but Deny carried him and laid him in the sun, while he loaded the dinghy. A week later, on an August day when the first daffodil came out, Nufty died in Deny's arms. The loss was felt by all the family, most deeply by Deny, the last link with his father gone.

The girls' attitudes to schoolwork continued to worry their parents and Margaret resorted increasingly to calling 'D. to the rescue. He did a wonderful job with girls' sums—done in no time'. With the children cooped up inside during 'beastly days' of rain, hail and gales, and unwilling to spend much time on lessons, the record player proved a boon. Deny's favourite disc was 'Pedro the Fisherman', a song he whistled to let Margaret know he was coming from the mine.

Visitors often commented on Melaleuca's tranquillity and envied the pace of life, but few had any concept of what was involved in maintaining that lifestyle and offering such generous hospitality. Deny and Margaret were a team, always ready to help each other with difficult jobs and to give moral support. They worked long hours. Often they were up till after midnight finishing various tasks, and rose in the small hours to avoid interruptions. Sunday was no different from other days for Deny.

He spent countless hours maintaining equipment for mine, boats and house. He always referred to his work as 'tinkering', but it was far more than that. He devised and invented, improvised, contrived and contrapted, using whatever was to hand. He never discarded anything, in case it might come in useful. He made washers from tyre tubes and turned the nose cone of a crashed helicopter into a tomato house. At sea he plugged holes in *Melaleuca* with bacon rind, and stuffed mutton-bird skins around a leak at the mast. There was rarely a problem he did not ultimately solve. Even in the most awkward and frustrating situations, he always maintained good temper and philosophical calm, often humorously attributing the problem to an imaginary character, the mischievous 'Quinkan'.

In 1958 Deny worked hard renovating *Blue Boat*, preparing it for the new engine, and making a pump. He built a slip and fitted new timbers cut at Bond Bay. Old bearers were removed, new fitted, and with Margaret's help on the winch the engine was hoisted into position. He installed cooling water pipes, bored holes for the exhaust pipe in the hard wood, puttied holes where the well had been, and 'tinkered' with the floor. They both repainted the boat and red-leaded the engine, and a month later relaunched it. At first there was only one speed—'FLAT OUT'—but after some adjustments the engine performed well. The boat now looked so smart and trim, Margaret wrote, 'We both hate the thought of getting wood.'

His next major task was cladding the chimney with new sheet iron, then insulating the ceiling. This involved dismantling some walls and shelves in storeroom and living room. 'Much scaffolding and many ladders! Awful chaos!' Deny, who had plenty of army practice erecting scaffolding, enjoyed the challenge. Charlie always called any useful contrivance a 'Jimmy Johnson', after a handyman he had known, so Deny's ladders were 'Jimmy Johnsons'. Scaffolding and ladders stayed in place for weeks, while they painted the living room. After restack-ing the timber and mending the garden camp blown down by gales, Deny rebuilt storeroom shelves and extended and remodelled those in the living room to accommodate radio and gramophone, Margaret's work box and books, using Huon pine he French-polished. He also made Margaret a sewing table, dressing-table, footstool and more shelves, Mary a dressing-table, and Janet a bed.

Because of insufficient water at the mine, Deny began digging a new race. At the house he repaired and replaced window frames, and did exterior painting, maintenance on the refrigerator, *Blue Boat*'s magneto and carburettor, and the Mines Department's and Win's radios. In the garden he repaired the storm-damaged greenhouse and built another peat shed. At the airstrip he made and installed a windsock. At the waterfront he began work on a new wharf and building a boatshed, rigging the derrick to install posts, and renovated *Nifty* and *Scamp*.

Downstream he had rerigged *Melaleuca*, varnished the wheelhouse he had built, and painted the boom, deck and rails. He made many trips for ten-metre poles for the boatshed, wharf and a new bridge, which required skilful manoeuvring as he towed them back. And, as always, wood for stove and fire had to be cut and transported to be docked with the Southern Cross engine. This had been relocated by means of the D2 and forky sled, winched down to the water-front sawbench with help from walkers. Trips had to be made to Bond Bay also to collect supplies Clyde had brought.

A day after the Mines men flew out for Christmas 1958, the next plane brought the first summer walkers, twelve Hobart Walking Club members, led by Leo and Jessie Luckman. Deny took advantage of extra muscle power for one of his tongue-in-cheek 'harbour cruises', another wood- and pole-getting excursion. The group and other male 'personnel', as Deny and Margaret always referred to non-family, helped Deny install the extra long pole to serve as the bridge on the Cox Bight track.

On Christmas Day Margaret fed eighteen people. With the number of walkers increasing yearly, Deny, never at a loss for a new project, decided to honour his father's life and work by building a large hut to accommodate them. On New Year's Eve with Margaret's help he pegged the site some distance from the house. Then all gathered at Kings' for probably the most southerly New Year's Eve party in Australia.

Deny and dorts started 1959 with a 'gift from the walkers—nasty nosey colds!' Like weeds inadvertently brought in, which flourished in the damp Melaleuca soil, introduced germs often struck the isolated family, an undesirable side effect of visitors.

Life at Melaleuca had its dramas. Even when away the Kings

always left the house unlocked in case of emergencies. In January 1959 after a 'tats' with Olive to Bond Bay they returned to see a helicopter landing on their strip. Two walkers had struggled in through difficult terrain to radio for help for a companion who had fallen from a steep ridge. In response the helicopter with a doctor had rescued the injured man. Only days later a flight brought the distressed skipper of a wrecked fishing boat, who had flown along the coast to see what was left.

Deny worked hard to finish the wharf and had the satisfaction of moving *Blue Boat* 'into her lovely new moorings' in January. He then started readying *Melaleuca* for Hobart, while Margaret began yet again the exhausting preparations for departure. After many sleepless nights she had decided to send the girls to the state school near Norfolk Crescent.

With help from Mines men, for once it was an easy getaway, and they had a leisurely, unusually sociable trip, enjoying the rare calm, warm conditions. After two nights at Kelly Basin, visiting Win and Clyde, they set off at dawn in company with *Pedra Blanca*, which had visited three summers before. They reached South West Cape after three hours' pleasant sailing, observing seals basking on the rocks and playing in the sea as they passed The Pyramids.

Free from seasickness, which usually beset Margaret, Janet, and sometimes Deny, they revelled in the sight of dolphins diving around the bows, cleaving the green-blue waters, dorsal fins in shining symmetry. Watching the albatrosses was another delight. The great birds swept slowly, scarcely moving their wings, tips just above the water. Gannets glided high with downturned heads gazing into the fish-rich waters. Suddenly, one would fold its wings and plummet, emerging with an unlucky fish firm in its dagger-sharp beak. Deny switched off the engine, as he occasionally did, so that they could just enjoy the sailing, its quietness, and the sounds so often muffled by sea, wind and motor.

They anchored in the lee of Maatsuyker Island, with the south-ernmost lighthouse in Australia, the only manned station along the wild southern and western Tasmanian coasts. After setting nets they took advantage of exceptionally calm weather to explore. All went in *Pedra Blanca*'s dinghy to the little landing stage at the base of the sheer eastern cliff. It was an exciting, even hair-raising, ride up the steep haulage which climbed 140 metres above the sea.

Deny took in every detail. The haulage consisted of two tracks over 300 metres long with a trolley attached to each end of a single cable. As one was let down the other was winched up by a diesel motor driving the cable. When the party reached the clifftop, a keeper met them and drove them through dense stands of tea-tree, melaleuca and banksia to the lighthouse.

Many times as Deny sailed by night he had been glad of its two warning flashes every thirty seconds, visible at a distance of forty kilometres, as far away as Cox Bight and the western end of New Harbour. So it was a special moment to enter the squat brick building, to climb the wrought-iron staircase leading to the third floor which housed the great cylinder of 540 prisms.

Deny was in his element as the keeper showed the mantle lamp and explained the original clockwork. It was thrilling too to walk round the outside balcony, with its breathtaking 360-degree panorama of Southern Ocean and coastline from South East Cape to South West. Like Melaleuca, Maatsuyker was an official recording station, but with an even more demanding schedule of regular three-hourly reports. Deny enjoyed discussing one of his favourite subjects with these men of Maatsuyker, which bears the full brunt of the gales from the Roaring Forties.

In Hobart Deny remained only long enough to see the girls settled into their new school. Slipping the boat, and obtaining and loading supplies, including the first building materials for the new walkers' hut, occupied most of his brief stay.

Invited passengers, Jack Symons, director of Mines, and Terry Hughes, chief geologist, remembered first impressions aboard:

> There was about a ton of iron and goodness knows how many 4x2s, the full length of the cabin floor, and a ton of coke on the deck in loose bags. I was most surprised and said, 'Deny, you haven't got those lashed down.' He said, 'Oh, they won't come off.' And they didn't. We landed at Recherche just about dark. Out came the fishing lines and we caught a meal.

In the morning they saw whales spouting south of Recherche, then after rounding Whale Head had 'rather a joggly time'. Deny sailed closer inshore than usual to allow his passengers to look at geological formations. With the wind strengthening to Force seven, thirty-three knots, they anchored just out from the surf, in company with three other boats sheltering in Louisa Bay, and Deny was sick. Symons, a yachtsman, was surprised to see Deny put a reef in the mainsail. Deny, however, knew what he was doing.

A north-westerly breeze kept *Melaleuca* at right angles to the south-westerly swell. But overnight the slop forced water up the exhaust pipe into two of the four engine cylinders. When the engine would not start the following morning, Symons realised Deny's forethought had been a precaution in case they had to get away in the dark without power. Deny patiently dismantled the engine, wiping each part dry, and finally it started.

The heavy slop persisted as they set off to cross Cox Bight, and conditions worsened as they rounded South West Cape in squalls and rain. *Melaleuca* had a marked tendency to roll, deluging the decks. On this occasion Deny recorded the cockpit half-full of water several times.

He spent four days drying sails and washing down engine, tools and everything else that had been drenched, before he could start on other matters. At the house the powerline from the generator was down and in the garden, the greengage plums were ripe and prunes were dropping. But his first tasks were to catch a voracious wallaby (his name for pademelons), whose night forays threatened the seedlings he had brought, and to repair the fowl yard, to forestall marauding tiger cats.

Deny hardly had time to be lonely. The Mines men were in and out for mail, meat and messages and often stayed for meals, or a cuppa. Symons and Hughes came to see the mine and try their skill on the nozzle. Deny also kept watch on their movements, lighting signal fires one night when two failed to return from Mount Counsel, and going down to North River to check when they were overdue on another trip.

They made several expeditions with him for crays, fish and mutton-birds, wood-getting and cutting poles and battens for the boatshed ridge-pole and rafters. A visitor gave a welcome hand putting galvanised iron on the boatshed roof, fixing the front panels from a scaffolding rigged in *Ark Royal*, and erecting the sides. There was work to be done too on *Nifty*, which was leaking badly.

Deny always saved the mutton-bird feathers, methodically washing them several times to remove their odour, for Margaret to use when she lengthened the girls' sleeping-bags. One night a tiger cat made off with a bag of feathers. As they represented so much effort, he spent an hour hunting to retrieve it.

Since Nufty's death garden invaders had become a problem, so in April he was up again at nights in pursuit, rewarded for his vigilance by splendid views of auroras. As well as fencing the vegetable garden against further intruders, he built scaffolding, higher each year, in order to trim the melaleuca hedge, a task he enjoyed doing to the strains of Julie Andrews and Handel's *Water Music*.

After enlarging the dam at the mine, Deny worked hard for a worthwhile load of tin. He was anxious to see Margaret, who had been in hospital, and he stayed in town over a month. The family went north to visit his old army mate Keith Heeney and wife Clemmie, and had a wonderful holiday, the beginning of an enduring relationship between the families. Deny and Margaret flew back to Hobart to prepare to return to Melaleuca, and gave the girls, at eight and seven, their first taste of independence, travelling back by bus.

They had completed two school terms and Margaret had decided to resume their correspondence lessons. So in June 1959 Deny sailed with more building materials for the new walkers' hut, while Margaret opted to fly with the children. Deny was delighted to have all his girls home again.

The South-West welcomed them with another fierce winter. Again they were without light and power as the wind was too strong for Deny on the generator stand. An exceptionally high tide flooded the wharf and the boatshed floor, forcing him to move all the timber and flooring for the walkers' hut, while the girls' bantams were sheltered in the playroom.

In August Deny helped Clyde, who had a contract to erect a light on Whalers Point, on the north of Port Davey. Clyde had brought the metal stand and gas cylinders from Hobart and Deny helped unload them. Like most South-West jobs it was no easy task. The site was above a gulch where it was difficult to jump ashore even in calm weather because of swirling kelp and a swell sweeping up the steep rocky sides.

Because of a 'rather big' sea, it took three days to land the equipment. They rigged a winch with a twenty-two-metre wire rope down to water level to haul up stand, cylinders and cement. Sand and water had to be brought seven kilometres from Bond Bay. They dug a hole in the peat and gravel for foundations, then went in *Stormalong* thirteen kilometres, to spend another day digging gravel. This was loaded into *Blue Boat*, towed back, and hauled to the clifftop in heavy seas.

They mixed the concrete by hand to make the stand's base, setting bolts in it as they went, and two days later, fixed the tower to them. 'Den's idea. Do it properly. No short cuts!' Clyde said. A week later Deny took his girls to see where 'the lighthouse' was to be. Clyde and Win collected the Swedish-made beacon on their next Hobart trip.

On these Port Davey trips, Deny made observations of intense interest to ichthyologists at the Australian Museum and the CSIRO in Hobart. Whiptails, usually living at ten to thirty fathoms, had penetrated into brackish water as far as Melaleuca Inlet. He also saw deep-sea whiptails, which live at 800 fathoms, in Bathurst Channel. It has since been proved that a high tannin content reduces light levels, enabling creatures normally found only at greater depths to live in these shallower waters.

In October he started in earnest on the walkers' hut, which he had decided to name the Charles King Memorial Hut. On a two-day trip to Old River to collect a load of beautiful flat river stones for their garden paths, Deny realised they would also make a handsome chimney.

On a mild spring day when the scent of sun-warmed earth and the aroma from boronia and tea-tree foliage were strong, when the gold of prickly wattles flecked the bush along the banks of Moth Creek and Melaleuca Inlet, and little 'grass parrots' were speeding like bright arrows across the blue sky, the family went to the site. Together they turned the first sods for the new building.

Deny dug drains, carried timber from his stockpile near the wharf, re-drew and re-measured his plans and dug the foundation for the fireplace. The soil was very deep, so he built a track for his barrow to the old airstrip pit 100 metres away, wheeling loads of gravel and stones to the site. Over the following week with Margaret's help he boxed up and finished the chimney foundations. Then it was back to the mine where he moved the tractor shed by sledge across the race to a new paddock and began building a new dam. He also burned off swathes along the mine race to try to lure the wallabies away from his precious vegetables with new growth.

Margaret's friend Elaine Pearce arrived in November for three weeks, and vividly remembered the happy family life. Everyone greeted her at the airstrip, the children gave her bunches of wild-flowers and Deny flew the flag in her honour. 'At night it was wonderful to be where there was no one within miles and miles, no lights, no signs of civilisation. You didn't have to draw the blinds. You'd just look out onto nothingness.' Elaine's visit was another excuse for more tats, exploring old whaling and pining sites, visiting stands of Huon pine, walking to the coast, beachcombing as Deny loved to do.

Elaine was amused by Deny's humour. When Margaret wore a new blue and white spotted blouse just arrived from David Jones, Deny remarked, 'If that was brown you would look like a native cat.' Native or 'nady' cat was his name for the eastern quoll.

Margaret decided to make a quick trip out with Elaine, for Christmas shopping and business. Hearing the booked aircraft arriving early, Margaret was annoyed, exclaiming, 'VIPs! The departure time has been changed to suit them!' Sure enough visitors arrived—novelist Nevil Shute's wife and companion.

Although Deny had built the airstrip for his own family's safety in emergencies, it had opened up Melaleuca to a far greater extent than he had foreseen. Used not only by Mines Department personnel, and by bushwalkers, it had also become a destination for day-trippers, who came on Aero Club mail and 'tucker' deliveries to the Kings.

After Margaret returned, Deny left with fifteen bags of tin and the tractor tracks for repair, pleased to be guest of honour at the Hobart Walking Club party. Home again, on Christmas Day he was up before dawn, not for the children or presents, but to catch a blackbird which had found its way to Melaleuca and was raiding the cherries.

On Boxing Day when the sandflies were 'vile' and the house was a 'Christmassy mess', fragrant with 'brews' of raspberry and strawberry jam and cherries bottling, an aircraft landed with five Melbourne University Mountaineering Club walkers. No sooner had they left next day with Deny in *Blue Boat* for Spring River, than another arrived with five Launceston Walking Club members. The day before New Year's Eve to the girls' great excitement, two aircraft were on the strip together, bringing more walkers and tourists. So it was a large group aboard *Melaleuca*, which set off for Old River.

Returning loaded with stones for the walkers' hut chimney, *Melaleuca* met two more boats. They journeyed together to Melaleuca where they were joined by another old friend of the Kings. Wilderness photographer Olegas Truchanas had arrived neither by air nor by water but 'on own feet'. As Joyce Denne wrote, it was a 'Grand New Year's Eve'.

CHAPTER 19

A responsible citizen

'An example of citizenship which might well be emulated.'

Fire was always a hazard in the South-West, and in 1951 Deny had expressed his concern to the Rural Fires Board. But a plan for a rural fire district with a local warden was not finalised. So Deny continued acting as firewatcher and fighter until 1959, when the Port Davey Rural Fire District was proclaimed. He was then appointed warden for the far South-West, which added to his load.

The summer of 1960 was very hot. Deny always took precautions to minimise risk around house and mine by systematic burning off at appropriate times and clearing where necessary. However, fires lit by irresponsible fishermen, boaties and walkers were a perpetual hazard and, after destroying bush, could burn for weeks in the peat. Deny therefore was continually watching for smoke and sniffing for fire.

One late March Sunday morning at the mine, Deny smelled peat burning. He hurried home to learn that on the 9.30 sked Win had mentioned a bad fire on Woody Island. Although still recovering from severe flu, Deny set off at once to investigate, towing *Scamp* behind *Melaleuca* over twenty-five kilometres.

In Bathurst Channel on Woody Island, now known as Munday, he found an extensive fire burning. Twenty-six years after the Sunset Ranch devastation, Deny had to deal with another potential catastrophe. This time his efforts took two weeks. He reported the fire had been deliberately lit in three places while crayfishermen were cutting potsticks to hold bait.

'The bush around the shore was very dry with a foot or more of peat under the trees,' Deny recalled, 'and if the fire got into that it would continue burning, regardless of weather.' He was deeply concerned because the island was a breeding place for the elegant little fairy prion.

Helped by Sid Dale and crew he tried to extinguish the fire. The next day he returned with pump and hoses from the mine and worked for seven hours, again with Sid's help. But the fire, burning to a depth of a metre, spread over a hectare in pockets. Its heat dried out the bush and the hoses were inadequate. Even Deny was disheartened:

> You could pump water all over the top of this burning peat and it wouldn't make any difference. It would just burn away from it. The only way to put it out was to feel along the edges and cut behind any fire with a mattock. But the slightest little bit left, you wouldn't see until six hours later. You'd think you'd got it out, then you'd see smoke and have to go over it all again.

Returning home Deny radioed Hobart urgently requesting sixty metres of large hose. Telegrams went to the Forestry Commission and back to Melaleuca. A Rural Fires Board assistant searched four suppliers for hose and fittings and, after dashing to the Aero Club, plaintively reported 'there was no normal flight to Port Davey'. Finally it was dispatched on an aircraft which first took Sir Edmund Hillary to Lake Pedder.

It arrived too late.

The fire, fanned by a strong dry wind, had spread over almost half the island. Returning, Deny anchored in Schooner Cove among eleven other boats, including that of the crew responsible for lighting it. To his disgust only five men from more than thirty helped, despite his repeated requests. This was one of the rare occasions Deny expressed disappointment in others. 'They only ever came because they were short of tucker and I had some. Otherwise I wouldn't have got any help at all.'

In showers and gales they trenched around the fire, then brought the boat into the lee to pump with two hoses. Deny doggedly battled the fire with little help for a further four days, trying to prevent trees being undermined and crashing on the rookery. After five days, Deny thought he had the fire under control.

He spent the next two days cleaning up the boat, washing the engine, pump and fittings, then returned with Clyde and Win, spending another three days cutting more trenches and pumping until all fires were finally extinguished. They had saved more than half the island including its tall timber and the fairy prions he loved.

Some twenty years earlier he and Charlie had collected specimens there. An August 1949 letter to Margaret reveals the thoroughness of his investigations, the exactness of his observations and the depth of his knowledge:

> After grubbing out some burrows we found one pair. They are such lovely things I did hate slaying them even for the sake of science. Do not expect the birdies will be much better off however much mankind knows or finds out about them. However I had to steel myself and not think of it any more. Those two were the only ones we found and no eggs.
>
> That night we went back to Island from camp 10 minutes away to try & find out more about birdies. Aug 10 last year they were there in hundreds after dark so thought they would be now, but there was not the sign of anything. This is strange as these sort of birdies are very strict on dates. Mutton birdies for instance are on the job same day each year.

Deny's voluntary firefighting efforts were motivated by his love for the environment he valued and respected. They cost not only heavy labour and use of boats and equipment, but also valuable working time. The brigade's chief officer commended Deny for his initiative and leadership in bringing a fire under control 'in conditions which few people could appreciate'.

Naturalists R. H. Green and B. C. Mollison, who visited the South-West for field work on their checklist *Birds of Port Davey and South Coast of Tasmania*, and valued Deny's detailed knowledge of local birdlife, acknowledged his and Clyde's contribution:

> The depredation by some elements of the fishing community has extended to lighting fires on the bird islands, and Clayton and King recently spent days quenching such a fire. Their commendable action no doubt saved vast numbers of breeding birds and was an example of citizenship which might well be emulated.

Yet even as Deny fought the Woody Island fire, others were lit on surrounding shores. This prompted Deny and Margaret to begin another campaign—writing to people in authority. In order to prevent the deliberate lighting of fires, they requested the foreshore all around Port Davey, Bathurst Harbour and along Bathurst Channel and the islands be declared a reserve.

A year later, in June 1961, all Port Davey foreshore to a chain's width (approximately twenty metres), was declared a scenic coastal reserve, totalling 547 hectares. In December 1962, the Scenery Preservation Board, forerunner of the National Parks and Wildlife Service, proclaimed all islands within Port Davey and Bathurst Harbour as scenic reserves. Triumph was not a word Deny would have used describing any of his achievements. Nevertheless, these were milestones, marking the first steps in recognising the unique value of the great South-West.

In its 1961–64 report, the Scenery Preservation Board recorded 'its thanks to Mr King for his honorary supervision of the Port

Davey scenic reserves over a long period of years. Mr King's deep appreciation of the scenic values of the South-West and its interesting flora and fauna is shared by an increasing number.'

Two years after the Woody Island fire, the board established a system of volunteer firewatchers operating from Schooner Cove in the summer. Pilots of aircraft flying into Melaleuca also acted as firespotters, assisting to identify boats. Deny commented, 'Gradually the fishermen woke up to the fact they were causing a lot of trouble and some of them stopped lighting fires.'

It was an interesting year for visitors in 1960. Returning from Woody Island, the weary firefighters took aboard some walkers, Sir Edmund Hillary and his party, led by Jack Thwaites. At Melaleuca, Hillary slept in the front room on the Huon pine window seat recently built by Deny and upholstered by Margaret. It was long enough even for him, so he declared it a rare bed.

Deny took them on *Melaleuca* for two days' exploring Port Davey, visiting the Aboriginal cave and middens at Kelly Basin. Because of Hillary's interest in thylacines Deny also revealed a spot where one had been sighted by a fisherman some years before. He was gratified when he eventually saw a copy of the *Mercury* in which Hillary, the first to climb Mount Everest, declared, 'The South-West of Tasmania provides one of the best walking areas I have ever seen.'

As well as walkers, boaties and a helicopter survey, a Tasmanian film crew visited twice with a Hobart Walking Club cast, making a documentary, *Five South West*, including landscape and life at Melaleuca. They filmed Deny on the D2 and at the weather box, Margaret at the radio, and the girls feeding the dusky robins which occupied the house as their own. Deny also took the crew out on *Melaleuca* and *Blue Boat* to film Bathurst Harbour and Channel. The ten stayed in the garden huts and Margaret provided many meals and evening hospitality, even more appreciated when two days of bad weather delayed departure.

The only unwelcome visitors were two blackbirds which Deny hunted morning after early morning. When he shot one raiding the raspberries, he carefully plucked it, stowing it in the refrigerator to await its mate and their final fate in a pie!

Deny was building the walkers' hut like the house, which had proved so successful in withstanding the strong winds. This involved constructing extensive scaffolding, so he was in his element, with 'much rigging of blocks and tackle and an old mast from *Arlie D* for derrick'.

Margaret helped erect and varnish the end wall boards; then it was all hands for the great excitement of putting on plywood and sisalcraft roof lining, followed by a celebration picnic in the hut. Next came the struggle over several days putting the galvanised iron into position, finishing in intense heat. Margaret was pleased the following day was too wet for Deny to work, as he badly needed a day of rest and she was stiff from helping lift the iron.

Deny also had a rare rest on Easter Day, though not before attending to *Melaleuca*, forced bow up into the bush when stern lines were broken by storm-force winds. But he could not relax for long. In the afternoon the barometer had fallen rapidly to an exceptional low. Storm winds raged gusting over seventy knots and a phenomenal high tide flooded the woodshed and tomato house, marooned the sawbench and swept right up under the orchard trees. Deny in thigh boots worked on the wharf while Margaret waded round collecting floating apples, as the waters surged over the plain between the lagoon and Melaleuca Creek.

Under such conditions the prospect of a long-planned Great Barrier Reef holiday was very appealing. In May at the first break in the weather Margaret and children flew to Hobart, leaving Deny to sail with the tin when storms abated, then join them in Queensland.

After a relaxing stay on Heron Island, Margaret and Deny, who valued friendships and nurtured family bonds, established a pattern of visits to Margaret's relatives and friends in Queensland and New South Wales. Visiting Tenterfield and staying at Kathleen Walker's Coolootai Station provided Deny and dorts with an insight into Margaret's early life.

In Sydney her old friend Nan confessed that when Deny appeared 'looking almost like a hobo', she thought, 'Heavens above, Margaret, what have you married?' But by the end of the evening she knew 'he's all right'. Deny's stocks soared even higher when his knowledge and searching questions at an engineering exhibition impressed Nan's husband and colleagues.

Deny never missed an opportunity to investigate machinery and work methods, be it canecutting, cattle raising, aeronautics or manufacturing. He was an observant traveller, listening, learning, visiting factories, museums, galleries and exhibitions, attending lectures, films, theatre, watching television, seizing every chance to broaden his knowledge. Never an idle guest, wherever he was he made himself useful—fencing, felling dead trees, cutting firewood, gardening, doing repairs, painting and stockwork. And he was always birdwatching.

Back in Tasmania in August a warm welcome from their old friends the Heeneys rounded off their holiday and a visit from Olive and daughter Little Olive brought Deny full circle. In Hobart it was lists and more lists as they prepared to return to Melaleuca. For Deny it also meant long hours on *Melaleuca*, cleaning and overhauling, then the usual loading marathon. But despite his painstaking repairs, trouble struck on the voyage.

They got under way in calm conditions and Deny took the boat downriver in darkness and dawn. Half an hour after leaving Southport, Deny discovered a leak in the fuel pipe. Margaret took the tiller while he tried to solder the pipe. When his efforts failed, he improvised a plastic bandage and caught the precious fuel in a tin which needed emptying every fifteen minutes. Margaret steered for six hours. They passed Cox Bight at sunset and fortunately the sea remained calm until they rounded South West Cape.

It was rough all the way to Port Davey and Deny was glad of the light on Whalers Point. 'Very comforting' he wrote in the log book. Relieved, he dropped anchor in sheltered Schooner Cove that night, twenty hours after leaving Hobart. Then on a fine spring morning they left on the last stretch past familiar and loved landmarks. On the otherwise empty page of 11 August Margaret wrote in bold: 'MELALEUCA—Home Sweet Home!'

Homecoming was indeed sweet. Even the roos' ravages could not detract. Silverbeet, celery and little cabbages had survived in the tomato house. Clyde and Win arrived, giving welcome help unloading. The windmill began charging without trouble, *Blue Boat*'s engine started at first try, as did the radio, and the fridge coped with the meat. The cherry-plum tree was in blossom and the first daffodil was flowering. Best of all, the children started their lessons willingly and 'had a lovely session of tables with D'.

Within a week Deny could not resist the call of his wild kingdom, setting off on a sunny afternoon for Moulters Inlet on Bathurst Harbour, where they tied up alongside *Stormalong*. Clyde had bought a chainsaw, impressing Margaret with the amount of wood he cut while Deny was back in his beloved bush, nosing up the creek in the dinghy, going ashore to boil the billy and taking the girls exploring.

Before long the girls' attitudes to lessons challenged Margaret so much that Deny took over more and more. Soon instead of her diary describing his help with school, Deny began noting 'M helped with school'. Margaret recorded Janet's preference for Deny, because 'he was more fun!'

By the beginning of October the first whip snake had already been seen, sandflies had started their torment, and petals of plum, pear and cherry blossom lay in snowy drifts. There were still frosts, so Deny lit fires under the trees to prevent the newly setting fruit freezing. As the month progressed Deny rejoiced in the 'grass parrots' return, and was tickled to find dusky robins nesting in *Melaleuca*'s cabin, while in the orchard the delicate blossoms of apple and quince trees were a delight. At the end of October they enjoyed their first gooseberry pie, but soon Deny recorded rosellas' annual inroads on the fruit, which evoked a favourite expletive, 'Paste the parrots!'

Life at Melaleuca was rich and full. No two days or nights were ever the same. October brought a satellite and a particularly unusual aurora in the east as well as the south. Deny enjoyed new discoveries and observations, new problems to be thought through and solved. In November the melaleucas were tufted in mauve, and flowers of bauera hung like thousands of tiny lanterns on banks and cuttings.

Deny had chosen good ground for a new paddock and began building new races and dams, a new sluice box and gate and moved all the equipment. Mary and Janet rowed up to inspect, often twice a day, sometimes transporting their mother with lunch and the faithful thermos of coffee for Deny. He appreciated help with sluicing from Margaret and even the girls, who delighted in the 'lovely mud' and the water 'play' of nozzling. Deny was picking up half a bag of tin a day so nephew Allan Woolley was welcome. He and Rose flew in on a day of gales, when all hands had to hold down the aircraft while pilot Nick Tanner unloaded.

Before Christmas house guests arrived Deny contrived an irrigation system for the parched garden and made more bathroom improvements. He flatly refused, however, to install a shower, declaring that having a shower was too much like standing in the rain.

Among the summer visitors in 1961 were the Newham family, Hobart Walking Club stalwarts. Ken provided welcome help completing the Charles King Memorial Hut. In January, despite back trouble, Deny, with Ken's assistance, finished the floor, sheathed interior walls with plywood, erected iron at the front, reset windows and triumphantly fixed the door in place.

As walkers from around the world lie there snug and dry, listening to rain pelting on iron and wind howling across the plain, few would realise what an intense labour of love the Charles King Memorial Hut represents. In the early sixties Melaleuca was still button-grass plain without the protection now provided by trees and shrubs planted and nurtured by Deny and Margaret, and bush, which has subsequently grown up as conditions became more hospitable.

The first to enjoy the comfortable accommodation were Hobart Walking Club members, Rhona Warren and Mark Creese, who had both already visited Melaleuca. They stayed for three January nights and after several outings on *Melaleuca* and climbing Mount Rugby, Mark fell under the South-West spell, returning twice that same year. Other HWC members, and some from the Van Diemen's Alpine Club, Launceston Walking Club, Tararua Tramping Club of New Zealand, and the Australian National University followed in quick succession, as word of the splendid new facility spread.

With double-decker bunks donated by the Hobart Walking Club, plenty of floor space for more bodies and gear, a great fireplace with wood, and a rainwater tank, the hut afforded an excellent weather-proof base for walkers commencing or completing their strenuous hike or a midway rest for those on extended walks. In Melaleuca tradition a visitors' book was part of the furnishings, and two pages were already filled before the hut was officially 'opened'.

Sunday 26 February, 1961, a day of drizzle and showers, was historic—the occasion of the first church service ever held at Melaleuca. With personnel from *Lyndenne* and *Stormalong*, whom the Kings entertained to lunch, a congregation of eleven assembled in the Charles King Memorial Hut. The rector of Clarence parish, the Reverend T. A. Cloudsdale, who had sailed round with the Kings' friends Rupert Denne and Bill Watson of base radio VIH, conducted evensong—an appropriate opening for the hut built to commemorate stalwart Christian and churchman Charles King.

A comment written at the opening describes the building as 'a worthy tribute by a Pioneer to a Pioneer'. Forty years on it still stands not only as a memorial to his father but also as a testimony to Deny King's care for others.

CHAPTER 20

To Hobart for school

'Sadly we parted.'

The family's last year together at Melaleuca, 1961, started with an adventure. In January Deny had his first helicopter flight. Two days later, Mines men came to report the helicopter overdue. A search was organised and Aero Club pilot Nick Tanner spotted it, crashed on the Spiro Range.

Margaret worked the radio for two days with skeds almost hourly, while Deny left immediately in *Melaleuca* to pick up his friend, Surveyor General Chris Butler, and the pilot who had walked out as far as Old River. Arriving home at 4.15 a.m., he left again three hours later for the rest of the party stranded at Kelly Basin. Then, emergency over, he seized the opportunity to set craypots and nets. The following day the airstrip was busy again with the arrival of five DCA officers and others investigating the crash, and another helicopter. With the drama over, Deny and Margaret cut and sewed sails, and he took the girls for their first sail.

It was another winter of very hard frosts. Mount Counsel, Mount Fulton and the Ray Range were bright with snow, and in the distance the snow-crowned Norolds and Arthurs glowed apricot in the sunshine. But things were not so bright at home in the school department. Many times Deny was called in to take control. This meant that maintenance jobs such as re-fitting Mary's leaking bedroom window, extending her bed, insulating the hot-water pipes with cardboard, soldering the preserving outfit which had sprung a leak, installing new plywood ceiling panels and making a new bench in the kitchen, building a peat box, cleaning out the chook-food bins, trimming the tea-trees, fixing the windmill, as well as reinforcing the race, tidying the oil shed, reconditioning and refitting the tractor rollers, assembling pipes for the suction pump, and of course mining itself, were all subject to interruption.

Then good news came. Bill Watson at VIH told them about the School of the Air and arranged Mary's and Janet's enrolment. They were thrilled to be the first Tasmanian students, and on 11 July the family listened to their first session.

Deny's teaching extended far beyond formal schoolwork and sailing. He made the girls toolboxes and gave them carpentry lessons. He encouraged their curiosity, powers of observation, their independence and interest in nature. Remembering his own reluctant sessions in the Sunset Ranch kitchen, he loved them to be outside.

There were exciting nights when he took them 'wobbledy' hunting or chasing prowling 'ger cats'. There were wonderful trips on *Melaleuca*. Once Deny planted a cherry tree on the island in Old River, thinking what a pleasant surprise it would be for some hungry hiker to find it in fruit! In return he collected Huon pine and myrtle seedlings to plant at Melaleuca, where they thrived. On another memorable occasion he took the girls to climb Mount Counsel. On reaching the top they lit a fire sending a jubilant smoke signal to Margaret.

At the end of July with Deny's encouragement, his girls visited Brisbane again, where Margaret took the dorts to the races, to the Show for four days of horse events, and for a week's riding at Patricia Marks' farm.

With gooseberries leafing and the first snipe arriving on 30 August, Deny knew spring was really on the way. A message on 1 September thrilled him that his girls would soon be home. Apart from seeing Win and Clyde twice, he had been alone for a month, and with poor radio conditions there had been little other contact.

While still alone Deny set out on an expedition planned for some time. He left at 6.30 a.m. for North River 'with equipment to put father's ashes on Mt King'. At midday, after almost reaching the mountain, he developed such severe cramp he had to turn back. It was a painful walk along the foot of the range, and a great disappointment to be still carrying the box of ashes. He arrived home in darkness and downpour, fourteen hours after setting off, mission unaccomplished.

He also helped Clyde and Win build a wharf at a sheltered anchorage now known as Claytons Corner at the entrance of Melaleuca Inlet, prior to their moving house there, as Bond Bay had proved too exposed. The forty-metre-long jetty was built from the bay to the shore. They felled suitable trees for piles and the ten-metre spars were hooked up on a line from *Stormalong*, dragged out of the bush and driven into the mud one by one from the boat, precisely anchored and tied to the shore. Deny blew the bank out with gelignite to make an approach. They put huge shore logs in place for a 'pigsty' abutment, a form of earthworks support used in mining. Later they decked the jetty with boards from the Bond Bay house. It still stands, a welcome haven for boaties.

Deny was disappointed day after day when weather conditions prevented the girls' flight from Hobart. He had the flag flying and eventually 'all were delighted to be home'. But they brought the inevitable town wogs which laid Deny low for three days. So it was welcome news from VIH that they had been approved as a Royal Flying Doctor Service outpost, a possibility Margaret had canvassed while in town, and the decision boosted her morale. Reception, however, had been consistently bad and Watson advised a new aerial, so Deny and Allan Woolley went to Bathurst Harbour seeking suitable spars. Frustrated by strong winds, they made three trips before succeeding in getting the poles aboard and back home.

On 17 October 1961 Tasmania's first Royal Flying Doctor Base was inaugurated. Three Cessnas with nine people landed on the Melaleuca airstrip. RFDS executive Ernest Mills, who piloted his own plane, gladdened Deny's heart commenting in the visitors' book: 'I wish that half the places I have to land were as good as your excellent airstrip.'

The group included a doctor, journalists and a photographer recording the occasion for the *Mercury* and television. The doctor handed over a chest of medical supplies, explaining their use to Margaret. He also brought a box of books for School of the Air, which operated from the same base. Next evening the family was thrilled to hear Margaret's interview on the news, but despite Deny's painstaking efforts to install the new aerial poles, it required two more visits from Watson and a technician before the radio functioned satisfactorily.

Among other visitors in 1961 the Kings entertained a diver investigating the wreck of the *Brier Holme*; members of the Tasmanian House of Assembly and Legislative Council, and the British House of Commons; and HMAS *Huon* with an army exercise. Port Davey also put its spell on Nan Chauncy, whose books Margaret and the girls had enjoyed.

While Margaret and the girls were busy 'Christmassing', Deny bricked in the walkers' hut stove, finishing it just before the first big group for the season arrived. On Christmas Eve he gave them tea and fresh rolls before ferrying them to Old River and Settlement Point. From then on it was cups of tea non-stop for all comers, including the first group of Boy Scouts to visit Port Davey. But New Year's Eve lacked the customary jollities. Margaret wrote, 'Personnel in and out all day. To bed very early—wearily.'

A regular visitor, fisherman Bob Pettman, wrote in the visitors' book:

> There are kinds of isolation
> Where the problem seems to be
> To cope with the population
> And to find a moment free:
> Here on Melaleuca's shore,
> The rule is as it's ever been—
> The world comes trooping to the door
> Where Kings are to be seen!

Margaret's concern for the girls' education ended full-time family life at Melaleuca in 1962. She had passed on her love of reading and literature and allowed their imagination to have free rein. She had encouraged their love of music and fostered their creative talents. They had learned domestic skills by example and tuition, so that cooking, sewing and knitting were a pleasure, flowers a delight and gardening a joy.

But with Mary eleven and Janet ten, Margaret felt they needed a more structured program, especially in subjects beyond her experience. She enrolled them for first term 1962 at St Michael's Collegiate School, Hobart.

The girls were aghast. 'We were absolutely horrified,' Janet recalled:

> It was such a shock. Our mother made us practise wearing leather school shoes. I remember us standing outside under the cherry tree, both feeling a bit dejected, with these shoes on our feet. It felt very strange, because we'd only been used to gumboots or bare feet. Wearing uniform too was strange, everything was strange.

Although Margaret was prepared to hand over her daughters for school hours, she could not contemplate complete separation. Her own boarding-school experiences had been too unhappy to consider that as an option. She now had to choose between Deny and the dorts. The prospect of city life again with its conveniences and amenities was not without its attractions. But for the girls it was a reluctant packing up and for Margaret sad and tiring.

Deny stayed in Hobart eight days, just long enough to do a host of jobs at Norfolk Crescent, help Margaret settle in, shop, and see the girls well started at school. After they went by themselves for the first time he set sail, with Doug Watkins for company.

They arrived home just in time for a unique event. The passenger liner MV *Anking* entered Port Davey, came up Bathurst Channel, and anchored near Woody Island. Passengers then disembarked into five fishing boats, *Melaleuca*, and lifeboats which *Melaleuca* towed to Deny's wharf where 'there was no room for any more'. The passengers 'went walkabout' to the mine and while Win and Doug boiled the kettle, Deny packed a box of flowers to send to Margaret and collected signatures in Chinese characters in the visitors' book.

Back at the liner all crews boarded by rope ladder for a tour and were entertained by the captain to a meal. 'The grog flowed freely' according to Deny, a very light drinker, and 'a good time was had by all'. Then, to his delight, the boats' masters were invited onto the bridge to travel as far as Breaksea.

A week later Nan Chauncy, whose first visit Deny had missed, returned aboard fishing boat *Tangara*. Deny enjoyed her company over three days—'There was much to be talked about'—with several expeditions showing her special spots, recording she was 'very thrilled with the place'. She developed a warm friendship with the Kings and later used Port Davey as the setting for two of her children's books, *The Roaring 40* and *High and Haunted Island*.

Janet surmises Chauncy found inspiration for the early part of *The Roaring 40* from Deny's tales of his first prospecting trip to Mount McKenzie. The subsequent part is set near Bond Bay. The book's dedication reads: 'In admiration of the true "South Westers", this story is inscribed to all the children living at Port Davey—to Mary and Janet King.'

There were still boats arriving and aircraft bringing visitors, so Deny always seized the opportunity to pack boxes and send Margaret flowers from the garden and bush, fruit, vegetables, fresh herbs, mutton-birds, jam, crayfish and frequent letters about daily life—anything to remind his girls of their Melaleuca home. In between visitors he worked long hours at the mine. But in mid-March he took another day off.

Setting out early in *Blue Boat* on a fine warm day he returned to North River to climb Mount King once again. Ascending from the steep eastern side, he reached the summit at 1.45 p.m., hot and very thirsty, then had to descend the west side for water. Returning to the pinnacle he scouted about until he found a ledge under a rock. There he cemented in the box containing his father's ashes, then sprinkled the place with white gravel from their old North River camping spot. Again he was badly afflicted by cramps in the three-hour walk back. It was a fine calm night, however, and *Blue Boat*, Charlie's pride and joy, 'steered herself most of the way over the harbour' back to Melaleuca, which Charlie had been the first to call home.

The house seemed even more empty than ever that night. Deny, stirred by memories, adopted his usual practice when sleep eluded him. He went outside and with long steady strokes pumped water from the bottom tank to the top one at the house, hoping the rhythm and exertion would induce rest at last.

Plum and cherry trees were colouring rapidly, and crescent honeyeaters were around in unusual numbers. Deny had finished autumn burning off, bottled ginger beer, made jam from good quince and pear crops, and often enjoyed sweet corn for tea, before recording the first frost early in April. The tin was 'light on', so Deny, eager to be in Hobart for the school holidays, continued to work long days trying for a worthwhile load.

At the end of April he dug all the potatoes to forestall the bush rats' inroads. He strengthened all the fencing, 'snugged down' his beloved D2 after removing its tracks for overhaul in Hobart, and made the house shipshape. He had finally struck a good patch of tin, so had sixteen and a half bags to sew up and load singlehanded, as well as digging bags of sand and gravel for concreting jobs at Norfolk Crescent, and plants for Margaret's town garden.

This time Deny stayed over four months, the longest he had ever spent in Hobart. He slipped *Melaleuca* and attacked the difficult, dirty task of digging out ballast and concrete to reset the keel, whose bolts were so corroded it was in danger of parting from the hull. When the boat was spick and span with new cabin floor, railings and paintwork, improved lockers, new folding table, and navigation lights installed on rigging and mast, the family set off to explore the east coast, with borrowed charts and plenty of advice from fishermen friends. It was another adventure after Deny's heart and the dorts were delighted to spend school holidays at sea.

It was strange heading down the Derwent to sail east instead of west. Deny was glad of the help of an 'old army cobber' to pilot them through the Dunalley canal, a headlong rush as the tide was running very strongly. They sailed out into the Tasman Sea with the fishing fleet and headed north towards Maria Island.

They continued to Freycinet Peninsula and anchored in the clear turquoise waters of Coles Bay beneath the red granite bulk of The Hazards. They stayed seven days, exploring and visiting more of Deny's old friends and making new ones. Deny was interested in the granite quarries and abandoned tin workings, and had long talks with the National Park ranger about the area's natural history. He took the dorts on walking expeditions to beautiful Wineglass and Sleepy bays and climbed Mount Amos, for memorable views of the coastline and its brilliant azure waters.

Back in Hobart for the new school term, the family had an active social life, entertaining and entertained by people who had enjoyed Melaleuca hospitality. Slide evenings were popular, and they enjoyed slides of others' travels, or invited people to view theirs. They often saw Melaleuca visitor Olegas Truchanas and his wife, and his superb images of the South-West were always a special pleasure. They met friends too at meetings of the Hobart Walking Club and the newly formed South-West Committee, a voluntary organisation formed to protect and preserve the unique South-West. The Kings were foundation members, and made an important contribution to the committee's submission to the government, proposing a new national park to protect south-western Tasmania. This included Lake Pedder and Port Davey.

Margaret wanted a new kitchen and other renovations at Norfolk Crescent. So the 'unholy mess', which Deny seemed destined to create wherever he was, began again as he pulled down the back verandah, and helped builder friend Mark Creese dig and pour foundations, rip out ceilings, knock down walls, clean bricks, and put up studs. He also dug trenches and drains and laid stormwater pipes. Inevitably there were problems and delays, which tried Margaret's patience sorely, but which Deny accepted philosophically. When she declared, 'Felt like giving the place away and buying a tent!', Deny smiled, remembering the camp at Cox Bight.

Margaret also wanted a car and took driving lessons. She and Deny renewed their licences and finally selected a Hillman station wagon. For the dorts, horses were still the passion and Margaret started taking them to riding lessons. A conscientious mother, she became very involved with school activities. Town life agreed with her. Wishing Deny to look the part, she bought him a navy blazer and white flannels to wear on *Melaleuca* on Regatta Days and at other yacht club events. But Deny, who usually acceded to her wishes, flatly refused, and they had to be returned.

Late in 1961 Deny had been distressed to learn that Olive had cancer. Family bonds were strong, so now Deny and Rose decided to spend a few days with their sister. Deny helped Jordan with his building project and did some prospecting.

Back at Norfolk Crescent Deny improved the garage, but he had no time to enjoy the finished renovations. It was mid-September and he was preparing for departure. Two days after his birthday the girls accompanied him down the Channel, and Margaret drove to meet them at Woodbridge. She helped stow cargo and hoist sails, and Deny wrote in the log book, 'at 3 p.m. we sadly parted'.

One fine October day he moved the Sunset Ranch piano for the third time, leaving home at 5.30 a.m. to go with Clyde and Win to Bond Bay. They manoeuvred the piano into a case which they slid down skids onto a dinghy, then hoisted it aboard *Stormalong*. Five hours' sailing later they reached Claytons Corner, but the tide was too low, and they had to wait until 10.30 that evening to unload, slinging the piano ashore in darkness. Early next morning, using block and tackle, they skidded it on boards up to the house, where it was in place by 9.30. Job done, Deny went home and by noon was sluicing in the mine.

For weeks Deny's only company was several gulls picking over the newly stripped paddock. Few aircraft came in and radio conditions were bad. He was distressed he could not get a message to Margaret for their thirteenth wedding anniversary. When a Mines Department friend arrived, they walked to Cox Bight, where Deny showed him the old workings, spent several days prospecting.

He scouted for hewardias to take to Dr Winifred Curtis of the University of Tasmania's botany department. Dr Curtis, or 'Curty' as Deny called her, was the scientist with whom he had his longest and most fruitful collaboration. Ten years earlier the Tasmanian Museum had passed on to her specimens Deny sent for identification. She was working on a book, *The Student's Flora of Tasmania*, and was interested to find that one of Deny's specimens, *Eriostemon virgatum*, a member of the waxflower family and found on the east coast and at Macquarie Harbour, also grew near Port Davey. She offered Deny help to identify plants at any time and some specimens Deny sent her made significant contributions to the field of botany.

In Hobart in December Deny planned a quick turnaround, to allow the girls maximum time at Melaleuca. Nevertheless, he did a radio interview to raise public interest in the South-West and its need for protection. With the same concern he discussed with Jack Thwaites of the Scenery Preservation Board the firewatchers' program to be inaugurated for the summer. Then somehow he made room on *Melaleuca* for all the firewatchers' gear.

It was a relief for Deny and Margaret when the first volunteers arrived just before Christmas. Although fires the previous summer had been less serious than the Woody Island fire, they had caused Deny much anxiety and cost many days' work. For many firewatchers it was their first visit to Port Davey, and Deny did much to assist them. A number returned in later years, and some became family friends.

The 1963 summer holidays featured some special expeditions. Deny had been asked by anthropologist N. J. B. Plomley to try to trace George Augustus Robinson's route in the 1830 search for the local Aboriginal people, ordered by Lieutenant-Governor George Arthur. Deny readily accepted the challenge.

From Melaleuca Inlet they climbed into the hills searching for a cliff of marl and red and yellow ochre Robinson had described seeing as he walked from Cox Bight to Horseshoe Inlet. They did not find it, which provided the excuse for four more 'Robinsoning' trips, unsuccessful but much enjoyed. Deny put his inimitable bushcraft to good use, imparting it also to the dorts, and sharing his respect for Aboriginal culture.

After his thoughtful search on foot, Deny wrote to Plomley, 'Robinson's journey to the Arthur Range is truly quite a feat . . .The difficulties of this undertaking cannot be fully appreciated by anyone who has not been through this country and experienced the type of weather that prevails.' Plomley replied, 'Your welcome letter came yesterday and the map and manuscript this morning. . .What you have done will be of the greatest help. I only wish I could have advice on other sections of Robinson's itinerary half as good.'

In the introduction to his book *Friendly Mission*, Plomley acknowledged Deny, also quoting his tribute to Robinson's seamen:

> Credit should be given to the coxswain of the whaleboat for finding his way into and up to Melaleuca Inlet when the area was practically uncharted and the dark water prevents anyone from judging its depth below one foot or eighteen inches. In places the Channel is narrow and runs through mud flats.

Two days before returning to Hobart Deny led Margaret and the girls on another expedition—their first ascent of Mount Rugby. So many times they had gazed on its grandeur, stark against a blue sky or swathed with scarves of cloud, or purple and gleaming gold in the sunset. So many times they marvelled at its symmetrical reflection mirror-clear in the silver waters of Melaleuca Lagoon.

Climbing it was a triumph and the fulfilment of an ambition, even a rite of passage for Margaret, Mary and Janet, as Mount Weld had been in Deny's youth. Although its height is little over 770 metres, its sides are steep and rocky, and the summit is a jumble of huge boulders intersected by crevices, so the climb required some effort.

The panorama from the pinnacle was its own reward—the great shining sweep of cornflower-blue waterways and shimmering sea, rugged mountains rising range on range to distant forget-me-not blue horizons, and in the middle distance their beloved Melaleuca— mine, airstrip, Charles King Memorial Hut, garden, home.

CHAPTER 21

Dreamland

'Watching and waiting for D.'

The year 1963 was full of comings and goings. After starting school in February, the girls were 'Nung-sick', so Deny returned to Hobart again in May, August, October and December.

Deny always noted milestones in local and world history, so February held a special thrill. The royal yacht *Britannia*, bringing the Queen and Duke of Edinburgh, arrived in the Derwent. Boarding *Melaleuca* early the family collected friends before joining the big fleet of small craft.

The great river with its backdrop of mountains dominated by the grand sentinel Mount Wellington, distinctive with tabletop silhouette and organ-pipe facade, was a fitting highway for the queen of a maritime island. The gathering of boats of all sorts and sizes, bedecked with flags and bunting, was a rare spectacle.

Deny, for whom the river was indeed a highway, was excited to see the sleek vessel approaching, and to be part of the welcoming flotilla. They saw 'Their Majesties passing' and at night drove up Mount Nelson for a fine view of celebratory fireworks.

Deny always enjoyed catching up with boatie friends on Regatta Day. So *Melaleuca* joined the yachts, but took part only in the last event, *Britannia*'s departure—an exciting finale before his own.

He reached Melaleuca to find prunes, plums and red apples ripe and that swallows had hatched another brood in the boatshed. He worked solidly, with scarcely a day's break, often sluicing six hours at a stretch. Always observant, while dozing a new strip he was intrigued to find 'numerous bits of charcoal in some very old grass like a tiny stream bed in the clay', and collected specimens.

First term was full for Margaret so her diary was neglected for several months until the telling brief entry on 7 May: 'Watching and waiting for D.' She was preoccupied, trying to make a cherished dream come true. She wanted a place in the country where the girls could keep horses, and where she hoped, quite unrealistically, she might persuade Deny to retire. The search for 'Dreamland' was on.

Returning to Hobart in May with eleven bags of tin, Deny arrived for the funeral of Herb Skinner, his mother's brother, so fond of her and so disapproving of Charlie. Perhaps with his father's ashes now in their chosen resting place at last in the heart of the great South-West, Deny felt free to search out his roots and renew old ties. Two days after the funeral the family went to the Huon district and Hartz Mountains to visit old haunts. He visited other uncles, Vic Skinner in a nursing home, and Carl Skinner for Sunday dinner. If there was any unfinished business in family relationships, Deny, who never held grudges and was expert in building bridges and repairing fences, took this opportunity to resolve it.

With 'Dreamland' on Margaret's hidden agenda, they went for drives, looking round other old haunts near Brighton Army Camp and Cambridge Aero Club. They walked up Mount Nelson and to Collinsvale, and visited Nan Chauncy at her wildlife sanctuary home near Bagdad.

Departure for Melaleuca was delayed by gales, so Deny had to unload all the perishables and buy fresh stock before he finally left. Sailing single-handed again, he faced the prospect of a long lonely winter. Win and Clyde, faithfully keeping in touch and staunch in offering assistance and hospitality, often invited him for a meal. He would always call at 'CC', as Claytons Corner became known, for a cuppa and yarn on any of his wood-getting trips, and sometimes join them for a day's fishing or mutton-birding.

In early August when a pair of scrubwrens had started nesting by the lawn and the first heath was out, Deny struck some good tin and worked solidly to get twelve bags before leaving for Mary's thirteenth birthday.

Margaret and the girls awaited this visit even more eagerly than usual, but Margaret's longing was mingled with considerable trepidation. Over the years she had taken the initiative and made many purchases to change or improve their lifestyle. Now she had made the biggest decision since acquiring the house and *Melaleuca*. She had taken the plunge and bought a property near the girls' riding school, without consulting Deny. She did not attempt to contact him, even when she closed the deal on 'Dreamland' a week later. By the time she had arranged the overdraft he had left Melaleuca.

When the girls saw *Melaleuca* rounding Sandy Bay Point, Margaret began to feel worried about her 'wild decision'. Despite their excitement Mary and Janet kept the secret, and it was not until next day that, on the pretext of collecting firewood, they drove out to 'The Rise' at Acton and broke the news.

The following day they returned with a picnic, boiled the billy and planted young melaleucas by the dam. The girls rode horses, and Deny cut the first of innumerable loads of wood to take back to Norfolk Crescent. His diary entry finished 'lots of birdies on the Rise', probably the seal of acquiescence if not approval.

Outflanked by the girls, in addition to all the jobs awaiting him at Norfolk Crescent, Deny immediately began necessary maintenance and improvements Margaret wanted at The Rise. They inquired at the Department of Agriculture how to clear the serrated tussock grass, a noxious weed useless for feed, prevalent in the paddocks. It resembles the native tussock grass and Deny was to spend many backbreaking hours trying to eradicate it. In October he left again for Melaleuca.

Margaret's life, full and satisfying, now revolved largely around the girls' pony club. She had also become treasurer of the South-West Committee. The group met in members' homes and Norfolk Crescent was often the venue. Margaret enjoyed the company and dedicated energy of the members, who included old friends and visitors she and Deny had welcomed to Melaleuca. The committee aimed to raise public awareness about the area by showing slides, including Deny's, to schools and public-spirited groups.

Describing the 'golden days of spring', and anticipating being together again at Christmas she wrote to Deny, 'How the years are flying by. We must make the most of them.' This was a poignant comment that they both later recalled.

At Melaleuca foxgloves on the bank were 'making a great show', with a hundred stately spires of mauve-pink bells. Rhododendrons near the house were a riot of bloom, and the waratah Deny had planted rewarded him with its first scarlet flower. In October he heard a fan-tailed cuckoo and in November the swallows were trying again to nest in *Melaleuca*'s wheelhouse and Deny put up shelves in the boatshed, to encourage them there instead. Flocks of 'stripeys', as he called New Holland honeyeaters, had arrived to feed on the wonderful flowering of mauve melaleuca and white tea-tree.

Late in October when the bauera was a pink fairyland and gums had started blossoming, Deny hit 'tin too good to cover over' in a place he was stripping to put overburden, so he changed his plan. Then he found more rich tin running across a patch he had thought 'would be only just worth cleaning up'. Even for an experienced miner, there were surprises, sometimes disappointing, sometimes exciting.

He was busy too with all manner of jobs making house and garden welcoming for his girls. But he took time to assist a Viennese ornithologist who arrived in search of ground parrots. The Canberra CSIRO Wildlife Research Division also sought his help, requesting his wartime observations on Papua New Guinea birds made twenty years earlier.

The family had a rare Christmas Day alone at Melaleuca, before personnel in their dozens started arriving by sea, land and air. New Year's Day 1964 saw another innovation at Port Davey, reducing its isolation, this time initiated by Win and Clyde. The Kings gathered at CC, for the switching on of their newly installed television. Now images from all over the world were beaming in, almost to Deny's doorstep, a far cry from old newspapers pasted on walls.

A few days later Margaret recorded seven aircraft arriving on the strip. In a week the tally had risen to twenty-six, with forty-five passengers in and forty-two out. With walkers and boaties too, every square inch of the Charles King Memorial Hut was occupied by bodies, boots and packs. Deny and Margaret also had house guests. Day visitors included the botanical collector Lord Talbot de Malahide and companions. He signed the visitors' book, but Deny, never impressed by titles or rank, merely recorded 'an aircraft came in from Launceston with 3 collecting plants'.

It was a wet, cold, windy January, but the rain meant water for sluicing. Margaret and the girls went to see him finish streaming and pick up the first tin for 1964, and sometimes helped. Remembering Deny's comment that he might call the business 'King and Dorts', 'Girl Power' worked well. When the tin was bagged and Deny and Margaret had sewn it up, Mary and Janet took turns driving the tractor towing the loaded sledge to *Blue Boat*.

Deny ferried two track workers to Spring River before the family continued their last summer tats to Port Davey for three happy days fishing, swimming, helping Clyde pull craypots and going to Breaksea for mutton-birds.

Back in Hobart in February 1964, Deny's first purchase was a chainsaw, and within days the family were at The Rise, where he sawed down a tree, cutting and stacking wood while the girls rode in a pony-club rally. As he watched them saddling up hoping to win ribbons, he remembered Rose and Win riding Sam bareback tandem to Judbury and back, to deliver the hard-won cream so vital to the family income. Sunset Ranch seemed another world, another lifetime.

He sailed back with firewatchers Charlie Vaughan and son Puck crewing. Rounding South West Cape into a stiff northerly, waves breaking into fifteen metres of pipe overhanging the bow sent water spouting out the stern end. Puck recalled Deny's quip, 'Prunes and cheese for tucker—they counteract each other.' Later when they took Deny some ducks they had shot, he teased, 'I should arrest you! They're protected. But the fishermen treat this place like a chook pen, so we might as well pluck them and have a good feed.'

In March 1964 Deny received a further request 'for help regarding information about Aboriginals in your district'. It came from the Australian Institute of Aboriginal Studies, where his name had been referred. Later, field worker Peter Sims returned for several summers investigating sites. In the same month, anthropologist Therese Belleau Kemp, from the Research School of Pacific Studies at the Australian National University, Canberra, made a field trip to Melaleuca. Deny did not need any persuading to leave the mine for a week and took her and bushwalking friends by boat to sites he knew.

They investigated the red ochre cave near Schooner Cove, then crossed Port Davey to Bond Bay, where Deny helped Kemp with excavating, and showed her the middens. On a second trip they sailed round to Stephens Bay. Along this vast wild curving bay open to the Southern Ocean, where the breakers pound in endless succession and the rugged spume-wreathed coast rolls south to the formidable pillars of South West Cape, the Needwonne people had made their home. They camped in the shelter of the great sand dunes north of Noyhener, the beach whose name still preserves a word of their language, and found good hunting and gathering at Stephens Beach. Seals and mutton-birds on nearby islands, and shellfish along the rocky headlands provided rich sustenance. Inland, game abounded: wallabies on the moorlands and button-grass plains and swans on sheltered waters in nearby Hannants Inlet.

The extensive middens consist mainly of abalone and warrener shells, and also contain stone tools, seal and wallaby bones. Deny mentioned large bird bones that he thought most likely pelican. They left for home next morning, where Deny 'helped Mrs K pack bones and stones' before her aircraft came.

For Deny, now in his early fifties, it was a special week, a rare interlude sharing some little-known and undervalued features of his world. He had found a kindred spirit, someone who understood and appreciated the treasures he was revealing, someone who could also hear the song this wild country sang to his soul, and with whom he had 'great laughs'. Kemp appreciated the Kings' hospitality and help, and continued corresponding for years from Sweden, Canada and Britain.

Margaret found Acton Rise's proximity to the Aero Club a bonus. Departures were always uncertain and sometimes she packed a parcel three times before a flight could take off, which meant buying fresh meat, bread and fruit each time. Now she combined trips to The Rise with delivering parcels and letters to be flown to Melaleuca.

Deny lived for his girls' letters. Margaret's were often lengthy, written late at night beside the fire or in bed early in the morning. Sometimes they were yearning, speaking of their 'longth' for him; or tenderly solicitous of his wellbeing, especially his 'backy', and hoping he was feeling 'frisky'.

Margaret recounted business matters, household events and dort doings with humour and original turns of phrase. Deny was pleased to hear how they enjoyed mutton-birds he had sent and was amused at her cooking them outside in the electric frypan, 'so that the stink-oh was not all through the house. What a pity thinks you.' He grinned on reading that Margaret had distinctly smelled the birds' odour in church—from the dorts' unwashed faces!

She always described the weather, frequently mentioning 'snoot on the moot' (snow on the mount). She tuned into VIH daily, hoping to hear him 'booming across the kitchen', but chided, 'You never say a thing—except about the weather', or exclaimed, 'All you talked about was the filthy barometer!' She discussed books he would like and exhibitions, especially those of artists who had visited the South-West. She also retailed news of family and friends, especially from the fishing fraternity, with whom they had so much in common.

A fair judge of character, Margaret tried to protect Deny from visitors whose motives she suspected and who, she felt, would abuse his hospitality and take advantage of his generosity. She wrote pithy sketches dismissing or approving people who called inquiring for Deny, or asked about the possibility of a passage or work.

Often her letters were just short scrawls written in haste on any scrap of paper as opportunity presented. Aircraft movements being unpredictable, mail deliveries were still erratic—dependent upon passenger demands as well as weather. On occasion parcels shuttled to and fro several times, not desirable for meat and butter, or flowers and mutton-birds, and very frustrating for Margaret, concerned for Deny's food supplies. One passenger delegated to deliver letters from Deny called at the pub on his way to Norfolk Crescent and arrived reeking of his stopover.

Sometimes the Aero Club forgot to notify Margaret of proposed flights and once, to Mary's great indignation, Deny did not get his three birthday cakes on time. Often, however, the pilots delivered Deny's letters and parcels themselves and many became family friends.

Deny derived both amusement and concern from the dorts' letters. Janet made no secret of her homesickness and how much she missed her beloved father. Margaret wrote to 'Dear our Bear' that Janet had a bad attack of 'Nungitis which will not be better until *Melaleuca* is on her moorings'. So Deny, having struck some rich tin, and insoluble trouble with the Thornycroft engine, which cost him many hours, returned to bring the girls home for the May holidays.

To give them as long at Melaleuca as possible, he spent just three busy days in Hobart, buying gumboots, parts for the tractor and engines, and paying bills. Then while their parents stowed the gear, Mary and Janet steered as far as Partridge Island where they anchored overnight, before an uncomfortable voyage. Showers and gales did not stop Deny mining, as he wanted another load of tin ready when he took the dorts back.

Three weeks later and back in Hobart, Deny's first job was to buy a length of chain for *Melaleuca*'s new moorings. His second was to arrange servicing for the Thornycroft engine. The boat's overhaul proved to be more extensive than expected. After the rigging was unscrewed the mast broke as he and helpers lifted it out. He discovered a rotten patch, and was very thankful it had not snapped in the big seas and vicious squalls of his last two trips with his family on board. Ever-resourceful he cut down and installed the mast as gateposts at The Rise.

When Mary was rushed off with appendicitis, Margaret was glad they were in town, and grateful for Deny's support. He already had a steady hospital round, visiting Charlie's old friend Sid Dale, as well as his Uncle Vic.

In late August, with snow on Mount Counsel and dusky robins nesting in the tracla house, Deny back at Melaleuca was dozing up pay dirt rich in fine tin, and within four weeks had twenty-seven bags.

Hobart end-of-year social activities were in full swing when Deny arrived. But he had been giving much thought to the next stages in modernising the mine and was more interested in investigating new machinery and welding equipment. He was also pleased to receive a request from Julia Greenhill, keeper in invertebrate zoology at the Tasmanian Museum. Recalling the land snails he had collected at Lake Pedder back in the 1930s, she asked him to collect specimens from the Port Davey area, which he did the following year.

The family enjoyed another quiet Christmas at home, their tree a branch cut from a myrtle Deny had planted years before. On New Year's Eve Deny greased the tractor as usual and filled the hydraulic pump with new oil. That peaceful Melaleuca night, as they listened to the familiar chromatic calls of ground parrots, Deny held his beloved Margaret close, rejoicing she was in his arms again, sharing memories and planning for the future.

CHAPTER 22

In sickness and in health

'M ill.'

New developments at Melaleuca in 1965 caused concern and divided opinions in the King family. Mining giant BHP Ltd had taken out exploration leases in the region, set up base at the Mines Department camp and wanted to airlift personnel, supplies and equipment.

To the girls' consternation, the Hydro Electric Commission was also investigating the area for possible water storage and a power station on the Davey River. In 1963, a pilot friend who expected to fly in the first HEC survey group had advised Deny they wanted him to transport them; and recommended charging them 'EXORBITANTLY'. Such antipathy was increasingly expressed by people concerned for the integrity of the remaining wild regions.

The pressure was on Deny to extend the airstrip.

Margaret and the girls were totally opposed. They valued their privacy and did not want to lose it. They wrote numerous letters trying to deter Deny. When it was first mooted in 1964, Mary wrote, 'It would be better to be getting some tin to have enough money for that new wheel for the mine. Isn't it lovely that you're not going to do the strip and make everything peopley?'

Margaret, who kept a close watch on tin prices and worried about school fees, uniforms, medical bills, The Rise mortgage and even the 'Wuppets' weddings, wrote in similar vein:

DON'T do it unless Nick [Tanner] agrees to give you an
annual subsidy. I just don't see why you should put yourself
out and wear out tractor tracks just so Aero Club can make
more money and BHP can fly in windier weather. PLEASE
Bear get it in writing this time. It's only right and fair. I
really think you should go flat out for tin (£1372 ton) and
put in your machinery.

'What's happening about the frightful strip?' she later wrote. 'TIN
now £1402 a ton. You should be flat out sluicing like mad for a jigama-
roo and an easier life ahead.' She added she was selling BHP shares to
meet the interest on The Rise and another big bill for supplies.

Janet, showing her practical nature and maturity beyond her
years, had written sternly. 'You should consider Moosie. She is not
feeling very well because of worry over her debt and you doing the
strip. Please don't do the strip. We don't want a sophisticated airport
at home.'

And when Margaret heard Deny was going ahead she did not
mince words:

We three feel very wild with you. Not a word said to Nick
either, I'll bet. I paved the way for you—told him it was
high time the Aero Club paid you either an annual £50 or
so much a landing. You should be getting out tin flat out
while it's so high, for your new equipment. Now you'll just
have to pay more interest on an overdraft—very bad
business—you've had enough of them in the past.

Deny, however, was enjoying the airstrip being 'peopley', interested in the number and different types of aircraft landing. Although
the airstrip could never be called sophisticated, the exploration
team's gear certainly was. Deny was chuffed that a big mining
company depended on using the airstrip he had built alone with his
little D2.

There were so many in the BHP team that some stayed in the Charles King Memorial Hut. This also gave Deny wry satisfaction, remembering the basic camps he and his father had endured over the thirty years since their first prospecting expedition to the South-West. Now these men, employees of a large company, were living in comparative luxury because of his labour. He spent evenings yarning with them, and the university graduates were impressed by the hospitality of this slow-speaking gentle bushman, and the knowledge and wisdom he so generously shared.

The BHPs, as Deny called them, relied on him not only for local knowledge of terrain and weather and for communications with the outside world, but also for use of his boats and assistance with their equipment. He delivered their fuel, fixed their fridge, brought them firewood, built a mailbox for their outward mail, and put his bridge-building skills to use on their behalf. And despite 'tracla trouble', he worked hard on the strip, starting at 6.30, grading and resurfacing it for the heavy traffic it was receiving.

To simplify exploration, a Haflinger all-terrain vehicle had been brought, in parts, by aircraft and helicopter. Deny was fascinated to watch it being assembled. The 'boys' took Deny for a ride up Kings Knob and halfway to New Harbour, and he was amazed at its performance, doing sixteen kilometres per hour over rough country. Later they transported Deny's tin for loading.

Much to his pleasure Deny was also often given helicopter flights. One fine clear day they flew over South West Cape, landing on top of the range and other places near the coast, a thrill for Deny to observe familiar topography from a different perspective.

In May Deny returned to Hobart for two months. He was ready to implement his long-considered plans for further mine improvements, so spent more time looking at machinery and obtaining quotes. He arranged a bank loan to purchase a new trommel, a large cylindrical revolving sieve for cleaning ore, which would eliminate much manual work, and ordered its manufacture locally to his specifications. He visited his old army commander Gordon Colebatch for information about an electric power plant, necessary for the extra pumps, trommel, conveyor belt and jig he wished to install.

Margaret had never enjoyed good health, and frequently recorded feeling tired and wretched. So Deny took her for tests and an X-ray. The girls were having their usual bouts of winter ills and Deny also succumbed. But for him this was nothing compared with the news that *Mariner 4* had reached its destination, and the excitement of seeing the first pictures of Mars.

When the new trommel was delivered in sections to the boat in mid-August, it was time to leave. Friends helped load it as well as curved iron, pipes and timber for the engine shed. He was at Melaleuca only days before he had to return suddenly to Hobart, this time a grateful patient with the Royal Flying Doctor Service. Clyde and crew had helped with unloading, but Deny strained a muscle and was in considerable pain. At Cambridge airport Margaret met him with an ambulance and took him to the Royal Hobart Hospital. After a week's physiotherapy he was working at The Rise.

Margaret decided to go to Melaleuca with Deny for a short spell. They flew back, leaving a friend looking after the girls. It was a rare experience to be alone together, as from the outset of their marriage Charlie had been with them. They enjoyed each other's company even in mundane tasks such as clearing up the mess where rats had been at the apples, jam and cornflakes. Deny was grateful for Margaret's help at the mine and in the garden, and appreciated coming home once more to the house fragrant with the smell of fresh-baked cake and sweet with the flowers Margaret loved arranging.

As they lay contented and close in bed on wild stormy September nights, listening to the rain running in torrents down the curved iron roof, they talked again of their hopes and plans. Then the distinctive Melaleuca smell of quietly smouldering peat with which Deny had banked the fire permeated their drift into dreams.

Deny had no need of a 'Dreamland'. His life was his dream come true. With Margaret in his arms, in this house built with his own hands, which could withstand the worst of weathers from Antarctica, in the fruitful Garden of Eden they had created, in his mine with its challenges and rewards, in this wild and wonderful land he knew as his own, he was totally fulfilled.

After eight days Margaret left and their idyll was over.

At the beginning of October strong south-westerlies brought hail and heavy snow as low as 300 metres, but the tin was coming quickly and Deny continued sluicing. Allan Woolley arrived to help, so with Clyde's assistance they cut bed logs for the new engine shed and had them in place after three days. A week later, the shed finally erected, he made several trips collecting hewardias and 'blandies' for Mary to enter in the Hobart Flower Show, and searched for more botanical specimens for Dr Curtis.

Those he had sent to the university in March had been well received. 'The whole collection was extremely interesting,' Curtis wrote. The 'beautifully pressed specimens' included a species of *Euphrasia* (eyebright), not yet officially named. In order to do so she had to draw up a full description in Latin. 'Before I can complete this I am obliged to ask if you can kindly give me some further help.'

Dr Curtis wanted to know whether the plant was annual or perennial, its flower colour range and locations. She also requested details about other *Euphrasia* species, and more material, including fruits if possible. In October Deny found a fine specimen with forty-two flower heads at the airstrip edge.

The distinguished botanist identified another specimen with delicate white starry five-petalled flowers as *Oschatzia saxifraga*, saying she had never seen fresh material before and very little had been collected. Referring to her own annotations of Rodway's *Flora of Tasmania*, Curtis stated that given Deny's information, perhaps her distribution description was inaccurate, and she should correct it in the next edition.

The third specimen was of even greater interest. It was a plant Deny had discovered in 1937 in only one location. In 1965 he found another elsewhere. Curtis wrote:

> I thought [it] might be a form of *Lomatia ilicifolia*, [but] it proves to be not that species. It is most likely to be quite new 'hitherto undescribed' but with some affinity to a species from Chile, *L. ferruginea*. I am most anxious to have fruits of this plant (and of course, any more flowering material in due season!). I am very appreciative of your interest and help.

Deny's curiosity and enthusiasm were well aroused and in spring 1965 he set about collecting the desired specimens, leaving early to return to the recently observed plant, an arduous walk involving much scrambling and crawling through thick understorey. He dug six suckers and cut a section of the wood.

It was a momentous day's collecting. Deny was elated by Curtis's letter acknowledging receipt of the specimens: 'The arrival of this box of treasures caused considerable excitement in the botany department. I do sincerely appreciate all that you and Mrs King have done to ensure that these plants shall reach us.'

Dr Curtis told him she hoped to visit the Melbourne and Canberra herbaria shortly and would take the opportunity to examine all available *Lomatia* species. Deny was excited by her comment, 'However, I shall be surprised if I can match your plant, I think it is an undescribed species.' His excitement increased on reading that she too thought the *Euphrasia* he had sent was a new species.

Both specimens indeed proved to be new to science.

The grevillea-like *Lomatia*, with glossy green leaves and crimson flower spikes, was later named *Lomatia tasmanica*. Deny was acknowledged in its common names, Kings lomatia and Kings holly. It has since been identified as the oldest known plant clone and is protected by an Act of Parliament.

The *Euphrasia* was endemic to the Port Davey area and duly named *Euphrasia kingii*. A member of the Scrophulariaceae family, it grows in the peaty heathlands and mountains in south-west and western Tasmania. In flower it is conspicuous and attractive, with small serrated dark green leaves evenly arranged, setting off the cluster of lobelia-like flowers at the top of the stem. The flowers, usually white, may be striated crimson or purple. Sometimes they are pale lilac or deep purplish blue. Curtis's description in *The Endemic Flora of Tasmania* concludes: 'The species is named in honour of Mr Charles Denison King who collected the specimen designated the type, and who has done much to increase knowledge of the flora of south-west Tasmania.'

There were many incoming flights in a Skywagon with BHP and HEC personnel, and timber for BHP works. But Deny's heavy equipment came by fishing boat, a load of over two tonnes—alternator, trommel frame, and conveyor belt, plus drums of fuel, at £50 a tonne. After Allan Woolley left, Deny continued alone rigging shear-legs and endless chain ready for the arrival of his new alternator.

The Haflinger was used to transport trommel parts from wharf to mine and to cart sand and rocks for the alternator base and concreting the engine shed floor. After days' work, the trommel was finally assembled. Then in November Deny was off to Hobart again.

After a taxing trip, the relief he felt on reaching the Sandy Bay moorings, seeing the dorts waiting, was shortlived. At Norfolk Crescent, Margaret was ill. She had been suffering from 'vile bilious attacks' for weeks.

Concerned for her comfort on the trip back for Christmas, Deny made arrangements for a new fitting on *Melaleuca*. An amenity Margaret had long desired was a proper ship's toilet. When they bought the boat, it had none. Deny had no problems with this. As a passenger recalled, 'I had never been on a boat in seas like those round South West Cape. There was an enormous swell and yet I recall vividly Deny leaning out the stern, with only a small rail against his shins for support, urinating into the ocean with great aplomb.'

Deny's concession to Margaret's different anatomy had originally been a tin can down below, later replaced by a plastic bucket. Despite repeated requests, Deny would do nothing about installing a proper head, concerned a hole cut in *Melaleuca*'s timbers would create a possible weak point. Now Deny took *Melaleuca* to have the head professionally installed.

Two days after he arrived Deny wrote in his diary, 'M ill cannot do anything eats very little' and took her to the doctor. Three days later, on Janet's fourteenth birthday, Deny called the doctor to the house and Margaret was admitted to St John's Hospital. The next day Margaret was told an operation was necessary. Four days later Deny wrote, 'report very discouraging'.

The diagnosis was cancer.

CHAPTER 23

Bereft

'I felt as though half the world had fallen away.'

Margaret was Deny's lodestar and he was devastated. But his diary reveals nothing of his anguish. Nor does Margaret's. She had stopped keeping hers six months before.

Neighbours, friends and family rallied to help. After two weeks Margaret was allowed home. It was a quiet Christmas, their first in Hobart for years, and Deny cooked.

He had already bought supplies and made all preparations for returning to Melaleuca. But even with Keith Heeney, Mary and Janet for company, it was with a heavy heart Deny set sail late on New Year's Day, and left Margaret. It was a difficult parting, each fearful of what 1966 held in store.

One of Margaret's new year resolutions was to resume her diary. Describing *Melaleuca*'s departure she wrote, 'Girls overjoyed to be sailing for home at last', but did not mention her own feelings. On 2 January she returned to hospital for chemotherapy. Deny and the girls sent 'lovely long letters' and big boxes of 'flowers from the button grass' as soon as they arrived, and by then Margaret needed all the comfort she could get as the treatment began to take effect. After eight days she asked to be allowed to go home, and her doctor agreed.

Deny wrote he had been 'hirried' (worried) about her as he baked bread early one morning, and she confirmed his intuition as she had then been 'well in the doldrums'. But mostly she showed a brave front, revealing little about her pain and the treatment's unpleasant side-effects. She wrote she hoped to join them and assured Deny, 'People have been kindness itself to me'—as indeed they had.

When finally she had permission to travel, to her disappointment bad weather kept aircraft grounded for a week. It was 5 February before she was reunited with Deny and the girls at the 'Forever and Ever Place', Melaleuca.

They had four happy days around their old haunts, Breaksea, Bramble and Schooner coves, Bathurst Harbour and the Celery Top Islands. Margaret stayed four more days at Melaleuca, valiantly making bread, marmalade and red-currant jelly, and entertaining visitors.

She flew out with Janet, and Deny and Mary sailed three days later, exploring on the way. Margaret met them at the moorings and Deny was delighted she felt well enough to drive again. Almost immediately he began rebuilding the sitting-room fireplace as she wished, and hope rekindled in their hearts. He supervised other improvements too, before going back to the tussocks at The Rise.

Margaret had lost so much weight that 'dear ringy' was very loose. She took it to master silversmith Harold Sargison for re-sizing. He was amazed at its fine moulding, and when he heard how Deny had collected the gold and made it, could not bring himself to touch it. So Margaret wound wool round it to hold it in place.

Deny stayed for Margaret's birthday. Her best present was doctor's permission to make a Queensland trip. In mid-March Deny saw her off, then sailed for Melaleuca, leaving a friend with the girls.

It was a taxing trip physically and emotionally for Margaret, farewelling people and places she loved. She wished to spare the dorts seeing her decline, so in Sydney she spent time with her cousin Kath Stephenson, and wrote to Deny, 'She is ready to come to our aid.' This reassured him after reading her admission, 'Feel I'm not really much good, dear Bear.'

'To Hobart' were the last words Margaret wrote in her diary. In

April she was exhausted after the trip. Her fears were indeed well-founded. The cancer was spreading. She quickly wrote to Deny, describing her plans for the girls, to which she had given much anguished thought.

Although she had lived life fully, she had always had a sense of the relentless passage of time. She had often written in her diary, 'nothing to show for the day', or after a frustrating episode, 'wasted whole day'. As the girls grew up she had been even more conscious of years passing, separated from Deny. Now she had to face the reality that there were no years left and even her days were numbered.

She wrote to her friend Nan, cheerfully newsy as usual. Then almost at the end of the letter her guard slipped, and in a cry from the heart she shared her anguish and begged her to come to Hobart for a final week together. 'I'm awfully ill dear—the cancer is inoperable. I'm just devastated at the thought of my three darlings without their Chief Advisor. Specially the girls in their growing years.'

On 13 April 1966 over 450,000 hectares of the South-West was declared a conservation area. But BHP and Hydro men and gear continued arriving and departing from Deny's airstrip. This helped distract him from the heavy pall of anxiety hanging over his own life and he spent many evenings yarning in the Charles King Memorial Hut with helicopter pilots from the US and New Guinea, and geologists from England and New Zealand.

When golden cherry leaves were whirling across the garden in autumn gales, he took the unprecedented step of sending out six bags of tin by air to maintain the cash flow and ease Margaret's mind. He also wanted to avoid another demanding single-handed voyage, conserving his energy for looking after Margaret and domestic affairs.

Cruelly worried about her, he decided to fly out to visit. He stayed only a week, just long enough to boost Margaret's morale.

Back at Melaleuca, where the cherry trees were now bare, Deny went straight to CC. He discussed with Clyde how they would unload the new jig, the latest piece of equipment he had ordered. When the power was connected the recently installed trommel would take the hardest labour out of separating big gravel and clods from pay dirt. The steel jig, a large box-shaped machine, would then separate the fine dense ore from the lighter sand, mud and gravel in the next stage.

Clyde had sold *Stormalong* and brought the jig down on *Reemere*, an old Derwent ferry he was remodelling. Landing the jig entailed moving the wheelhouse, so they tackled this first. They then unloaded the jig onto the wharf and rolled it on pieces of pipe to the shore.

The girls' company in the May holidays cheered Deny, but after they left he confessed to feeling lonely without them. He was alone more than usual as Win and Clyde were having *Reemere* re-decked in the Huon, so there were no daily radio chats. As always in his solitude he found solace in the birds, which he fed with cheese. Six blue wrens and a young grey thrush, 'young Richard Tauber' which kept him company at the mine, were his particular delight.

On 1 July, a day of dark skies blotted with fog, he sailed solo again. He was shocked at Margaret's appearance, and despaired for his beloved. She had lost her hair and wore a wig. With Deny to do the housework and look after Margaret and girls, cousin Kath returned to Sydney to sell her house and finalise her affairs. It was now clear she would be needed at Norfolk Crescent for a long time.

Deny stayed home with Margaret as much as possible. How glad they both were he was his own boss and could spend his time as he chose. After taking her to the doctor he wrote briefly 'report not encouraging'.

He dealt with his despair in the only way he knew. At The Rise he cut down dead trees, sawing and stacking them. He brought many loads of wood back to Norfolk Crescent, where he split and stacked it day after day. He tore into the garden too, front and back, dismantled the street wall and cleaned the bricks before rebuilding. He took the dorts to the university Open Day, as Margaret had been worrying about Mary's higher education and future. He also escorted them to the school dance. But Margaret, who had always taken such pride and delight in dressing the girls, now had to let Kath buy their clothes.

After Kath's return in late August, Deny left. Margaret wrote, 'I hated to see you sail away into the black night.' It was indeed a black night of the soul for them both, as they wondered how often they would be together again.

Nor was it easy sailing, as *Melaleuca* ran into a rain front with freshening south-westerlies and a big slop. After passing South West Cape the exhaust pipe broke off and Deny, cold, wet and miserable, had to make temporary repairs. Twenty-four hours after leaving Margaret, he reached Port Davey. Exhausted, he spread bags on the engine room floor and curled up for desperately needed sleep.

Home again, it was time to tackle the vegetable garden and plant the summer crops. But Deny's heart was not in it, as he wondered if Margaret would live to enjoy his succulent lettuces and tender peas.

Clyde and Win were back, and many hours and much effort went into reloading the jig to transport it to the mine. They unloaded it at Deny's wharf, and with typical ingenuity lashed a forty-four-gallon drum on each side, then towed it up Moth Creek and canal.

It was a wild bleak spring. September snow on Mount Counsel, and hail and sleety rain at the mine made conditions cold enough on the hands for even Deny to consider knocking off, but driven by the thought of the overdraft, he persevered. A few days later strong south-easterly gales delivered four centimetres of rain, causing another flood.

After a two-day trip on *Reemere* Deny reached Norfolk Crescent to find Margaret's condition had deteriorated. She persevered with treatment, and Deny accompanied her each day to the Royal Hobart Hospital. He also went with prospective buyers to The Rise, which was now on the market. Two weeks after arriving, on 5 November Clyde was ready to sail. It was Deny and Margaret's seventeenth wedding anniversary, a particularly poignant leavetaking.

This time Deny spent only four weeks at Melaleuca. He cleaned up the waterfront ready for the dorts' summer frolics, built a new timber rack above flood level, and did a fine job on *Melaleuca*, painting her cabin-sides turquoise blue. What undoubtedly gave him the most pleasure was going out twice onto the hills gathering hewardias for celebrated Sydney wildflower artist, Thistle Harris.

Sailing single-handed in early December with six bags of tin, it was almost midnight when he arrived at the moorings. Although longing to see Margaret and take her in his arms, he stayed aboard so as not to disturb her. But by 4.30 a.m. he was ashore.

Margaret was having another series of injections and had to be taken to the Royal Hobart Hospital, so they saw little of each other. A few days later she was re-admitted to St John's Hospital. Deny attended the girls' Speech Night and between business calls and collecting supplies, visited Margaret twice a day. Then he and the girls visited on the mid-December morning they sailed.

Teenagers Mary and Janet were overjoyed to be home, revelling in their freedom. Their effervescent letters were a delight and comfort to their 'Dear Moosie'. Most precious of all to Margaret were the exuberant accounts of the joking, laughing, bantering and teasing between Deny and dorts.

Deny entered into the holiday spirit for their sakes. They had not been told, and did not realise, how serious their mother's condition was, and Deny did his best not to let the shadow of Margaret's illness spoil their carefree mood. Although his heart weighed as heavy as the tin he dug day after day, the dorts' sense of fun and their adoration cheered him. He told them stories of his childhood, which they always loved, composed songs to popular tunes, and played practical jokes.

Deny sometimes enjoyed pulling the leg of an objectionable visitor. An Englishwoman, who thought he was a labourer and ignored him, inquired why the water was so brown. Deny said they'd been chucking tea leaves into it. When she remarked it was brown everywhere, Deny answered they'd been doing it for years.

She then asked whether the Kings came to Melaleuca by car or rowing boat. Deny and the pilot couldn't resist replying that they rowed, whereupon she suggested they should have motor scooters. Told as she boarded the aircraft that it had been a leg pull, Deny said she qualified for a Sunset Ranch term the girls loved—a Red Cheeks Chook! Afterwards he declared they should have just pretended they couldn't speak English.

When a walker asked Deny what he used the tractor for, he replied it was for dozing up the dirt to the nozzle. The man looked blank, so Deny, tongue in cheek, drawled, 'We haven't got to the stage yet where the dirt comes by itself.'

At the end of January 1967 Margaret's cousin Elsie flew to Melaleuca at her request to remind Deny to return in time for the new school term. Full of admiration for Margaret's courage, Elsie was also filled with concern; Margaret was failing fast, and it was her sad task to tell Deny. They stripped the garden of fruit, dug potatoes, loaded the tin and prepared to leave.

On the eve of departure Deny woke in the night 'with a feeling of impending disaster'. As they rounded South West Cape on 6 February they saw the cause of his foreboding. A great cloud of dense smoke was drifting along the coast. With clear sky behind and thick smoke ahead they sailed on to anchor at Recherche for the night.

Deny could not sleep for long. He was up at 2.30, weighing anchor an hour later. It was an eerie dawn through heavy haze with the glow of big fires on the hills further up the channel. The hot wind began to freshen and by the time they reached the Derwent it was gale force. A coppery glow suffused the sky and the strong smell of burning brought back terrible memories to Deny.

The sky grew dark and a pall of smoke blotted out Mount Wellington and even Mount Nelson behind Norfolk Crescent. Deny was desperate to reach Margaret. Elsie brought the station wagon to the yacht club where willing hands helped *Melaleuca* berth in the fierce wind. They drove to the house where Margaret, thin and weak, anxiously awaited their arrival.

Margaret was nearing the end of her own battle for life. At night, sick at heart, Deny walked back to the boat where he stayed, alone with his anguish.

The February 1967 fires were the worst in southern Tasmania's history. Sixty people lost their lives, over six hundred homes were destroyed, highways were blocked and power was cut.

Over the next few days as stories emerged about the damage— homes in ruins, stock and poultry burnt, as well as the human toll of injuries and death—Deny relived the dreadful days of 1934 and the fire which destroyed Sunset Ranch. He and Elsie took goods to the fire relief depot and then went to The Rise to find everything burnt except the cabin and a couple of paddocks. Immediately Deny came home he cleaned a neighbour's gutters as a fire precaution.

Deny counted every moment with Margaret. His diary entries for two weeks were minimal. Although there was work to do on the boat, business to be dealt with in town, fire relief bales of hay to be collected for the horses and fences to be replaced at The Rise, he contrived to spend as much time as he could 'looking after M'.

On Sunday 26 February 1967, when the bells of St David's Cathedral were ringing for morning prayer, Margaret left Deny, four days before her fifty-sixth birthday. She lost consciousness when she tried to get out of bed and was taken by ambulance yet again to St John's Hospital, where she died an hour later in Deny's arms. 'She was so brave right to the last,' he wrote.

The depth of his own feelings received a rare mention in his diary. 'I felt as though half the world had fallen away and for the first time I feel old and inadequate.'

CHAPTER 24

Life goes on

'Feel depressed—what is it?'

Margaret's funeral took place the following afternoon in the Nixon Chapel at St David's Cathedral where Deny and Margaret had been married.

In the mistaken belief the girls were being protected from some of the trauma of their mother's death, it was decided that Mary, sixteen, and Janet, fifteen, should not attend the funeral. They were sent to play tennis by Kath, who had been encouraging them to improve their game.

This well-meant decision compounded rather than diminished their long-term grief. So did Deny's reticence about what had happened after the funeral, and his inability ever to talk about his own grief, let alone share theirs.

Deny hurriedly dealt with business matters, investigated some new machinery, and started repairing fire damage at The Rise. In his diary he did not refer to Margaret's birthday, three days after her funeral, simply recording 'not feeling very well'. He spent the day writing to her friends and relatives, whose letters had always meant so much to her, and stacking wood, remembering how she had always exulted in a big pile.

Two weeks after her death, Deny, widowed at fifty-seven, retreated to Melaleuca like a wounded animal. As he berthed, his mind returned to Margaret's first visit, and to the second time, when she came as his wife. But grief apart, this was not an easy homecoming.

The tide was too low to row across the lagoon, so he had to walk around, carrying the meat. Swarms of blowflies, even more numerous than usual, were in possession of the porch, and when he tried to light the big kerosene fridge it refused to burn.

Walking up the path to the house Deny experienced perhaps the loneliest moments of his life. The bitter knowledge that his beloved would never come again or be there to greet and welcome him weighed more heavily than any bag of tin or stores he had ever carried. Nevertheless, her touch was evident everywhere—in her favourite tender blue forget-me-nots rippling through her precious flower garden; through the house which radiated her taste and homemaking skills. Outdoors and in, Deny was surrounded by reminders of Margaret, evidence of her care and love.

Deny sought to blunt the keen edge of his pain by immersing himself in work. Day after day, week after week, he trimmed, slashed and cut every accessible tea-tree. He dug and dug, driving the spade sharply into the peaty black soil, unearthing the potatoes which would sustain his body but not his spirit through the long winter ahead. When the south-westerlies brought wings of weeping rain and driving hail like frozen tears, tormenting the shivering dark waters of Moth Creek in its twisted bed, he stayed inside to make quince or pear jam, and to answer condolence letters which arrived by the score. Sympathy came from all over Australia, as news of the death of Melaleuca's gracious hostess spread through the walking and boating communities.

There was always the tin to be won too. Although he felt 'down and tired', Deny had plenty of incentive to work harder than ever, with the mortgage on The Rise, and loans for his new equipment still to be paid off, and the dorts to be provided for. There was also much yet to be done on the new plant before it could become operational: installing motors and piping for the pressure and gravel pumps to be used with the jig and trommel, prefabbing and welding, making an adjustable chute between trommel and conveyor belt.

Early in April he admitted to a 'very depressed and sad feeling' and drew a small pen sketch, rare in his diary, of the ranges. He wrote to a friend, 'I am so much looking forward to the May holidays when the girls will make this once more like the real home it used to be.' With Mary and Janet home, his spirits lifted and he joined them in drawing and painting sessions. He appreciated their help at the mine and delighted in their enthusiasm for making apple pies, jam tarts, cakes and even cream puffs. They sailed to Hobart with the tin, and after two weeks of the usual chores at Norfolk Crescent and The Rise, Deny returned.

As always the birds were a comfort in his loneliness. Droppings on the diary cover testify to their company in the house. In the garden a little owl slept on a post beside him all day as he cut dead canes from raspberries and planted broad beans.

Deny made two more of the gruelling 115-nautical-mile trips alone in 1967, delivering tin. In August he made a point of getting to Hobart for Mary's birthday. It was Saturday morning when he arrived at the moorings. Margaret had kept an eager lookout when she thought he might be coming and she and the girls always gave him a great welcome. On this occasion three little words bleakly tell the end of an era: 'Arrived house unobserved.' Now it was only a house, where a wife no longer watched and waited.

Deny busied himself with repairs to the temperamental Hillman; driving practice for Mary, now seventeen; and school interviews about her future, Margaret's long-term plans made with such forethought having fallen through. He also painted the house exterior before returning to Melaleuca.

The tin yield was a poor return for Deny's labours. One day ten hours of the cold wet job sluicing yielded only one bag. Then sluicing stopped when the dam wall collapsed, the second time in months, necessitating immediate repairs.

There were problems too on *Melaleuca*, where rats had got into cupboards and chewed through the radio aerial, and the engine had become clogged and corroded, requiring many days of hard work to restore. At the house the hot water system developed a leak, which Deny fixed only with Clyde's help. Then in his absence, helping Clyde with a problem on *Reemere*, the large refrigerator, already temperamental, completely defrosted. On his return Deny found the meat was 'smelling to high heaven' and had to work swiftly to salvage it, washing it, soaking it in brine, cooking some and storing the rest in the small refrigerator, also unreliable.

After a bitter winter when snow often shrouded Mount Counsel, it was a wild, cold spring, short on promise. Even the migratory snipe, harbingers whose arrival Deny loved to record, were scarce. A total eclipse of the moon in October was of keen interest, but held an aching symbolism. Among the customary ink diary entries Deny wrote a rare unfinished pencil note: '9 a.m.—feel depressed—what is it?' A week later the answer is apparent. 'This is our 18th wedding anniversary. Have been feeling so sad today, have felt the loss of M so much. Have shed some tears throughout the day.'

As Deny looked back over his marriage he reflected, with even deeper understanding, on its similarities with his parents'. At Melaleuca he and Margaret had, as far as possible, replicated for their daughters the childhood Ollie and Charlie had created for him and his sisters, allowing unusual freedom but also developing responsibility and sturdy independence. To maintain such a lifestyle had demanded long periods of separation for Ollie and Charlie, and very hard work for both. Ollie was a year younger than Margaret when she had died, after twenty-eight years of marriage. Charlie had lived alone for twenty-one more years.

Even with Win and Clyde's support in Port Davey and help from many others in Hobart, 1967 was the worst year of Deny's life.

CHAPTER 25

The mine

'Deny very much the skipper in charge of his operation.'

The mine was the reason for Deny's existence in the South-West. It had given him the opportunity to make this wondrous region of untamed land and wild waterways his kingdom, where his soul could breathe. Its problems and difficulties, its challenges and rewards were the fabric of his being. It required brain power as well as muscle, and Deny was well endowed with both.

Mines Department officer David Jennings visited Melaleuca numerous times over twenty years from the mid-1960s, both in his official capacity and as a bushwalker. 'Sometimes when people got into dire financial straits, I had the job of trying to assist them to improve their performance,' he said. 'But I was never requested to do this with Deny. He was an astute miner, always very much the skipper in charge of his operation.'

Deny was not a rapacious exploiter of finite resources. His philosophy was to mine just enough to meet his needs. Jennings recalled asking why he was working a particular paddock when evidence showed there was better value elsewhere. 'I might need that at some future time,' Deny replied. 'Meanwhile I'll clear up some of this other which is good enough for my present requirements.'

There was barely a day when Deny did not go to the mine. In fine weather he dug and stacked pay dirt. In wet weather he processed it, sluicing and streaming with the abundant water. On a dry day he walked straight across the button grass with his unerring stride. On a sodden day he detoured to avoid the swampiest parts.

Whatever the weather, wild gale or serene sunshine, he was aware of his world—black mud squelching or dazzling white quartzite gravel crunching beneath his boots; button grass swathing the plain with its crowns of bobbing heads which twitched at his eyes; bushy tea-trees knobby with nuts, dainty sequinned sundews, showy trigger plants, reefs of coral fern, tussocks of reeds coarse and fine, tuffets of golden moss like little echidnas burrowing into the peat, from which protruded skulls, knuckles and bleached bones of tea-tree stumps.

He would lift his gaze to the chaos of clouds which were his constant companions, merging and parting, draped round the shoulders of the mountains like feather boas, filling the sky with celestial cauliflowers or tumbling bales of unscoured wool. His keen blue eyes would watch the circling of a big black cormorant arriving to fish in a dam or the silent stalking of a heron in the sedges; and delight in swooping swallows feasting on clouds of gnats hovering above the water, or secretive scurryings of mouse-like emu wrens through the button grass.

His ears were attuned to every sound which made up the ever-changing symphony of his surroundings—varied croakings of frogs, the dull drone of blowflies and joyous twittering of swallows, the distant murmur or roar of the sea, and the wind singing or sighing, whispering or whining, screaming or howling.

Deny would head straight for the engine shed, another Nissen-style building open to the north-east, with its warm smell of oil and grease. As he checked the big Southern Cross engine and started it, swallows which built their mud nests on the rafters went about their business, as did dusky robins which also nested in the shed year after year. With his love of birds' company but aversion to excreta, Deny had nailed sections of oil drum as 'poo trays' under their nesting sites.

For his own 'housekeeping' he had made a time clock for recording hours of engine use, enabling him to calculate fuel consumption.

He had a coke-burning forge with hand-turned bellows, in which he heated steel; an anvil on which he sharpened his tools and made parts and an oxyacetylene welding set. Coils of wire and electrical cord hung from nails on the walls, as did long strings of metal washers, and a clipboard listing parts to be ordered. An old frying pan and several billy lids made convenient trays for assorted nuts and bolts. One shelf and several wooden half cases all painted yellow stored D2 parts. Tools, shovel blades, crowbars, picks, spanners, wrenches and brushes of all kinds, wire, bristle and even old tooth-brushes, lay in heaps. Because of harsh conditions for machinery and tools, more days were devoted to maintenance and repairs than in operating the plant. Deny threw nothing away, because everything had to be brought in, and often parts ordered were incorrectly supplied. When dorts or friends had a clean-out, Deny said nothing, but gradually each discarded item found its way back from the dump.

Under ideal conditions natural forces do much of the work of alluvial tin mining. But Melaleuca's flat terrain was far from ideal. This necessitated three operations: pumping water, moving the pay dirt to the sluice-box site, then moving the tailings afterwards, which caused Deny constant problems.

Alluvial tin in the Cox Bight–Melaleuca area is found mainly in quartz gravels, sometimes very shallow, sometimes quite deep. The ore is usually dispersed towards the bottom, generally in the lowest parts of the undulating rock beneath, and the best tin lies in the depressions. Deny was always probing, reading below the surface, trying to locate depressions in the bedrock. It had to be very rich dirt to pay and in sufficient quantity to justify setting up all the equipment.

Weather was another problem Deny faced. With strong wester-lies, high tides and heavy rain from the hinterland, the Moth Creek water level would rise, submerging lower and more productive workings. No wonder Deny always noted extra high tides. The water table rose and remained high, so he could dig and stack pay dirt only in summer. The next phase, sluicing and streaming to recover the ore, requires copious water under pressure. But even in this area boasting one of Australia's highest rainfalls, only in winter was there sufficient rain to allow him to do this regularly.

The swampy nature of button grass meant time and energy were expended to extricate bogged equipment. In working new ground Deny dug off the button grass in fine weather, because the D2 would bog if the ground was wet. The peaty overburden was put to one side, while the next layer of ground was excavated. This probably was not ore-bearing, but Deny always had a panning dish handy and frequently checked for tin. In shallower ground away from the creek the cassiterite might be about a metre down, but nearer the creek it was often three or four metres deep. The barren earth was removed to backfill a previously worked area. The pay dirt was dozed into a heap and removed to a stockpile for later sluicing.

Deny always kept a close eye on the west, watching for change. The frequent passing showers did not stop him working. If they were very heavy he retreated into a shed, where there were always jobs to be done, until the squall passed. On days of persistent rain he worked in the sheds. When he anticipated fine weather, he started the pumps so he could bring in machinery.

The deeper holes required frequent pumping which could take all day. Deny had several portable pumps, including one for mud flow and one submersible, as well as pressure pumps for trommel and jig. Stones and gravel were hard on them and they often required service when conditions proved too tough and they jammed.

In 1968 with trommel, jig and conveyor belt finally in place, Deny began work on the electrical plant to run them. It was a task taxing patience, stamina and ingenuity to the utmost. In January Keith Heeney came to help and together they built the shelter for the new switchboard Deny had made. Then with walkers' help they carried it to its new home adjacent to trommel and jig. The switchboard had controls for pressure and gravel pumps, trommel, jig and conveyor belt, and a fixed sequence for switching. There was another switchboard in the engine shed for the generator, alternator and voltage regulator controlling the mine machinery.

Another major removal was also accomplished in January. Win decided her piano-playing days were over and gave the historic instrument to Janet. Deny and four firewatchers carried it down to the CC wharf and loaded it aboard *Melaleuca* with a derrick. At her wharf it was swung down into *Blue Boat*, transported across the lagoon at full tide, swung ashore by derrick re-erected at the waterfront, then carried up to the house 'without mishap'. All in a day's work for Deny!

On a 1967 Hobart visit *Scamp* had been stolen, and he had spent many anxious days searching until he found her. When he took the girls back for the 1968 school year in February he was even more anxious when *Melaleuca* disappeared. Noticing before dawn she was missing, he and Keith searched downriver and back to the wharves, then reported to the police. Life without *Melaleuca* was unthinkable. Deny's relief on spotting the Marine Board launch towing her upriver was profound. A few days later he stayed in bed 'feeling sad'. It was the first anniversary of Margaret's death.

The load for the return voyage was heavy and awkward, including two large concrete pipes for the new dam outlet. After laying them and concreting the intake he worked steadily to increase the height of the dam wall. He brought loads of peat sods to reinforce the wall on the inside, and constructed a spillway. He also rebuilt the lower dam.

At the end of April, after two months of intensive adjustments to cables and belts, Deny threw the switches a second time. Still two pump motors did not function. He sent a message to his electrical engineer friend Ken Newham, and with Ken's help the machinery was put to work for the first time and 'on the whole all went fairly well'.

Now there was a new procedure on sluicing days. Deny scooped up a load of pay dirt with its mingled smell of peat and diesel, drove it up to the timber nozzling platform and dumped it. Then he squirted the pump-driven hissing water jet to wash the dirt along the wooden-sided platform. In his gumboots Deny jumped on clods to smash them up and remove rocks, before they got to the trommel.

The mud was washed into it, to be sprayed again from a perforated metal pipe. All material less than a centimetre, mud, tin and water passed through the screen as it rotated, dropping into a hopper below, connected by a pipe to a metre-deep sump hole. From the end of the rattling trommel a conveyor belt hurried the mullock five metres along to tip over the platform edge. Before the tailings heap grew too big, it had to be removed by dozer, either to backfill previous excavations, or to a stockpile for roadmaking and other earthworks.

The gravel pump located by the sump hole was fed with dam water by a pipe with a butterfly valve and float to regulate the level. When the primed pump was switched on it sucked up the slurry to be spewed over the top of the jig. The metal jig, as big as a bed, comprised two chambers filled with water, covered by two perforated metal screens. Beneath the ragging, a layer of coarse hematite gravel, rubber diaphragms bolted to a rod driven by an eccentric wheel caused the water welling up through the hematite to pulse intermittently, keeping everything in motion. Being heavier, cassiterite sank through the hematite into hoppers below, while lighter quartzite gravel moved on with the slurry to a raised peat slab drain.

At day's end Deny switched off the machines. Quiet returned. Then he opened the valves at the bottom of the hopper and estimated the day's yield as the cassiterite poured into cut forty-four-gallon drums beneath, to await streaming.

Skipper Deny and deckhand dorts on a *Melaleuca* cruise in 1971. Janet is at left, Mary at right.

Deny in typical stance. Mount Brock in the background with Mount Rallinga under rain.

Expeditions to Bathurst Harbour were always multi-purpose. Janet's easel left, Deny's woodpile, right. *Blue Boat*, *Melaleuca*, *Tin Dish* and the Rugby Range can be seen in the background.

Mount Rugby and early-morning reflections in Melaleuca Lagoon.

In the studio overlooking Mount Counsel, 1991. Behind the painting of South West Cape is a cloud image from a photograph of Karina's. She received this gift the day she heard of Deny's death.

The iron barque *Svenor* wreck was one of Deny's favourite painting subjects. He often included oystercatchers in his coastal scenes.

Janet described her father and his mine with feeling:

> The mine was a busy, changing, shifting, pulsing work environment, constantly evolving. There was a satisfaction in watching his system functioning—a moving flowing rhythm of muddy brown water. Eyes and ears were constantly alert for any small changes, which could require adjustment.
>
> When mining on his own, he was on the move constantly. He stood at the nozzle for a while, then trotted down the clod embankment and onto the dozer for another load of pay dirt. Back at the nozzle platform, then off checking pumps and water flow. He galloped down a gravel heap and shovelled stones away from the conveyor belt. There was a companionship in the whirr and hum of pumps and electric motors, the pulsing of jig and rattle of trommel. When he switched off all would be still except for the drip of water from recently active machines and the gentle lifting of steam from warm motors, as he opened the hoppers to see if he 'had a good haul'.

By September 1968 Deny's perseverance in getting the new plant to function efficiently was paying off. He had thirty-five bags of tin.

Melaleuca gave Deny more anxious hours in Hobart when her moorings broke in gale-force winds which swept her downriver. Deny, alerted by a phone call, rang the Marine Board for a tow. Meantime two men had already boarded and just saved her from running aground. Deny's relief shows in his diary entry. 'It's a miracle how she missed the Manning Reef.' They got the engine started and brought her back to the yacht club, where Deny thankfully took over.

In July, because Kath worried about him alone at Melaleuca, Deny had taken on a husband and wife as minehand and housekeeper. It was not a success. Deny's grief was still too raw and he needed his solitude. He even 'had a barney', a very rare occurrence for him, and was relieved when they left.

It was busy in Hobart in December with Mary doing final exams, Janet practising for her driving test, and the noxious serrated tussock grass going to seed at The Rise. Most importantly, Deny, who valued Departmental advice and good working relations, had an interview with the Director of Mines concerning his long-planned purchase of a second-hand loader which he made two months later.

In preparing for the loader's delivery Deny installed mooring posts downriver where he planned to unload from *Reemere*. Then in April he flew to Hobart again to finalise the loan and insurance. He purchased heavy timber beams and hired a crane to position them on *Reemere*'s deck to spread the loader's weight. It was a 'big day' at the dock when, wheels removed, it was lifted aboard. But that proved just the beginning of the marathon.

The weather deteriorated, with storms and snow heavy on the mountains, so Clyde put in to Southport where they stayed six days before proceeding to Recherche to wait four more. *Reemere*, a solid old craft, carried her unusual load well, but Clyde was not taking any chances. When a fisherman radioed that conditions round South West Cape were bad, he put into New Harbour for two more nights.

A strong north-westerly created a 'nasty roll' and after attempting to leave they returned until it subsided. There was still a 'humpy sea' from the south and a big fast-moving south-westerly swell, but *Reemere* 'did not lurch excessively' as Clyde kept well offshore. Fourteen days after the loader was put aboard Deny wrote 'thankfully we entered Davey' and *Reemere* tied up at Claytons Corner. Even then it was still not plain sailing.

It took thirty-six hours to get the loader ashore upriver with help. First it had to be jacked up for the wheels to be replaced before it could be driven off up the bank, where it ran into deep mud, requiring another twenty-four hours' slog to free it. And it took sixteen more days to manoeuvre the great machine metre by hard-won metre across the button grass and creeks.

Even with the D2's help, much still had to be done by hand with pick, crowbar, fork and shovel. Clyde and Win pitched in, but despite their ready assistance it was a testing time, and the gremlin Quinkan was in his element. Shovel handles broke, and a new rake and shovel slid off the tractor to be mangled in the mud which held the big machine captive for hours on end. Deny celebrated the loader's arrival at the mine spending two days cleaning and greasing it and finally had the satisfaction of trying it out.

Soon he found that as well as being 'wonderful for stripping', the loader had other important uses. Removing the submersible pump, previously a dank and difficult task; moving bigger loads of pay dirt and tailings than the D2; and shifting gravel for a new road were all made easier with the loader.

In other ways too 1969 was eventful, both at Melaleuca and abroad. Unusual conditions had brought shoals of mackerel up the inlet and into the creeks, where both wedge-tailed and sea eagles gathered for weeks to feast on the teeming fish. Deny recorded ten eagles on one occasion, eight circling together, and Clyde counted eleven on another. At Claytons Corner Deny watched *Lunar 10*'s telecast from the moon; and Prince Charles' investiture as Prince of Wales. He listened with great excitement to the broadcast of the moon landing by *Apollo 11* and the astronauts' first moon walk. And Alice had three black pups in the wood box.

In Hobart it was the end of an era. Deny decided it was time to replace *Melaleuca*'s sails, which had served so well for twenty years. Kath, who had looked after the two feisty teenagers loyally and conscientiously for over three years, was preparing to return to her own daughter in Sydney. Tenants had to be found for the house as Mary and Janet were preparing in high spirits to return to Melaleuca for the whole of 1970.

CHAPTER 26

A new lease on life

'Girls and boys.'

On New Year's Day 1970, *Melaleuca* left Hobart under new sails and the year started well. Deny enjoyed Keith Heeney's company and help, and with 'dear darling dorts' home, Deny was happier than he had been since Margaret's death. They were capable, cheerful house-keepers; competent, experimental cooks, even converting part of the cherry and apple crops into liqueur and cider; and enthusiastic, intelligent gardeners. Willing helpers at the mine, they quickly learned to use the loader.

Early in February an irresistible reason for tats arose when Clyde proposed they should peg two old antimony leases. Deny needed no urging. They wrote claim notices and left immediately in Clyde's new powerboat to erect them, arriving just in time to forestall another hopeful. It was the first of many forays to Long Bay.

After Easter the family returned to Hobart, where Deny finalised documents for the antimony lease, attended a Save Lake Pedder meeting and a rally, and took the girls to the Weld.

Bigger companies continued to investigate South-West potential, taking advantage of Deny's airstrip to access new sites, and his walkers' hut for accommodation—facilities he did not begrudge. He also freely gave advice and practical assistance, while enjoying discussing their work and new technology. The January arrival of Offshore Navigation and Western Geophysics personnel and their efforts to establish a base on Mount Counsel by helicopter provided considerable interest, as both terrain and weather were helicopter-unfriendly.

The airstrip was in constant use by both commercial and private planes, and Deny recorded all movements—Piper Cherokees and Comanches, Cessna 172s and 182s, Skywagons and Skyrangers as well as little Austers and Tiger Moths which had pioneered the first flights from Hobart, Launceston and other airfields.

HEC men continued Davey River investigations and Ludbrooks Ltd (later Qintex), which had leases nearby, began revisiting old Cox Bight workings. It was expensive to remove equipment and supplies when operations concluded, so sometimes Deny scored perks, although they often required considerable effort to retrieve. Because transport for fuel was so expensive, Deny was prepared to climb 800-metre Mount Counsel to carry down a forty-litre drum of oil, such was his stamina.

Deny also observed visitors of a different kind; a wedge-tailed eagle feeding on a dead heron near the mine, a black snake fleeing July floods, and little fish appearing in the airstrip drain after rain. A wombat seeking winter lodgings in the playroom was evicted with difficulty, but returned in October. Deny dumped it in the creek, but instead of retreating to the far side, it sought sanctuary under the house. So Deny tied up the dog and let it be. He accepted a ground thrush feeding on the last cherries in autumn, welcomed dusky robins nesting in the amenities shed in spring, and cared for an off-course homing pigeon which alighted at the engine shed during June gales.

The sight of three swallows in late July and the sound of a cuckoo early in August enticed Deny and dorts on another challenging tats, climbing the Norolds. Up before dawn, they reached Rowitta Harbour in warm sunshine. Then thick scrub and Deny's cramps delayed them reaching Mount Norold's summit amid wind-whipped snowdrifts. A bonus during a difficult descent in failing light was hearing a masked owl, then seeing it 'hovering and soaring like a sea eagle'. Reaching the plain they fired button grass for light and pushed on. It was dawn again before they reached the dinghy and could boil *Melaleuca*'s kettle for 'the long wished for cup of tea' and snuggle into their bunks.

Exulting in their freedom, the girls went on many walkabouts, climbing mountains, jaunting in *Tin Dish*, the new aluminium dinghy, exploring waterways and visiting favourite beaches. Inspired by light, landscape and picturesque vegetation—twisted tea-trees, bonsai banksias, and wind-sculpted eucalypts—they sketched wherever they went, later translating drawings into paintings.

Deny, delighting in their happiness and joyous artistic response to his 'back yard', took up his own brush again, experimenting with oil paints. As winter's battering gales and scouring rains beset their cosy home, the three, snug by the fire, spent blissful days painting, working individually or sometimes all together, encouraging, criticising, chiacking—'What's that bunch of mashed 'taters doing flying across the sky?'

To create more space for their painting passion, Deny altered the front room, built a Huon pine cabinet for their gear, and constructed easels for Janet and himself. As more visitors were impressed by their talents, talk of a Hobart exhibition soon turned to serious planning, and Deny and Janet began framing.

Deny's birthday was rarely celebrated, either because he was at sea or alone at Melaleuca. In 1970 the dorts made his sixty-first a special occasion, with presents and birthday dinner, complete with candles, pavlova and his favourite Swiss roll, decorated with flowers and myrtle sprigs. His best present was probably the trusty Southern Cross engine's return to service. The head had cracked, and after telegraphing for spare parts and long hours of unsuccessful work, he had to airlift it out for repair. He had struck good tin and in October the girls made a cake celebrating two tonnes, his biggest yield ever. The loader was proving its worth. When they left in late November

Melaleuca carried three tonnes and Deny looked forward to reducing his loan on the big machine.

In Hobart Deny attended an army reunion. Then he began the search for a gallery to exhibit their work. A pre-Christmas flight to Lake Pedder with pilot photographer Bob Mossel, the girls trying the controls, was very exciting, and a dramatic contrast to Deny's first visit on foot. After spending New Year's Eve 'dining out' at CC, watching the Edinburgh Tattoo on TV, Janet wrote, '1971 begins not with the feeling of a new year, but the end of an old—a happy year, a family year. Our paths turn different ways, but long may they return and converge in family unity.' It was a sentiment Deny endorsed.

Early in January Deny began preparing for the dorts' return to Hobart. Janet had enrolled for university in 1971, and Mary for art classes. There were more paintings to frame and three packing cases to make for them, and a vain sad search for Nufty 2, who had disappeared. But Deny found time for a trip up the coast so the girls could explore the *Svenor*, a 1300-tonne Norwegian iron barque wrecked in 1914.

The family, accompanied by 'Nicky pupsie', made another challenging six-day walkabout, this time to South West Cape. In the early 1970s, before the practice was discontinued for environmental reasons, walkers still organised airdrops of extra supplies for a long trip. They could not always retrieve these, and often advised Deny of their possible whereabouts. To walk to the end of South West Cape was a rainbow dream for Deny and dorts, and now the lure of three 'bags of goodies' was the pot of gold.

South West Cape dominated every trip Deny and *Melaleuca* made. Its fierce peaks rearing from treacherous waters where cross-currents met symbolised the hazards of the wild coast. Inimical leaden-grey, sullen arcane-green, or inscrutable inky-blue, surging, roaring, crashing white-maned waves gave no quarter.

After two burning hot days' slogging over the South West Cape Range through button grass and bauera, up steep slopes and down deep gullies, climbing 'mountains that just kept keeping on', refreshed by mossy-cool creeks, inspired by myrtle rainforest, marvelling at majestic views and awed by nights under the stars, they reached comber-crested Window Pane Bay and looked south to their destination, stark and mysterious in late light.

After another day of biting sun, hard going with Deny ahead track-cutting, and tough terrain, 'surely this must be the last ascent/descent', they reached a ridge where another view of the cape beckoned, sky meeting sea. Spirits soared as progress improved over burnt button grass. Mount Karamu's summit was reached and the long spur to South West Cape stretched downward.

Mary spotted the airdrops and, feasting on rare delicacies, including tinned chicken, lychees, mandarins, shortbread, nuts and wine, they watched the sun's red orb slowly vanish. Then, lying in sleeping-bags on a clear calm night under a star-strewn sky, they marvelled at the miracle of candles stuck into the fresh green sward of this most dreaded cape, not even flickering in 'the windiest, the most wild-weathered place in Tasmania'.

Next morning they explored the cape, 'truly an artist's paradise', with its weathered grey granite forms, and awesome cliffs with white foam seething at their base far below. From a different perspective they gazed on the spume-stippled seascape of familiar islands and coastal peaks and 'it seemed strange looking at the cape from the land, when we know its features so well from the sea'. On the long tramp home Deny introduced the dorts to more bushcraft, sucking nectar from banksia flowers, as Charlie had taught him.

Deny and his choice of lifestyle in the rugged South-West were becoming increasingly known and he received a letter from the ABC asking permission to make an episode about the family for their new program, 'A Big Country'.

In February 1971 their crew arrived for a week. Deny took them for a 'harbour cruise' to Port Davey, wood-getting, setting nets, dropping walkers, even sticking in the mud at Claytons Corner. They filmed at the mine for two days, then at the house where the girls were cooking, making bread and painting. Returning in March, from *Reemere* they shot *Melaleuca*'s departure and passage down the Bathurst Narrows, then boarded her for the voyage and arrival at the Hobart Yacht Club. 'The sea was a bit rolly, especially at the Cape' and Deny noted 'a couple of cot cases'.

In town Deny's main focus was their art exhibition. They finally hired an auditorium and Deny continued the framing marathon and stayed to see the girls settled. Within a week of Janet starting her arts degree at university, she had attracted admirers. She particularly liked the company of quiet, thoughtful engineering student, Geoff Fenton. Auntie Win humphed about boyfriends, but Deny realistically changed his diary entries from 'girls' to 'girls and boys'.

After Easter Deny made a flying visit to check on Melaleuca, revelling in aerial views of Mount Anne, the Weld Valley and Judbury. Back in Hobart for Anzac Day, he joined the march, which became his custom, and continued framing. The exhibition was opened by Jack Thwaites to a capacity crowd on 28 April and twenty paintings sold immediately.

'A Big Country' fortuitously screened the Melaleuca program the following night, resulting in crowds of up to three hundred a day. Within three days all but one painting wore a red sticker, and a thousand catalogues sold within a week. When the exhibition closed after a fortnight there was a healthy list of orders. Deny was overwhelmed at the response. 'Everyone so nice and appreciative of our works. Genuinely impressed and pleased.'

While Deny and Mary sailed round in May in seas which 'hardly wet the deck', Geoff Fenton, walking with Janet and other Tasmanian University Mountaineering Club members, made his first visit to

Melaleuca. Deny appreciated Geoff's technical knowledge and unobtrusive, efficient assistance with engines and electrical wiring.

On Christmas Eve visitors, many and varied, started arriving as word continued to spread among universities, walking and climbing clubs Australia-wide of the unique challenges of the South-West, and fabulous King hospitality. Others came from Europe, North America and Asia. In 1971 Janet, arriving home from a solitary day's sketching, complained the place was 'thoroughly over-populated' with the hut overflowing, garden camps full, friends in the house, and meals, maté, snacks, fruit and drinks for all. Many Australians who stayed in the Charles King Hut over the years, such as Milo Dunphy, Bob Brown, Geoff Mosley and Karen Alexander, later became active conservationists.

In January 1972 the arrival of round-the-world sailors Eric and Susan Hiscock in Port Davey in their ketch *Wanderer IV* prompted 'a tidying up bee' in house and on *Melaleuca* before their visit. The Hiscocks' return invitation delighted Deny, who took his usual fresh-baked loaf and was amazed at all the Dutch-built yacht's fittings.

In February Deny decided on a track-cutting expedition with the dorts towards the Arthurs. After an idyllic cruise across Bathurst Harbour at dusk, Deny and dorts crossed Rowitta Plains early next morning to North River Gorge where they camped. Deny found traces of a brush-tail possum, the first he had seen in the South-West, and noted the rapid regrowth and sundews flowering after the previous year's fire, which he had spent five days fighting.

A week later they returned to Wreck Bay attempting unsuccessfully to retrieve *Svenor*'s figurehead remnant. Then they continued track work, hot, thirsty labour, through dense tea-tree, dogwood and cutting grass, with 'the March flies something terrible', returning later in fierce heat for another gruelling stint to extend what Deny often called 'our track'. The reward was 'an overwhelming wonderful view' from Pegasus Minor, though marred by dam construction at Scotts Peak to flood Lake Pedder.

Because twelve or more aircraft were arriving in as many days, in March Deny decided to make a parking bay and passenger shelter at the strip. In April Nick Tanner, now TasAir's chief pilot, renewed the search for an alternative landing site. So Deny took him to Spain Bay and Kelly Basin for two days.

The summer was long and hot. Deny noted even the dusky robins felt the heat, and drought precluded any sluicing. With mid-March rains the dams began filling, but a platypus had tunnelled through a wall and much precious water was lost. With the first frost Deny started burning off at night, sometimes working until 1.30 a.m. In the garden he contended with currawongs at the plums, parrots at the pears and bandicoots at the carrots. But he left the cabin door open at nights for a swallow which followed the loader. He confined a marauding roo in the chookpen and a wallaby in the dinghy to protect them from tiger cats, and spent two mornings building cages for their 'sea voyage' to a drop-off en route to Hobart.

He arrived for Anzac Day and to farewell Mary leaving for Launceston Art School. She took Hillman 'Waggy', so with Geoff's advice, Deny bought a Kombi van, ideal for the girls' and boys' trips away. He had great pleasure in the company of Janet and Geoff's student friends, joining some of their expeditions, providing passages to and from Port Davey, and jobs for some. He thrived on their lively talk and laughter, and intelligent interest in and concern for the South-West's natural diversity. He appreciated the girls' cakes and puddings and welcomed the boys' ready help with work on the mine, boat and garden. He watched with satisfaction as Janet and Geoff grew together, so happy and well-matched.

Early in May he travelled north for a weekend trip to Ben Lomond with Launceston Walking Club friends, joined by Janet and friends. For Deny it was exciting to discover and observe new country, and he detailed its topography and vegetation in three crowded diary pages.

In Launceston he saw Mary, Olive, Tom Coles who had helped at the mine, and Queen Victoria Museum curator R. H. Green, known to Deny as Bob, and for whom he had been collecting marsupials since 1963, and assisting with bird observations. Out of the ninety native bird species in Green and Mollison's Port Davey checklist, forty-two had been recorded only by Deny, and of the five introduced species, three only by Deny. Some of his descriptions were very graphic, such as the call of Lewin's rail sounding like a small motor boat. The masked owl which can be heard at Melaleuca in autumn when it is attracted to feed on a species of large brown moth, he described as 'flying with a roar like a distant motor'. He could even distinguish the call notes of shrike-thrushes and olive whistlers from different areas.

Deny was keenly observant of birds' feeding habits, recording bald coots at Moth Creek pulling up reeds to eat the soft white base. They also enjoyed his potatoes. Olive whistlers too acquired a taste for fresh vegetables, pulling up sprouting peas, and pipits, summer visitors, snipped off young sprouts. He saw black duck, grey and chestnut teal, black currawongs, blue wrens and waders feeding on kelp fly maggots in the deep rolls of bull kelp tossed up on the beaches by storms. He recorded the late summer migration of flocks of black currawongs to the high country for berries. He observed that ravens, plentiful in pairs, especially along the coast, gathered on the mutton-bird islands in summer to feed on eggs and young chicks and that they followed hunters for wallaby offal, which led him to surmise they may have accompanied man from Aboriginal times. They also visited the mine to feed on worms and yabbies but, being cautious, only after Deny left his bulldozer at lunchtime.

Silver gulls occurred in flocks of thirty to forty, with only three or four venturing up Melaleuca Creek for table scraps. Black swans, seen in flocks of hundreds in the early days of European presence in Port Davey, had been greatly reduced in numbers by whalers and piners, and according to Deny's estimates, totalled little more than two hundred and were seen usually in pairs or small groups.

The checklist also contains Deny's observations on the territorial dusky robins which 'attended the bulldozer' to harvest worms and insects it turned up, and frequented the house where they helped themselves to the butter and performed a more useful role catching blowflies.

Another daily helper reducing blowfly numbers was the tame yellow-throated honeyeater, also thoroughly at home. Deny wrote, 'In the house it seeks out sugar and examines every crack and cranny for insect life. When feeding young he catches blowflies on the wing two or three at a time, and if sugar is left out he dabbles the flies in the sugar before taking them away.' Mollison speculated that the honeyeater had developed this quirky habit because insects caught on flowering shrubs are nectar-coated. Deny had already written that the yellow-throated, widespread across the South-West, and other species of honeyeater 'feed on a sweet substance that oozes from the branches and stems of one species of tea-tree'. A banding program by ornithologists confirmed another of Deny's observations:

> It appears the male drives away the female and young after nesting, as we do not see anything of her until early spring, when he gets on a tall pole of a fine morning and calls loudly, I assume, to attract the attention of the female. When well-fed and contented, with nothing to do, he perches on a beam in the house and warbles away softly to himself.

He also recorded nesting locations throughout the region, on the islands in Bathurst Harbour and Port Davey, of a number of species.

He was amused by a pair of scrubwrens, which nested in a bag of onions hanging in a shed.

Deny's precise data had made a substantial contribution to knowledge of three species of bush rats, pygmy possums, and dusky and swamp antechinus (formerly known as marsupial mice), their distribution and feeding habits. His specimens were the first velvet-furred rats, broad-toothed rats, long-tailed rats and antechinus collected from the Port Davey area. Green particularly appreciated his description of a long-tailed rat's nest in the house wall, 'a very interesting observation, the first record I know of anyone ever finding its nest'.

Winter rain, gales, and hail justified Deny's staying home to indulge his painting passion, working on commissions portraying 'lovely reflections at sunrise' and 'grand snow-covered mountains'. He also worked from photographs taken on his new polaroid camera, investing each work with his deep feeling for the scene.

He enjoyed another airstrip search with Nick Tanner, and left again in August with his best haul ever—seventy-one bags, over three tonnes. In Hobart he worked less at The Rise grubbing tussocks, instead spending days with young people visiting Sunset Ranch, Scotts Peak dam and Lake Dobson. Most evenings he enjoyed return hospitality from friends. Driving north on a trip to Mary and Olive, they called at a Midlands bakery, where Deny, unquenchably curious, asked to see the set-up. Expecting a wood-fired oven, his face fell and his companions heard him mutter, 'Oh, diesel.'

In Hobart in late November with plants collected for the university, Deny met Mary's student friend Ian McKendrick, who sailed back on *Melaleuca*. Mary flew in a week later, while Janet and Geoff arrived on foot on New Year's Eve, in time for the biggest party ever at the Memorial Hut, with twenty-four in residence plus those from five nearby tents.

The summer of 1973 was happy with a house full of young

friends. Deny, equally observant of persons as he was of nature, had a knack of assessing capabilities and potential, giving people jobs they could handle, allowing them to use valuable equipment, providing opportunities to learn new skills. Many enjoyed a first success and gained confidence—driving the tractor, manoeuvring the loader, operating a dinghy or steering *Melaleuca*.

There were research expeditions after Deny's heart, looking for oysters for CSIRO, collecting reeds, and most rewarding of all, searching for a species of orchid not seen since 1893 and finding it.

This orchid (*Prasophyllum buftonianum*) only once before collected in the Port Davey area, by the Reverend John Bufton, had never been found again. Bufton had sent specimens to Ferdinand von Mueller at the Melbourne Herbarium, where they remained unidentified until 1949, when they were at last officially described. The plant was finally published as a new species in an article by J. H. Willis.

Then the search was on.

Orchidologist David Jones wrote to Deny, on the advice of Winifred Curtis and Willis. The eight-centimetre-high orchid was said to grow only in heathland, bearing small insignificant greenish-brown flowers, a mere two to three and a half millimetres, in autumn. Jones encouraged Deny's collaboration—as if he needed to be encouraged!—by telling him Curtis had expressed considerable interest in rediscovering the species and wished Mr King the best of luck.

Deny accepted the challenge.

Mary remembered in February 1973 they were returning from a four-day walk to the Western Arthurs when their father said, 'We'd better start looking out for Curty's orchid.' Only minutes later he spotted a colony of the tiny flowers on the Rowitta Plains north of Bathurst Harbour. He had recognised a likely location—a bare patch burnt several years previously, on an elevated well-drained site, rocky with rather poor soil. Dr Curtis sent two of the precious plants to eminent Australian artist Margaret Stones at Kew Royal Botanic Gardens in London to draw for *The Endemic Flora of Tasmania*.

The Kings went on pilgrimages each year to see the orchid, until one autumn Deny discovered it growing on the bank near the airstrip, in a firebreak—a few hundred metres from the house!

Deny enjoyed a two-day trip to Ketchem Bay and sailing on *Reemere* up the coast to Giblin River, which they navigated by dinghy, returning to collect *Svenor*'s figurehead, later deposited in a museum; and inspecting the remains of *Alfhild*, wrecked in 1907.

Visitors at this time included members of the renowned Californian conservation Sierra Club, with whom Deny had interesting talks. But he had no time for pretentiousness and played the hillbilly with Australia's patronising Chief Justice. Arrivals needing assistance beyond tea and sympathy for blisters and bruises included a walker with injured spine, a fisherman with gashed hand, and a boatie spiked by a hammerhead shark. Each added to the growing number of persons grateful for Margaret's foresight in installing radio communication and first aid equipment.

Bad weather delayed his March departure and it was a turbulent trip with 'verandahs on the waves'. Deny stayed almost two months, as the boat needed a new rudder and keel. With Ron Woolley's help at Lonnavale he obtained a blue gum log and took it to a local mill for sizing, writing nostalgically, 'have never seen or heard saws go so sweetly as these'. Ian rewired navigation lights, Geoff made a new wheel, the wheelhouse was partly rebuilt and other parts renewed or repaired.

It was a long winter in 1973, made more solitary because Nicky pupsie died, another link with Margaret had been broken. Once again the tea-trees bore the brunt of Deny's grief. He was also sad he had to replace the radio she had bought. And sad when bad weather prevented his flying out to support Olive at Jordan's funeral. Record high tides brought floods to the mine, the windmill ceased functioning because of corrosion, and a determined tiger cat refused to be dislodged from under the chimney, even biting the end off a glowing firestick, until Deny resorted to his mother's Sunset Ranch trick of hot water. At the end of July he finally shot a currawong which had been around all winter, so that 'the little birdies could have their tucker in peace'.

Tin was poor, radio reception was poor, but Deny brightened when he heard the first pipit, saw the first daffodils, and Janet and Geoff arrived in August. In Hobart in September, Mary and Ian told him they had been secretly engaged for months. Deny had private misgivings about the match, but, always unwilling to disappoint his adored Petty, only said, 'It's been pretty obvious.' Next morning he and Mary left for ten days, visiting Kath and Nan in Sydney and Margaret's relatives at Deepwater Station.

Even out of his own setting Deny made a lasting impression. Donald and Sandra Macansh remembered his visit:

> He was so unassuming. He and Mary were so happy in their own company. Every day they walked all over the property and found their own amusement. It was cold but he didn't wear many clothes. Unlike most visitors he wasn't impressed by the pedigree stock. He was more interested in the birds and what he found, and the effects of super on the pasture. Every evening he'd come in with his treasures from the day—leaves, grasses, rocks, and ask to have them explained, like a child. He was so at one with nature.

In October Deny returned to Melaleuca. Sailing alone in big seas he confessed it was 'a struggle to keep awake'. After 'a 25 hour day' and three hours' sleep at Bramble Cove, he awoke on 'a lovely am and the beauty of the hills and shore struck me as so much nicer than most places'. Port Davey was home. A TV series on South

American wildlife attracted him to Claytons. For Deny, though, nothing could surpass his birdies' dawn chorus, 'the yellow throats all around the lagoon, and a blue wren on a bush much encouraged when I whistled to him'.

In Hobart in December Janet and Geoff announced their engagement, and plans for Mary's Melaleuca wedding gathered momentum. While buying provisions and loading wine under *Melaleuca*'s floorboards, he recalled Margaret's admonition to work and save for 'the Wuppets' weddings'.

In Deny's absence thirty-two boys from an exclusive Melbourne school had abused garden, camps and mine. The 'barbarians' bogged the loader in flood waters, burned sawn timber, heinous in King eyes, cut wires, smashed globes and batteries, left switches on, used *Blue Boat*, broke its starter and strewed equipment everywhere. The Kings were incensed at such vandalism—the first in their long tradition of open hospitality.

On Christmas Day blue wrens and dusky robins with young arriving for cheese, and Richards nesting in the boatshed restored Melaleuca joy. After 'the day of the cherries', followed by 'the day of the raspberries' and the dreaded task of tank cleaning, preparations for the unique wedding began. The garden camp underwent major reconstruction and refurbishment for the 'bridal suite', and Janet and Geoff painted the house passage, kitchen, fireplace and chimney.

A trip to collect two sacks of crayfish from Clyde was followed by a night's boiling and a day's shelling. Then the girls began baking for the feast; the boys struggled to make the wedding ring from Melaleuca gold in Deny's tradition; early guests were set to tidying the garden, picking fruit, erecting tables, and digging loos.

It was a joyous occasion with eighty-five guests coming on foot, boat and plane. One walker arrived in tailcoat, shorts and boots. The Hut, garden camps and two tent villages filled rapidly, the strip hummed with aircraft and the radio with telegrams.

To everyone's relief and delight 12 January 1974 dawned clear and blue. After frantic last-minute food preparations and work on the ring, everyone gathered on the bank above the house to await the bride. Mary, dressed in traditional white, with hewardia corsage and leatherwood and Huon pine bouquet, and her two attendants walked up with Deny in shirt-sleeves, tie and thongs, serenaded by violinist friends, for the service performed by another friend. Deny pronounced the navy grace, 'Thank Gawd', and the party began. Hours later the newlyweds rowed off into the sunset to spend the night on an island beach, while guests yarned around campfires until dawn. Melaleuca's first and only wedding was over. Next day Deny organised one of his famous 'harbour cruises', for fifty-two people—for once without axes and chainsaw.

Janet's Hobart wedding two months later was by contrast a low-key event. While Geoff and Janet made the ring, Deny went to the Weld and north to Lord Talbot's Malahide estate for a special collectors' luncheon celebrating the book on Tasmanian endemic flora. At the wedding on 12 March in the Nixon Chapel at St David's Cathedral, Deny had a 'good chat at the door with all the people'. Then after 'a grand tea' at the Fentons', he went with Janet and Geoff on a trip to the west coast—an opportunity not to be missed for its scenic and mining interest.

They toured the huge Mount Lyell copper mine at Queenstown, explored the abandoned township of Crotty, and made two visits to the splendid mining museum at Zeehan. Camping overnight at inhospitable Trial Harbour, port for Zeehan's silver-lead, increased even more Deny's appreciation of Port Davey's sheltered anchorages. However, it was seeing Tullah, where Charlie had gained much of his mining expertise, and listening to the postmistress reminisce, that meant most to Deny.

CHAPTER 27

Good neighbour

'A totally generous man.'

At the end of March 1974 Manx fisherman Peter Willson arrived on his boat *Flickan* to take up the lease adjoining Deny's, which he and his teacher wife Barbara had bought from Win. They had called in January and Deny had showed them around, but Mary's wedding preparations allowed little time for further hospitality.

Now Deny welcomed Peter. It was the beginning of a staunch friendship and mutual co-operation which lasted until Deny's death. 'From when we first started here, he helped us in every way he could,' Peter declared. 'Right until he died we got the most of his generosity. I think everyone who came in contact with him felt that, because he was a totally generous man.'

In April Deny and frequent visitor Ray McKendrick helped Peter erect an A-frame house on a concrete slab. Then over the months Deny stripped the Willsons' first paddock, built their dams and a road from his mine to their house. 'We call it the King's Highway,' Barbara said. 'Best road in the South-West!'

Deny supplied vegetables until Peter could establish his garden, and fruit until his trees began bearing. Loaves of bread and jars of jam often went Willson-wards and Deny frequently called to check on progress and enjoy a cup of coffee. Peter was glad of Deny's advice and his radio to keep in touch with Barbara and his school-boy sons in Hobart. Deny often invited him to a meal and they would yarn by the fire until late, Deny relishing Peter's stories of copper mining in Zambia and fishing in Western Australia and Tasmania. Together they went wood-getting, fishing, exploring and helped each other load and ship tin. Peter was astonished at Deny's strength and fitness. 'I was in my late thirties and he was in his sixties, and he could lift things that I never could.'

Deny also had the pleasure of Janet's company for some months. Her ongoing field studies of freshwater invertebrates were of great interest to him. His pride in her painting continued, particularly when one tourist group bought all her pictures. He appreciated her help with dreaded accounts and correspondence, and at the mine, when pumps frequently blocked and the jig was once jammed by an eel! He welcomed Geoff's visits too, valuing his creative problem-solving and inventive abilities. The prospect of going to Papua New Guinea with them had engaged Deny's thoughts during winter.

When they sailed for Hobart at the beginning of July with thirty-seven bags of tin the decks were icy, they hit a log in the dark and met fog in the channel. With only two hours' sleep during the nineteen-hour trip, Deny was very weary and it was a big disappointment to learn that tin prices had slumped, significantly lowering his income. He also had to go Judbury to be with Rose for Ron's funeral, before leaving for New Guinea.

Once there, flying in light aircraft over the ranges, up deep 'luscious green' valleys, along great rivers, Deny revelled in the spectacular scenery. In his diary he meticulously described vegetation, weather, topography and geology, commenting on limestone plateaus with lakes and sinkholes like the Huon hinterland. More than most people he appreciated all that the tiny declivitous airstrips carved from jungle meant.

Instead of dispensing hospitality, he now received it from a network of patrol officers, miners and others. One had visited Melaleuca the previous summer, and in the Chimbu Highlands they had the unlikely experience of viewing his film of the South-West.

Deny thrived on the company of these people who had also chosen to live in remote places, and yarned most nights till after midnight, absorbing local information and wisdom. Yet he was always up at daybreak making his own observations, sketching, birdwatching and listening, comparing some species with those he knew, describing others he did not. The tropical vegetation delighted him and he noted mosses, tree ferns and other flora similar to Tasmanian species.

They ascended Mount Wilhelm in the Bismarck Range, at 4700 metres PNG's highest peak. It was a stiff day's climb up a frozen track. Travelling with swags and tent, they were amazed at the density of settlement along the mountainous ridges. Deny enjoyed talking with the villagers and was impressed by their gardens, particularly 'a fine patch of potatoes'.

At a mission he was delighted to find a Southern Cross engine powering their sawmill. He and Geoff also investigated mining operations, including the Porgera gold mine, where Deny understood well the difficult terrain. They marvelled at abandoned giant dredges transported over the ranges in three-ton segments by Junkers cargo planes for the Bulolo goldfields in the 1930s.

On a rigorous trip they visited Edie Creek, Zenag and Wampit. Deny recognised wartime campsites, and was thrilled to find a plaque commemorating the Royal Australian Engineers' roadmaking effort near the Snake and Bulolo rivers' junction. Visits to Wau agricultural research station, Lae botanic gardens, war cemetery and RSL club, and Port Moresby university completed a significant experience for Deny, looking back, remembering, always learning.

Arriving in Brisbane, still hungry for others' memories of Margaret, Deny spent time with her family and friends. In New England he met the Tenterfield chemist who remembered Margaret and John, and stayed with her cousin Norah. They were welcomed at Deepwater again, and spent several days too at Coolootai Station. In Sydney Kath and Elsie provided opportunities for Deny to reminisce over old photos. Near Armidale he delighted in seeing Antarctic beeches; from Canberra he visited Mount Stromlo Observatory; and in Melbourne a curator friend showed him the museum's fossil collection.

It was 'a bit of a shock' on arriving in Hobart on Mary's birthday to find the bank had reduced his overdraft from $3000 to $650, forcing him to sell some insurance to create a contingency fund. Then with Mary, Janet and Geoff as seasoned crew, he left for Port Davey in September. Two days later he wrote, 'Everyone very happy at being home again.'

Each spring he eagerly awaited the arrival of the 'grass parrots', which in 1974 he described for the first time as orange-bellied parrots. Over the years their diminishing numbers had caused him concern. This season his concern was that they had developed a liking for the seeds on the strawberries!

At the mine Deny made another important botanical discovery. Intrigued by ancient banksia cones that he had found in excavated soil, Deny compared them with live specimens, decided they were different and dispatched them to the university for investigation, as he believed them to be undescribed. Postgraduate students had sought his help in collecting a species of banksia, described as *Banksia insularis* by Matthew Flinders' botanist, Robert Brown in 1802, and also to locate fossil leaf material.

Scientists, however, thought they were probably the common species *Banksia marginata*, so they joined the uncatalogued backlog. Analysed shortly before Deny's death, they were recognised as a hitherto unknown species, now extinct. They had been preserved in a sedimentary bed at least 38,000 years earlier. The species was named *Banksia kingii*, in recognition of Deny. Palaeobotanist Dr Gregory Jordan, who wrote of the amazing find in several journals said, 'He discovered the deposit, encouraged its study and gave freely of his local knowledge and hospitality.'

In December 1974, when he and Geoff had almost completed a shed for the loader and with forty tin bags sewn up, Deny wrote, 'Getting ready to go to Hobart is near and we don't feel a bit like it.' To forestall a repeat of last year's vandalism he took the precaution for the first time of hiding the loader's key. He had decided to put compensation offered by the offending school towards building a second walkers' hut, which he was now planning. On Boxing Day 1974 with walkers' help he laid the new hut's foundations. In the garden he noted a particularly prolific patch of potatoes where the crayfish remains from Mary's wedding had been buried!

'With the mountains blue and their shadows deeper blue', Deny enjoyed the summer bird life. The lagoon was alive with cormorants, ducks, grebes and coots, flights of swans passed over daily, and herons 'rising in small circles to over 2000 feet, then swooping back to ground near mine' provided a skyshow. He was extra pleased to count fourteen orange-bellied parrots, 'have not seen this many for years'.

In March a couple wearing binoculars walked in to Melaleuca. Deny was delighted that Victorians Bob and Cons Lowry were keen birdwatchers, and befriended them at once, giving them food and warmer, more weatherproof clothing. Cons remembered:

> We'd been living mainly on rice and dried soup for eight days. And the first thing Deny does is offer us fresh fruit from his garden. That was our first impression of him: his generosity, warm hospitality and friendliness.
>
> We were absolute novices at bushwalking and he did his best to teach us all sorts of things, like how to find dry stuff to light a fire, and water by inserting plastic tubing in the ground or down a yabby hole.

Other welcome visitors over this period included Syrian campaign army mates, *National Geographic* photographers, ABC teams, and old friend Jack Thwaites. Less congenial was the Qintex leaseholder. He left a new chum English family at Cox Bight without supplies for months, so Deny and Peter had to help.

Helicopters, always a source of interest, had begun using the airstrip fortnightly to service Maatsuyker lighthouse. Sometimes in bad weather crew and passengers stayed overnight. Deny helped Qintex personnel rescue their lost dinghy, lent equipment, did their welding, advised them on problems, and sent and received their radio messages, regardless of interruption to his own work.

In April 'roos and wals were getting past a joke'. So was *Melaleuca*'s persistent engine trouble. After countless hours' work, Geoff and Deny discovered a cracked cylinder head, so Deny and Peter decided to sail in convoy to Hobart.

Flicken towed Deny's boat on a line shackled to *Melaleuca*'s anchor chains 'to help stop any jerks'. In thickening weather they met a big swell and Deny let out forty-five metres of chain hitched round the samson post to act as shock absorber against the waves. After passing South West Cape in darkness, he set the staysail, but a strengthening northerly with rain made it a slow trip until they thankfully arrived at the yacht club twenty-four hours later.

Deny stayed two months in Hobart while a new Ford Dolphin engine was installed and tested. Mary and Ian were living at Norfolk Crescent, and Deny often accompanied Ian on electrical jobs. Geoff's parents' kept open house for him, as did Janet and Geoff. They had bought a property at Sandfly, south of Hobart, where Deny made a vegetable garden and grubbed blackberries.

In June 1975 Charles Denison King was made a Member of the Order of Australia, for his service to the community. He was one of the first of only fifty-three AMs Australia-wide, yet with typical modesty, he did not mention it in his diary.

During winter, visits to and from Peter, seven olive whistlers, a solitary blue wren, a gathering of currawongs and a resident owl provided Deny with company. On wild wet days or when snow fleeced the mountains he was very content to stay home painting and making Huon pine picture frames. He brought inside a ringtail possum 'nearly done with cold' and put it on warm bricks to recover. When Peter's family arrived for holidays, he enjoyed the boys' help at the mine, and appreciated Barbara's care when he had flu.

At short notice he flew out to visit Olive in hospital, returning later to help while she convalesced. In Hobart he cleaned Mary's blocked chimney, then assisted Janet with a chapter on early mining settlements for *The South-West Book* she was compiling with Helen Gee and Greg Hodge for the Australian Conservation Foundation.

Winter burning off had been largely unsuccessful, so in September Deny advised National Parks that conditions were suitable. With help from Janet, Geoff and seven Rural Fires Board and Parks personnel, he recommenced a major burn to New Harbour and from Melaleuca Inlet to Horseshoe Inlet. He also gave permission for a rangers' hut to be built on his lease. In November he took another survey party to inspect a proposed airstrip site at Bond Bay.

Clyde gave Deny a baby yellow-throated honeyeater. Because it was always hungry he spent much time unearthing grubs, even tackling a bull ants' nest for larvae and taking *Blue Boat* to get grub-infested wood. He took 'Chicky Boy' down the garden while he dug, but had to take him back when duskies attacked. One dawn grub-getting foray Deny returned for his jacket and Chicky Boy, who always greeted his arrival with great excitement, flew out. Falling underfoot, the little bird was fatally injured. Deny was devastated. 'I felt so sad and upset as he was such a good mate, even though he was so time-consuming to look after.'

A week later, on 11 November, Deny stayed home to follow the political crisis when Governor-General Kerr dismissed Prime Minister Whitlam, and invited walkers to listen to the news. He always derived intense interest from radio news, interviews and documentaries and much pleasure from classical music, noting works and performers in the back of his diary—including Mozart's *Jupiter Symphony*, flute and piano concertos, Beethoven, '*Pastoral Symphony* not to be missed', Schubert, Mendelssohn and Haydn symphonies, and singers Maria Callas and Elisabeth Schumann. 'Singers of Renown' was a favourite program. A very light sleeper, Deny frequently rose at 3 a.m., baked bread or brewed jam, listened to BBC broadcasts, wrote letters or read, preferring travel accounts in remote places and stories of people achieving against odds. He always had a supply of books from the state library, and lent his own to weatherbound walkers.

He was very tired throughout November, heavy perhaps with the prospect of yet 'another one of those rotten bashes round the Cape'. Despite a leaking oil gasket, however, it was uneventful under mainsail, and *Melaleuca* was the first to lie up at the yacht club's new wharf, as well as the only boat ever to unload cargo, a practice to which an official blind eye was always turned. Once, a club member, feeling sorry for the barefooted old chap in ragged shorts hefting two bags off his boat, went to help, only to find he could not lift even one!

The 1976 summer was busier than ever, with many visitors returning for their third, fourth or fifth time. Lighthouse families, police officers, yachties doing their laundry and baking at his house, Deny welcomed them all. One day he recorded five parties totalling forty-one people. Especially welcome were walking club groups, including some from Hobart, Launceston and even Hamersley Range, Western Australia, who assisted with maintenance on the Memorial Hut and building the new one.

Less welcome were others whose campfire near the huts invaded the peat after they departed, and those who left one burning at The Narrows. Several walkers wood-getting with Deny formed a bucket brigade to help extinguish it, but Deny was upset because he had only his good axe to cut away the peat, smouldering over an area of ten metres by six. 'What he thought of people who DID NOT PUT OUT campfires, was "just nobody's business", one helper wrote.

After the tragedy of Lake Pedder's flooding in 1972, the South-West's wilderness values were becoming more widely recognised. In 1976 a group including Tasmanian university botany professor Bill Jackson and Launceston Museum director Frank Ellis, came to assess conservation needs. The Sierra Club returned for their second visit, as did archeologists doing field work for the Australian National University. Deny took Western Australian botanist Alex George and Victorian botanical artist Celia Rosser, who came to collect banksia specimens, towards Bathurst Harbour and was gratified they were so impressed with the country.

In January first-time visitor, Peter Hodgman, member for Huon in the Legislative Council, wrote:

> I was told the only way to know the South-West was to live in it. So for about a month I have roughed it! I am not a bushwalker, I hadn't ever really camped, but now I like camping, and I think the South-West is the greatest. I consider it to be one of my political priorities.

'The South-West of Tasmania has no rival,' a Floridan wrote two months later. 'Here's hoping fellow bushwalkers will bond together to hold back the thirsty desires of HEC, woodchipping, mining.' Belgian mining photographers, a miner from Greenland, visitors from Holland and the US, and a walker who had explored South America as far as Tierra del Fuego aroused Deny's latent desire for travel and adventure.

Meeting an organic farmer from northern Tasmania also influenced Deny, who subsequently adopted his methods. Now he became even more keen to put back as much as his crops used: he burnt prunings and cartons on fallow beds, planted cover crops, applied ashes, shell grit, compost and kelp, and mulched with reeds, tree fern fronds, seaweed, orchard leaves, and even cocoa-bean husks brought from Cadbury's, as well as grass. In strawberry and pansy beds around the mine he put mud from the works and mulched with fibrous roots from overburden. He specialised in liquid fertilisers: a particularly unpleasant-looking and noisome brew from small and spoiled potatoes soaked in a drum of water, 'hoot' from fish heads and guts, and 'crayfish soup'. And he enjoyed the birds attracted by flies round his compost heap.

A trip on *Reemere* in March proved to be the second last of many with Win and Clyde. In April they decided to sell up and move north. Deny did all he could to help them pack, but privately it was a bleak time. Their departure broke the last major connection to his father and Margaret. Unusual rainbows and brilliant auroras were a solace; and with Peter's staunch help Deny got his twenty-two bags of tin to Claytons Corner to go out on *Reemere*'s final voyage.

Native cats or nady cats, and tiger cats or ger cats, as he called the eastern quolls and spotted-tail quolls, were unusually bold, raiding the bird feeder and chewing socks left out in the rain for pre-washing. Worst of all, several came on board *Melaleuca* and 'messed' on his bunk. Not surprisingly his favourite expletive was: 'Cats!'

More winter ills than usual beset Deny in 1976. He was often fatigued, and although he helped Janet on mammal and bird chapters for *The South-West Book*, he frequently remarked, as Margaret had, that he didn't have much to show for the day. His diary for the year is a catalogue of malfunctioning equipment and in November he admitted 'very depressed about all the frustrations'.

Yet Deny found pleasure in small things: a well-risen loaf, a solid backlog for the fire, a colourful sunset, a patch of beautiful moss and lichen, the sound of swans at dawn, the sight of black cockatoos clowning in the banksias by the waterfront, a platypus in the creek. Then after a mail-less month, letters from 'the chooldren', Lowrys, and other house guests lifted his spirits. He was pleased when two of the big cheeses he regularly bought specifically for the birds were delivered, 'so birdies will not have to be rationed'.

It was a cuckoo spring, with both shining bronze and fantailed among the usual harbingers—welcome swallows, tree martins, pipits and snipe—though orange-bellied parrots were 'not about here much now'. 'Birdies were all around' when he dug out an original wooden house stump and replaced it with a concrete pier. A 'Young Richard which comes inside and sings so sweetly and happily' took cheese from his hand and played with a pencil and a coin on the table as Deny wrote and painted. He worried that birds which frequented the house might inadvertently be trapped inside in his absence, so artist Hilma Tyson painted a poster for the door, featuring Deny's favourites, requesting visitors to ensure all birds were out before closing it.

In January 1977 with Mary and friends he did a three-day walk from Bond Bay to *Svenor*, rising early to cut a track for the others through thick scrub along the shore. Then he led ten on a five-day trip to South West Cape, before accompanying the Willsons to Cox's to show them the old workings.

He spent two days aboard tourist vessel *Mascarin* with the federal Minister for the Environment and party, then returned to greet more groups, including an Adult Education party of twenty-two, to whom he gave an evening talk. Deny had collected moths for the Tasmanian Museum in 1975 and sandflies for the CSIRO in 1965, so was interested to meet an entomologist collecting wasps. He was also pleased to welcome fellow artists, including Max Angus and Patricia Giles, and a couple from the Tasmanian Agent-General's London office.

Early in February 1977, five yachts tied up beside *Melaleuca*, including Sydney–Hobart maxi *Anaconda*, while thirteen more anchored in Port Davey. It was a bad summer for fires. Fishermen lit several on islands and on shore. So Deny was thankful for Rural Fires Board and Parks personnel taking charge of firefighting. When another was lit at Louisa Bay, he reacted angrily. 'Those frightful fishermen, how mean can they be?'

In March, wearing a hired suit and borrowed shoes, and accompanied by Mary 'looking very sweet in her new hat', Deny flew to Canberra to receive his AM in a 'beknighting' ceremony from 'Missus Queen'. Her yellow dress, his favourite colour, met with his approval, but he could only manage 'Yes' when she commented, 'You come from a long way away, don't you?' Karen Alexander drove them to Government House in an unwashed borrowed VW Beetle and they 'partook of drinks and sandwiches very small' on the Yarralumla lawns afterwards.

While in Canberra they also visited the Botanic Gardens, and the War Memorial where Deny searched out Margaret's brother John's name on the Honour Roll. They looked up old friends, including Roy McAndrew, and went bushwalking where Elyne Mitchell set her Silver Brumby series, favourite of Margaret and dorts. They also drove to see the home of Gwen Meredith, author of the 'Blue Hills' radio serial, another favourite of the girls.

Arriving at the Anglican rectory at Adaminaby to stay with one of Mary's old school friends, Deny was delighted to see a Rayburn stove. But because of a particularly green load of firewood, the chimney had gummed up and the stove smoked. Always keen to help, Deny was up on the roof in no time, cleaning the chimney with snow chains, then down again in the kitchen dealing with the stove damper. And soon afterwards the satisfying smell of bread baking filled the kitchen.

The next day in the Snowy Mountains, Deny, Mary, Karen and Roy visited the old gold mining town of Kiandra, an underground power station and the Tumut dam. They made frequent stops to boil the billy, investigate wildflowers, birdwatch and photograph views. They climbed Mount Jagungal, enjoying the sunset panorama of mountains dominated by Kosciuszko, and camped, drinking 'lots of maté', his favourite South American tea, by the fire. For Deny it was bliss.

Deny and Mary then stayed four days with the Lowrys near Wangaratta, birdwatching and exploring the historic gold mining town of Beechworth, returning proud and excited in time for Mary's graduation.

Six weeks later Deny was back in Hobart for urgent business concerning the airstrip.

During July and August, wet, wild and freezing at Melaleuca, with ground-shaking, window-rattling thunder, Deny worked on repairing the trommel. Poor radio conditions were unusually worrying as Mary was expecting a baby within weeks, so Deny was uncertain whether to sail or fly out. *Melaleuca* left late on 1 September and next morning near Big Witch he received news of the birth of 'Mary's babe'.

Memories flooded back—hearing of Mary's birth at the same time twenty-seven years before and his urgent longing to be with Margaret. Weary with emotion, he stopped overnight at Partridge Island, and arrived next morning to hurry to the same hospital to see mother and daughter Kylie Margaret. Then, after unloading, he went to Norfolk Crescent, to find 'quite a party'. Friends had come to celebrate. At sixty-eight Deny was a grandfather.

CHAPTER 28

A new generation and new horizons

'He was way in front of everybody else in seeing things.'

Since 1957 Deny's airstrip, built for his own family's convenience and safety, had been used by fishermen, walkers, Mines Department, lighthouse and rescue personnel, rangers, firefighters, media, government officials, mining and exploration companies as well as VIPs, scientists, tourists and sightseers from many countries. Because of it, lives had been saved, the South-West had become better known world-wide, and it had opened up opportunities for other miners, abalone divers, and especially for TasAir, the commercial offshoot of the pioneering Aero Club of Southern Tasmania, with charter business. Deny logged over 200 landings a year.

Lake Pedder had been a popular destination for light aircraft, but after its 1972 flooding more private pilots began to use Melaleuca's airstrip. Then competititon with Tasmanian Aviation Services had led to TasAir's seeking a site for an independent strip. No alternative had been found, so in March 1977 chief pilot Nick Tanner talked about extending Deny's strip. But widening as well as lengthening it was a major job which Deny considered beyond his resources.

The strip had an unblemished safety record. Only months earlier Deny felt vindicated when a Britten Norman Islander, the largest plane to use it, had landed, and on take-off had become airborne within 150-odd metres. But in April TasAir complained to the federal Department of Transport that the strip's length and width did not meet regulations.

After lengthy lobbying by TasAir, the Department wrote to Deny on 28 April 1977 advising the immediate closure of the airstrip. But the letter, posted the day before the official closure, of course could not be delivered!

Radio conditions at Melaleuca were poor, so while Deny noted several planes passing over during May, and pined for letters from the girls, he resorted to sending his out with walkers. He remained uninformed of the new development until 28 May. When he received a message from Barbara and Ian, that they could not come as arranged, because the strip was now to be used only for emergencies, Deny and Peter were incensed.

After receiving the month-old news Deny struggled with poor conditions to radio the Department for permission for supplies to be flown in. To add insult to injury he then heard that a plane was arriving so that some passengers on *Mascarin* could fly out. The injustice provoked Deny into protest. He drove the loader with a log in tow onto the strip and parked it in the middle.

When a message from Tasmanian Aviation Services advised that their plane for the tourists was bringing in Barbara and Ian, Deny moved the loader. He had lost a day's work, but received his first mail in six weeks. Next day Nick Tanner, having brought supplies and two DCA surveyors, tried to conciliate him.

Deny was to lose many more working hours and much sleep before the situation was resolved and he could be sure his airstrip would remain operational. He and Peter spent several days surveying and measuring it before they left on *Flicken*. Because city-based officialdom rarely understood the problems of isolation, he spent days in Hobart consulting with Tasmanian Aviation Services, Mines Department, National Parks and Wildlife Service and the South-West Committee. He wrote letters until midnight lobbying for the strip's retention, as life now at Melaleuca without it could scarcely be contemplated.

In August, Parks officers flew in to discuss the situation. Deny and Peter, who was equally concerned, spent more time investigating extension possibilities. Deny, thinking ahead, began reorganising his pump to direct tailings stripwards for construction. In Hobart in September for Mary's baby, Deny was interviewed by the *Mercury* in an article fittingly entitled 'Red tape has a long reach'. He wrote to the Premier several times, spoke to Peter Hodgman MLC, and had an interview with the Transport Commission about finance for the required extension, which was finally passed by Parliament in November.

Deny visited VIH to meet new operator Phil Jones. He discussed the forthcoming change from AM to single side band radio, costing over $1000 to replace equipment, commenting ruefully, 'The Commonwealth gets more use out of it than we do because we send in the weather reports daily and act as a Royal Flying Doctor Service base.'

In November he began preparations for the mammoth task of extending the airstrip yet again, by another sixty-odd metres. In mid-December he burnt off at the end, then started digging out banks, backfilling with stone, pushing dirt and peat as a base for gravel covering, and forming a bench from which Peter could operate his digger.

To utilise the dry weather he declined a day trip for Christmas at Mary's, instead working seven hours ripping and dozing gravel. Four days later he was rewarded, finding a good patch of tin. A comment in the visitors' book on New Year's Day 1978 probably echoed his sentiments: 'A prosperous New Year to all at Melaleuca and confusion to all bureaucrats.'

For the next three months Deny averaged nearly ten hours a day on the strip, sometimes starting at 4.30 a.m. Mary, Ian and Kylie, plus dog and puppies, came in January and for several weeks Deny and Ian worked with the D2 and loader, taking lunchbreaks in shifts so work did not cease. In places where the ground was too soft for machines, they levelled it with pick and shovel. They burnt off to make clearing overburden easier and Peter dug drainage trenches and moved spoil with his excavator.

Only an emergency with Olive made Deny stop work. Late in February he flew out as soon as he heard she was ill. It was a rough flight back even by the pilot's admission, and Deny had to hang on to his seat. So the sight of the flag flying in welcome and the garden glowing with his favourite yellow dahlias was particularly sweet.

Just as Deny had adored watching Mary, he was now enthralled by Kylie, carrying her on walks, nursing her on boat trips, watching her crawl 'like little Tracla in a bog'. After the family left he appreciated the company of a solitary egret which became very tame, feeding on insects and yabbies exposed as he bulldozed. It even came into the garden, catching blowflies round the fertiliser bucket, standing by for worms while Deny dug.

Early in April, when 'winter was knocking at the door and the quinces were getting a good sniff', Deny finished the strip's north corner with help from Peter's son David, and began at the south-west end, with Roy McAndrew.

When seven CSIRO scientists came to investigate peat soils and take timber samples around Bathurst Harbour, not even the demands of the airstrip could keep Deny away. McAndrew was amazed at his detailed knowledge of features not visible from the water, what to look for and how to find things in specific spots, and how to differentiate species quickly by seeking small details and clues usually overlooked. Deny guided the botanists to one of the biggest Huon pines. Wishing to take a sample, they assured him it wouldn't cause harm. 'But there was no way he'd let them touch that tree.'

Deny 'spent some time grubbing up worms because the egret looked cold and hungry' before flying out for Anzac Day, an interview in Hobart with the Transport Commission about the strip, and visiting Olive and Win in hospital in Launceston.

Back at Melaleuca early in May, keen to achieve maximum hours, Deny was frustrated it was too dark to work before 7 a.m. When the loader windows were iced over he had to wait until nine to start. Sometimes the ground had turned to 'pudding' after rain. The ripper teeth and bucket blade had worn so badly they needed replacement and the ordered parts took a week to arrive. Commission inspectors, however, were pleased with progress and Deny was chuffed when a pilot used only half the extension for take-off.

A family visit mid-year was very welcome. Deny was glad of Ian's and Geoff's assistance replacing the windsock destroyed by storms, procuring and setting up new radio aerial poles and getting the new transceiver working. And he delighted in Kylie, 'a busy little scrap', who crawled exploring everything. He was pleased too with Ian's 'dorgy'. After it had barked under the house for days, they lifted floorboards and discovered a tiger cat's nest, which Deny immediately dismantled.

As his tin yield was very light Deny flew to Hobart. He spent six snowy weeks at Sandfly helping out, and took close interest in the final stages of *The South-West Book*, on which Janet, who had graduated from university and gained librarianship qualifications, was still working. He spent another four weeks at Norfolk Crescent mainly on Mary's workshop and investigating kilns. After conferring again with the Transport Commission about the strip, he signed the contract for further work before leaving in late August for a spectacular coastal flight to Melaleuca by float plane.

Mid-December brought two visitors who were to develop a particular affinity for Melaleuca and become special in Deny's life. Karina Menkhorst remembered Deny's greeting to her and a friend arriving from Cockle Creek: '"There's some raspberries in the garden. Help yourselves, then I won't have to make so much jam." With those simple words he won his way into our hearts forever.' Their feet, like many before them, were blistered, so as they recuperated they turned helping hands to garden, fruit, house and strip, while Deny awaited Karen Alexander, who was also walking in.

The next 'great excitement' was the unexpected arrival of Janet and another of Deny's favourites, Helen Fletcher, 'who is such fun'. The McKendricks followed for a great family Christmas. Kylie's prowess 'almost walking' was Deny's last entry for 1978.

Karen quickly learned to drive the loader and Fergie, the newly acquired second-hand Ferguson tractor, and started work with Deny on the strip on New Year's Day 1979. Deny noted her aptitude with equipment repairs. Capable too in house and garden, she gave the piano a much-needed tune and mended Deny's pack which prompted his appreciative comment, 'Busy little girl always doing.'

In late January the party walked via Ketchem Bay and Wilson Bight to join the Willsons and Lowrys, back for their third visit, on a five-day trip to South West Cape. On return Bob helped on the strip while Cons gardened, and at night they discussed an expedition through Central Australia along the Gunbarrel Highway to the west.

After Karen left on a prolonged walk, Deny worked twelve hours a day on the strip in waterlogged conditions. When the D2's hydraulic hose burst, insufficient clamps were flown in with the replacement, evoking his usual matter-of-fact response to disasters, 'Dear Bill, what a bastard!' As someone who helped him change the loader's wheel stated, 'That was as angry as Deny King ever got!'

Even though yabby holes in the gravel made driving difficult, Deny did not lose his dry sense of humour. In February zoologist Eric Guiler arrived and finding Deny deep in a very muddy hole on the airstrip, remarked, 'It's pretty nasty down there. I don't suppose even a yabby would enjoy that, would he?' Deny looked up whimsically and replied, 'No. Come to think of it, I've never seen a yabby laughing.'

Deny had long been concerned by the dwindling numbers of the migratory orange-bellied parrot and now mainland concern for its threatened status was mounting. He was heartened when the Chandler family from Westernport Bay, where ICI planned a petro-chemical plant adjacent to the parrots' main Victorian wintering site, spent two weeks searching the area and observing the orange-bellied parrots in Deny's garden. They were deeply impressed by Deny, his generosity, hospitality and 'practically inexhaustible knowledge of the wildlife of the area'.

A crew from the Australian Film and Television School returned several times, filming a documentary for the South-West Tasmania Committee of New South Wales. With the looming threat by the HEC in 1978 to flood the Franklin River, Deny collected visitors' signatures on a NO DAMS petition. Concern for the preservation of the South-West was growing steadily, as many impassioned entries in the Memorial Hut visitors' book by walkers from across Australia and the world testify. Sydney conservation activist Bob Burton railed against apathy, declaring, 'We only have wilderness once. SAVE IT.' And for Steve Bracks, later Premier of Victoria, the South-West wilderness was 'the best walk I have been on yet'.

Deny happily anticipated Karen's return in March. He raised the flag, washed and polished the floors, and placed flowers in the house. Working in shifts with her enabled him to deal with machinery repairs, yet maintain progress on the strip before the next inspection, and to record the weather and still do his morning radio sked.

In a voluntary commitment begun in January 1946 he served as one of Australia's most southerly weather observers. Each day he meticulously measured and recorded Melaleuca's diversity of cloud forms, winds, rainfall and other conditions. With a weather station containing anemometer, wet and dry thermometers and rain gauge, checked daily at 9 a.m., he reported 'as regular as clockwork at 9.30 a.m.' to the Commonwealth Bureau of Meteorology's Hobart office, and lodged official returns monthly. He also recorded full details of the day's patterns in his diary. His ability to forecast accurately was of inestimable benefit for bushwalkers and boaties, and Melbourne and Hobart air traffic controllers sought his information for search and rescue operations.

He attended the Anzac dawn service and marched in Hobart. Then the following day, carrying bottled raspberries and jam for friends, he flew to Alice Springs for the two-month Gunbarrel Highway expedition. The party, collecting data for the Royal Australasian Ornithologists' Union bird atlas, consisted of the Lowrys, Rob Drummond, nephew of Deny's commander Major Dick Drummond, Doug Humann and Karen Alexander.

Deny and Karen travelled with the Lowrys, enjoying frequent stops and walks for observation, sometimes noting sixteen to eighteen species different from Melaleuca's, but always delighting in the familiar welcome swallows.

'Travelling the Gunbarrel Highway was adventure enough in itself,' Doug Humann wrote, 'but to be sharing it with Deny and his vitality and love for natural places and living things was better still. His diary-writing was an inspiration and his recitations and stories a delight.'

They explored Kings Canyon, Ayers Rock and the Olgas, where the artist in Deny responded to the vibrant reds and ochres of the rocky ranges and sandy dunes, so different from Port Davey's blue and grey waters and mountains. Uluru, where circling hawks looked like swallows, awed him with its size and ancient sculpted surfaces and secrets, while Kata Tjuta's extraordinary formations, 'like giant cottage loaves', fascinated him, as did fiery sunsets and sunrises, gleaming salt lakes, desert spiked with anthills, and every detail of unfamiliar weather patterns.

He waded waist-deep along some creeks, dug for water in dry beds of others, swam in waterholes, scrambled up stony slopes and along steep gorges. He observed the different plant life—spinifex, cycads and succulents instead of button grass, mulga instead of manuka and melaleuca, elegant ghost gums and 'noble desert oaks' instead of Huon and celery-top pines; and tried bush-tucker fruits. He revelled in the abundance of dry firewood, quickly learning the burning properties of different species. Slow-burning mulga was a favourite, producing superb ashes for damper. Rob Drummond was amazed at Deny's strength. 'He would take off his shirt, grasp a fifteen foot tree with his big hairy hands, wrap his arms around and lift it straight out of the ground with a bear hug.'

He often slept under the stars, getting up to stoke the campfire, boil the billy, bake bread, write his diary and letters, or read. Adept with camp oven, he took his turn cooking, making scones and his specialty—curried sardines and rice. He put his mechanical skills to good use too, crawling under the vehicles each morning to check their roadworthiness and do maintenance. He kept the water containers filled, and was always the first to grab the shovel when their vehicles became bogged or encountered washouts.

A memorial to the fabled Lasseter stirred Deny's prospecting spirit. At Giles Weather Station in Western Australia he was thrilled to be shown equipment and procedures, including the graphs and release of balloons, and photographed the grader used in constructing the highway.

They traversed flat expanses of spinifex 'looking like fields of over-ripe grain' stretching to the horizon, with the road disappearing in the distance 'straight as a die'. 'Stark and bare without decent rain for over four years', it was totally unlike Tasmania's South-West. Deny was always interested in former mining areas, though the rubbish which often surrounded them shocked him, and he enjoyed fossicking in amethyst and rose quartz mines. Along the way he observed modern ore carriers, windmills, bores, mechanical installations, and outback airstrips and aircraft.

In south-west Western Australia highlights included a foray into the haunts of the noisy scrub bird, a very elusive endangered species, and several days at the RAOU bird observatory at old Eyre telegraph station, helping with netting, banding and counting.

Deny, now nearly seventy, had the travel bug, further fed in Sydney by seeing 'Ed Hillary's' film of his latest expedition, and in Melbourne a film on Patagonia made by Karen's friend David Neilson. Deny had plenty to remember but even more to plan. He spent three weeks in Tasmania, 'taking notes' about Argentina and Chile from Tom and Helen Coles, before returning to Lowrys' for a reunion.

In August Karina assisted with work on *Melaleuca* in Hobart and sailed with Deny to help at mine and airstrip. The house, uninhabited for four months, was dank and mouldy, and someone had left the gate open, so the garden had been devastated. But the first swallows had arrived, one melaleuca was in flower, and apricot, cherry and plum trees were blossoming. Deny was home. And Karina made good apple crumble!

Early in October, when 'Daddy blue wrens' were flaunting their brilliant breeding plumage, Parks personnel, led by Peter Brown, arrived to monitor the orange-bellied parrots. With resident birdos on site for the season Deny was in his element, chuffed that his meticulous diary entries since 1959 recording the orange-bellied parrots' arrival dates and relevant weather conditions were valued data. He made many trips with the rangers by boat and on foot, in search of the parrots' feeding, roosting and nesting sites. The only nesting birds observed, however, were at Birchs Inlet up the coast where Deny kept regular radio contact with another Parks team.

In November, always Deny's favourite month, fine weather brought 'a dawn to dusk curfew on house except for essential services—eating and midday nap'. Again Deny passed up a flight to Hobart for Christmas, and was on the spot to hoist the flag for the

Willsons returning in their new custom-built boat, *Rallinga*—an exciting finale to an exciting year.

The early weeks of 1980 brought grief. In January news of Olive's death shocked Deny. He arranged to fly out for her Launceston funeral. While he was away a walker collapsed and died in Hidden Valley. Then, only a week later, Karina's father, Peter Menkhorst, fell and died on Mount Rugby. The airstrip Deny and Karina had been working on from dawn to dark twice became busy with Search and Rescue aircraft and personnel. Appreciation expressed by the regional director of Civil Aviation for 'the sterling work done by you and your family during a number of emergencies', was well-merited.

Summer visitors included two from an Israeli kibbutz, a Norwegian student, a British couple who had sailed their nine-metre concrete yacht from Malta, and German and New Zealand walkers. In Melaleuca tradition many showed practical appreciation of Deny's hospitality and assistance, so two loos were dug, and windows installed to complete the new hut, which was already occupied to capacity.

Peter Hodgman walked in again, bringing another parliamentarian. Two men from the big tractor firm William Adams 'on a memorable visit to our southernmost customer' came to do a story about 'Tasmania's most noted "CAT" operator' for their house magazine. Then at twenty-four hours' notice, Lord Snowdon arrived to take photos for his book, *Tasmania Essay*.

Janet went into tidying mode, mending Deny's socks, cutting his hair, and preparing morning tea. Royalist Deny hoisted the flag in honour of his visitor, but kept his matter-of-fact calm, interested in observing yet another professional photographer at work. When Snowdon asked to look through the house, Janet was embarrassed, as everything had been bundled into the back bedroom. But Deny grinned when the visitor confessed he too had a room like that!

Trevor Wilson who wrote the text accompanying the photos said:

Snowdon thought the whole trip was worthwhile to meet Deny King. The photographer was greatly moved by this man who lived in the rugged south, in an environment of self-sufficiency which could hardly be imagined in a city. Living there in isolation, Deny King has a certain regal dignity about him, moving, sitting, standing in his formidable kingdom.

In April when Deny was 'busy with the fly banger', and the pay-dirt heap dwarfed the loader, he hoisted the flag again for Karina's return after two months' absence. She had settled well into the Melaleuca lifestyle, proving naturally adept at anything mechanical, with the energy and willingness to do whatever else needed doing, be it weeding, washing, housework, or mending the fishing net.

Deny appreciated her intellect and encouraged her to pursue correspondence studies in mechanical subjects, as he had done, as well as gaining practical skills on the job, such as welding. 'I've learned so much and I'll never forget or regret it,' Karina said. 'Deny is a mine of knowledge on doing what seems either an impossible or horrific job.' In leisure hours Deny enjoyed her vitality and zest, her excitement over the mail bag's arrival, her reading aloud of *Winnie the Pooh* and *Snugglepot and Cuddlepie*, and of course her cooking.

In May a Parks team arrived to construct the 'new International Airport Reception Centre', a storage and shelter shed, donated by the parents of missing walker, David Troedel. The airstrip throbbed with helicopters, transferring lighthouse personnel and stores, and making seven landings with building materials and supplies.

That same month one sleepless night at 3 a.m., spurred by Olive's death, Deny began his memoirs. At first he found pleasure in writing by the fire in the small hours, retelling his parents' stories of earlier years. But later he had difficulty recounting his own life, declaring, 'the most exciting parts are B-Me and when I come on the scene it seems rather dull'.

Deny had long cherished a dream of a Himalayan trek to the base camp of Mount Everest, and had obtained his passport and made plans with the Lowrys. In July 1980 he flew to Hobart for a medical check, and was told he was unfit for the trek because of high blood pressure. However, an even more 'specky' flight to Melaleuca than usual lifted his spirits, and Deny was exhilarated by the splendour of the snow-shawled mountains and metallic, frozen lakes in his own 'back yard'.

In August when clouds dumped nearly 400 millimetres of drowning rain and 'stopped play' at the mine, he took up his brush again and 'had a glorious time painting'. He was not a quick painter, often 'fiddling' or 'tinkering', dissatisfied with his results. But he finished a painting begun three years earlier, and one of South West Cape which he presented to the yacht club. Roy McAndrew had given him a pantograph with which to work from photos, and he enjoyed looking through many old prints.

After many planeless weeks, September stores were uncomfortably low, even for the birds, which did not appreciate a concoction of old evaporated milk and parmesan cheese. After recording the first orange-bellied parrots' arrival in October, Deny and Karina sailed to Hobart, where he heard about a December trip to Nepal planned by David and Fran Pinkard, who often visited Melaleuca. Their goal was the Annapurna region, over nine hundred metres lower than Everest base camp, so Deny returned to his doctor and extracted a clearance.

In November Deny's grandson, Tony Denison, was born to Janet and Geoff. It was a difficult birth and for three weeks his life was in the balance. Deny visited the hospital, consoling Janet, declaring he had 'a feeling it would be all right.' Tony lived, but Deny was shattered to learn that he had cerebral palsy. Tony, however, had inherited his grandfather's genes for survival, and sense of humour, and would grow up encouraged and strengthened by Deny's example.

Deny returned home battling a bad leak in *Melaleuca* all the way, 'a horribly slow disorganized messy wet trip'. At the start of the season's orange-bellied parrot survey he appreciated a visit from RAOU President, Norman Wettenhall, and eminent parrot artist Joseph Forshaw. He also enjoyed the Menkhorst family coming. Then in mid-December, leaving Karina in charge, Deny, now seventy-one, set off for his Himalayan trek, led by John Chapman, another frequent South-West walker.

Deny's ability to find interest in any place or person, his encyclopaedic knowledge from his wide reading, and his dry sense of humour made him an ideal travelling companion. The Pinkards were making their last expedition as a family, and Deny fitted in well with the teenagers. 'We really appreciated having Deny along,' Fran Pinkard said, 'because he added another dimension. He enjoyed our kids' company. He made them feel very special and they could relate to him better than to party members in their twenties and thirties.'

'He was way ahead of everybody else in seeing things,' David Pinkard remembered:

> He had a keen way of observation and keen eyesight. He was looking all the time to see what was different. He carried his darned travel bag containing binoculars, camera, bird book and writing materials all the way up and all the way back.
>
> The sherpas and porters were impressed because he wore shorts and you could see the size and power of his legs, which is what you notice with a lot of Nepalese people, because they're so used to carrying huge loads. Deny's calf muscles flexed like theirs and they noticed it because Westerners don't usually have muscles like that.

Chapman said that they called him 'The Strong Man', and that even those porters who carried double loads were in awe of him.

They trekked for six days to a snow-covered camp by a glacier at 3750 metres for a spectacular view of Annapurna towering above the snow cloud, gleaming in the sun. Next day they watched the tiny figures of climbers ascending the peaks before beginning their own descent. With reduced oxygen Deny felt as though he was half asleep 'like I get when I have had many hours on the boat', but it did not detract from his interest in new birds, vegetation, geological formations, and naturally, the weather, which even he found freezing.

Flourishing village vegetable gardens, the practice of burning off uplands for summer pasture, and building methods, varying in each village according to local materials, also interested him. He was particularly impressed by the Nepalese ability to build stone square and plumb by eye; with the stone shingled roofs; and with timber houses insulated with bamboo matting.

On a sleepless night he was thrilled to watch Mount Machhapuchare in the moonlight, and the following day, sunny and clear, Annapurna South with plumes of snow blowing off was a dazzling sight. Forests of Himalayan cedars 'with nice straight spars' and rhododendrons with their understorey of mosses, ivy and ferns delighted him. But litter and faeces left by trekkers disgusted him, as had Kathmandu's squalor.

New Year's Day 1981 provided a sighting of a Nepalese sunbird and an encounter with mule trains jingling with bells along the caravan route between Tibet and Pokhara. A whitewater rafting trip down the Trisuli River was an exciting new experience, when Deny coped better than most with the paddling. The adventure finished with a visit to Gaida wildlife camp, for more leisurely birdwatching, walking, and travelling by elephant, 'not a smooth ride'.

The weary but enriched traveller arrived back in Hobart. Nepal and the Himalayas were now part of him and other places awaited. Deny was possessed by wanderlust.

CHAPTER 29

Later years

'Losing horsepower.'

In mid-January 1981 Deny returned to Melaleuca to find house spick, boats span, garden tended, and mine ticking over. It was another happy 'girls and boys' summer with Karina and friends, and Deny thrived on their company. One visitor spoke eloquently of life at Melaleuca:

> There is no pressure, yet things are done. Ingenuity is often demanded to perform something that would be so simple in the city. Values are so different here. There are jobs to be done simply to ensure survival. One cannot give up because a task is distasteful. Self-sufficiency means having to do all things.

Deny, still collecting signatures for the NO DAMS petition, welcomed more Americans and Israelis, an opal miner, a Bushwacker band guitarist who made music, and wilderness photographer Peter Dombrovskis. A pilot who 'never tired of flying into Melaleuca' brought CSIRO botanists, on a *Phytophthora* survey, with whom Deny talked 'plants past and present'. Melaleuca had become a mecca not only for adventurous spirits, but also for media now taking interest in the orange-bellied parrots as well as in their protector. During the summer Deny was interviewed and filmed by the Tasmanian Film Corporation crew, an ABC Nationwide team, and another *National Geographic* team.

During a family visit Deny took four-month-old Tony on his first

Melaleuca fishing trip to Breaksea Island and Kylie bestowed her grandfather's final nickname, announcing she was 'pleased to be at Gerr's house'.

On a six-day walk to South West Cape, Karina recalled Deny had a pack nearly as big as himself and 'hand luggage' containing lettuce, tomatoes, parsley and white sliced bread. Although, as Deny wrote to Janet, his boots were 'gnawing at his toes', Karina marvelled, 'Deny was like a spring chicken while the young'uns looked like a pack of geriatrics'.

Beachcombing, investigating Aboriginal sites, sighting orange-bellied parrots, boiling the billy beside enticing creeks, even one 'long lunch with 5 boil-ups', and sleeping out under 'amazingly starry skies', when Deny told Greek myths of Orion and Zeus read in childhood, were his idea of heaven.

Campers' peat fires, continuing trommel troubles, exceptionally high tides and pump problems caused concern and much hard labour, while TasAir's failure to deliver mail upset Deny and Karina.

Even more worrying, however, was *Melaleuca*'s worsening leak. For weeks one or the other went daily to pump her out and pour copious quantities of sawdust into the bilge trying unsuccessfully to stop it. When water rose above the prop shaft Deny was deeply concerned.

In earlier days he used to dive to check the hull underwater. Now amid July storms, gales and unabating high tides, he decided to investigate by emptying the fuel tank and winching it out. On pulling up the floor Deny found fourteen portside and five starboard timbers had cracked at the same level from mast to bulkhead and water wept right along the seam. It was a disaster.

Deny discussed the damage with Peter and immediately started emergency repairs. Karina cut out steel straps for reinforcing broken timbers while Deny took patterns of the needed bends and began sawing Huon pine to make them. Meanwhile pumping out

Melaleuca took longer each day. On removing forward lockers and cabin floor they found more broken timbers. Working through sharp freezing showers they removed the slag ballast.

Weather conditions prevented Deny speaking with Geoff by radiophone, and were too severe to seek needed bush timber. But the catastrophe had even further impact. Already distressed by Mary and Ian's decision to separate, Deny's blood pressure rose. Unable to eat, he admitted he had 'not felt at all well lately, very weak and short of breath as if at 13 000' altitude'. On the first frosty day when the mountaintops glistened with snow, Deny finally got a message through asking Geoff to come.

Geoff and Karen, who also came to inspect *Melaleuca*, were even more concerned for Deny and urged him to seek medical attention. In Hobart his doctor diagnosed he had suffered a coronary attack and Deny was admitted to hospital. Discharged after four days, with his irrepressible desire to help he was digging potatoes and felling trees a day later.

Deny also consulted a shipwright, who agreed with his belief that *Melaleuca* had been crushed by a large boat tied alongside at the yacht club or her own wharf.

Returning to Melaleuca at the end of July, with 'birdies clamouring around the door', Deny wrote, 'It is good to be back home again.' Jeanette Collin, now walking from Hobart regularly, helped Karina at the mine and stayed for a timber-getting expedition seeking naturally curved branches or 'knees'.

To construct a slip was impossible, so with Mary's help too, throughout August all work on the boat had to be done from inside, an awkward, uncomfortable, labour-intensive procedure. From the wooden knees they cut, drilled, split and fitted replacement parts. Rigging a forest devil winch they passed cables under the keel and across the deck to tighten the timbers, using blocks to prevent wire cutting into the decking.

Leaks were caulked and new timber screwed over old. Steel strips were then fixed over broken planks, steel straps over broken ribs, and flannel padding under boards affixed over leaking seams. After bilges were cleaned out and ballast restowed, on a trial round Breaksea, to Deny's huge relief *Melaleuca* scarcely made water.

For the second time Deny, again unwell, was grateful to travel in convoy, but was dismayed when Peter decided to leave on a day of wild weather. As a precaution *Rallinga* carried Deny's tin, radio and precious granddaughter, while Mary and Karina crewed on *Melaleuca*. Relentless gales and rain forced them to wait two nights in Southern Cross Bay where Deny celebrated his seventy-second birthday and worried about *Melaleuca*'s anchor holding.

When they reached Recherche four days later, fishermen still sheltering there were incredulous at Deny's ingenuity in repairs which had held through such formidable conditions. So was the Port Huon shipwright who made the professional repairs.

Work on the boat could not start at once, so Deny flew to the mainland, spending time with Karen at the Wilderness Society's Melbourne office, where the fight for the Gordon and Lower Franklin rivers was in full spate, while he 'snoozed' on the office floor. He browsed in art galleries and outdoors shops, enjoyed another Gunbarrel Highway reunion and stayed with the Lowrys. He also visited the Heeneys in Queensland, where his first sight of hang-gliders recalled memories of his own youthful attempts to fly.

With *Melaleuca* on the Port Huon slip, Deny delighted in Jeanette's exhibition of 'marvellous SW paintings', but not in 'a terrible diet—no meat, taters, dairy products or processed foods, sugar, salt, tea or coffee', advised by the clinic. He said 'a few words re No Dams' to a TV crew, cast his NO DAMS vote, and made a nostalgic visit to his birthplace, Clifton Grove, before sailing in his restored boat in mid-December.

The 1982 summer brought more aircraft, boats and people than ever. One walker recorded having met 228 others on the south coast track in four days. There were visitors from Alaska and Germany, more CSIRO scientists, and another *National Geographic* team. Deny enjoyed discussing his passion with a Melbourne Supreme Court judge and his wife, also keen birdwatchers. Bob Geeves brought fourteen groups, 'Bob's mobs', to his new tourist camp on Bathurst Harbour, using one of Deny's garden huts as a base. More fishermen too arrived by dinghy at the mine to walk to Willsons'. French skipper Jean Poncet and his Tasmanian wife Sally spent weeks cruising in Port Davey and Deny avidly absorbed their stories of Antarctica, while their plans to sail to South America stimulated another cherished dream.

In February Deny rejoiced when Janet and Geoff's daughter, Sally Margaret, was born, on the fifteenth anniversary of Margaret's death. Deny was naturally comfortable in female company and women always responded to his unselfconscious charm, grace and easy humour. Many young women who had ventured into his kingdom ill-prepared and ignorant of its rigours were befriended by Deny. In response they often fell under its spell and his, and were pleased to work for days, weeks, sometimes months, around the place. He loved their spirit and zest, and they cheerfully provided the domesticity he yearned for, company, cooking, cleaning, clothes mending. He especially appreciated their smaller, deft hands, able to accomplish tasks now beyond his own, large and increasingly arthritic.

When Annie Ball, a young Western Australian architect, arrived late in 1981, Deny was away. She fell in love with the house and garden he had created, so flew to Hobart to offer to work. 'It just seemed the obvious thing to do. One minute after meeting him I felt as if I'd known him all my life. And I felt very at home in the mine.'

With Karina in Nepal, Deny was glad of Annie's help for airstrip maintenance too. For her it was a life-changing experience:

I'd worked a lot with men in my profession. Deny was the only male I'd ever worked with who could just share work without ever needing to put you down. If he foresaw a problem, he'd say, 'Now this is the very situation Quinkan would be watching. Any moment you lost concentration he'd snap that spanner out of your hand and drop it into that deep well.' That was his way of saying, 'Be careful. You're standing over water now, and if you drop that spanner we're stuffed.'

He would never instruct, never say, 'This is the plan and this what we do.' You'd just hang around watching, and as you picked stuff up, you'd do it. You couldn't have worked with Deny unless you were prepared to wait and discover. Even when he made mistakes he'd just laugh. Really laugh at himself.

So when Annie decorated him with stars and tinsel, filling his bushy eyebrows with glitter, Deny entered the spirit of a boaties' party at CC. Standing in the dinghy, hair swept back in the wind, he sang all the way. Always out of tune, he joked he should be quiet lest he was heard and sent to Covent Garden. She also remembered:

Anything you did was greatly appreciated. He always thanked you. He was very humble. He'd been doing a lot of TV and radio interviews and someone said, 'G'day, Deny. You're a bit of a star these days.' He replied, 'Yes. A falling star.'

He never lost sight of how other people would feel. Everybody felt so special. It was the perfect communal home. Everybody was welcome. He never felt ill at ease with anybody—except people who were a bit pretentious. He would laugh heartily when Karina and I sent them up, but it was something he rarely did himself.

Sometimes we felt too exhausted to offer the hospitality

> Deny wished. One day I heard people coming and thought, 'I can't answer the questions again! So I hid in the cupboard.'

As soon as Deny didn't feel like talking any more, he would just lie on the window seat and close his eyes. And visitors who picked their chop bones met with his quiet disapproval. Bones were for the birds and were duly affixed with battery clips to the fence for Richards' and the olive whistlers' delectation. On Karina's return, in addition to the constant visitors, Deny's habit of leaving his radio on all night induced her to move to the furthest garden hut, so they all worked for weeks on renovations in autumn.

His painting was inspired by the winter reflections in the tranquil dark waters of Bathurst Harbour, the rose-pink and pansy-purple lights of sunset on snow-flowered mountains, and exquisite ice patterns on the lagoon and he had five 'on the go' in August.

But in 1982 he again felt the chill of grief and bereavement. In April Deny flew out when Rose was unwell. In late August, preparing to leave with forty bags of tin, he heard that she was gravely ill. Despite a strong wind warning Deny set off. It was a very rough trip without radio connection, whirlies tossing water across the deck, and the boat lunging wildly as waves broke over the stern.

Rose died three days later, just before Deny's seventy-third birthday. Seeing old friends at her funeral and staying with Win and Clyde while *Melaleuca* was slipped at Port Huon, Deny had many opportunities to reminisce. Then at Sandfly 'enjoying the children' was an occasion to look to the future. He was proud of Mary studying horticulture, and Janet art, and Geoff's work on his new steel-bending invention and company, Magna Bend.

For Deny, though, the future was less promising. He underwent melanoma removal, 'waking to feel them cutting and sewing—a bit of an adventure'. Moreover, since 1980 his finances had been 'well below water level', because he forfeited months' mining to work on the strip, incurring substantial fuel and labour expenses, and he had to borrow to pay 'all that fool income tax'. But the Transport Commission remained tardy in reimbursing him because the official responsible for payments, who disliked flying in single-engined aircraft, postponed inspection.

'Sometimes he wished he was a smoker,' Mary remembered, 'so he could give it up and suddenly have piles of money!' Now news that small tin producers would be put on quotas was of serious concern. He had only $2000 working capital, four drums of fuel cost almost $500, and framing timber was 'alarmingly expensive'. In addition he was very conscious of paying his helpers low wages, and grateful for their forbearance waiting until tin payments were received.

News of Kath's death three weeks after Rose's was a shock. She had visited Hobart only months earlier and Deny had taken her to Melaleuca. In September he flew standby with Mary to Sydney to condole with Elsie, then to Brisbane to see Kath's daughter, before going to Tenterfield. Travelling south he was interested in irrigation in the Riverina, but concerned at the dying eucalypts. In the Dandenongs with Karen he enjoyed a trip on Puffing Billy. As Annie Ball said, 'He never let go of the child within.'

Back in Hobart with tin payment now in the bank, Deny bought equipment for the mine, a new anchor chain for *Melaleuca*, and attended the Wilderness Society's headquarters opening in mid-November. Then with Mary and Jeanette crewing and a two-tonne load, Deny headed home through 'big white heads and white squalls' and was glad to give Mary the helm on reaching Port Davey.

At Christmas 'Karina came Home', and in January 1983 Deny welcomed another new hand. Lynne Davies, who had visited the previous summer, impressed him. She drove big machinery on the Pilbara mines, kept a diary and was a birdwatcher. He had maintained contact and invited her back to work.

With the South-West listed in December 1982 as a World Heritage Area, Deny, an unwitting arch-agent of change, watched as daily landings on his airstrip increased and up to fifty people packed his huts at night. In addition to bushwalkers, 'stewed ants', 'towerists' and 'customers' in organised tours of up to thirty were now arriving. More and varied aircraft came from further and further afield. Dick Smith arrived on his round-the-world helicopter flight. Deny, however, was more impressed by a North-West joiner who fulfilled his dream of flying, building his own low-winged plane over three years, and who gave him a flight.

In February Deny was thrilled to see the elegant forty-metre brigantine *Eye of the Wind* riding at anchor in Bathurst Harbour, her longboat *Eyelet* dancing on the wind-ruffled waters, and exclaimed, 'I've always wanted to see a square rigger here!' He marvelled at her size—'our mast scarcely went up to her lower yards', commented 'I'm two years older than her!', and appreciated a guided tour and yarn with master Tiger Timbs.

That winter Deny luxuriated in cheerful evenings of cosy fireside chat and chuckles, chocolates and cherry liqueur, stretching contentedly on the window seat while the girls knitted and tackled crosswords. Lynne read aloud from *The Thousand and One Nights*, Karina from Saki and Paul Gallico, then *The Magic Pudding* and *The Little Wooden Horse*, childhood favourites of Margaret and dorts, which brought back many memories. These feisty new-generation girls challenged him with their choice of music and their taste for Asian and other exotic cooking, but he also affected them. Lynne declared:

> He brought into being my appreciation of the wilderness, and influenced where I live and what I do with my life. Living with Deny was easy, very much living from day to day. The seemingly slow unhurried way of doing things, very flexible. And you never knew what he would come out with—the funny twists to the way he put things. He showed

that face to everyone. Only a few people got the Deny that was worried. If there was something he could do about it, he did. If there wasn't, he didn't dwell on it. But there weren't many things like that. He was incredibly self-reliant.

He always had so much love to give, but he lacked that special person to give it to. He really missed that. Late winter nights he would sometimes get a bit sad. He loved to hear the piano played. I was just learning, but Deny loved it.

It was another white winter. Snow transformed the garden into a hushed world. Then frost brought diamond-bright days, crisp ground brilliant as a salt lake, leaves and ferns sparkling in seductive sunshine. With 'the far Arties [Arthurs] calling' Deny could not resist 'lovely tats weather'.

Three times they set off wood-getting, *Melaleuca*'s decks and shrouds veiled in frozen snow, rejoicing in the gleaming glory of the mountains. Clear star-strewn nights, waves lapping, dinghies gently knocking against the hull, anchor chain creaking and windsong in the rigging nourished the soul, while fiery sunrise haloes on the mountains inspired the artist.

After finishing sluicing mid-July and bagging the tin, Deny dreaded returning to Hobart—'all that rushing about town all hot and bothered hunting for things and shopping'. He did, however, spend three months there. In late October, with Mary crewing and mine helper John Hughes, 'Snapper' to Deny, *Melaleuca* left for Port Davey.

During November, with 'snow upstairs' and 'bees having a great time in the seeding turnips', Dave Watts spent days in the garden photographing orange-bellied parrots, Peter Brown taped the dawn chorus, Mr and Mrs Richard nested in a cake tin on the porch, Karina returned and Deny lent his camera to Snapper for his walk out. In December when the garden was swaying with three-metre-high foxgloves, Janet, Geoff and 'the biters' arrived, followed by Kylie and Mary. With a bough from a Huon pine planted for a Christmas tree when the dorts were tiny, they had the first full Melaleuca celebration in years.

Lightning and earthquakes had always fascinated Deny and in January 1984 specky storms brought lightning strikes on nearby mountains, and he felt an earth tremor at The Narrows. Closer to home there was excitement on the airstrip. One morning three TasAir Cessnas arrived in quick succession, followed immediately by two RAAF Caribous. As each Caribou landed and took off using only half the length Deny again felt his original strip vindicated and smiled at the crew's amazement 'as people came from everywhere to watch'. Even dusky robins investigated the aircraft.

In March three events added further drama to the strip's history. An RAAF turbo-jet powered helicopter, 'much quieter than others', brought RAN officers and gave their Port Davey coastwatcher a ride. Then within a week Peter Willson had to be flown out. Unable to walk because of an injured knee, he was carried to the plane on a chair lashed to poles, 'looking', Deny said, 'like an important Eastern gentleman with a large procession of attendants'.

Ten days after this, Deny himself was fortunate to escape injury. Returning from a day with botanists at Cox Bight, the Cessna 206, caught by a gust from a fluky north-easterly, ran off the end and overturned. Emerging unscathed, Deny nonchalantly remarked, 'I've never been in that position before.' Calling radio VIH for assistance he said with customary understatement, 'Just a spot of trouble down here.' Deny, Lynne and Karina fed and bedded down twelve people that night.

The waterways also provided more than their usual share of summer interest, with a regatta in Bramble Cove on 2 February to celebrate the 125th anniversary of the first Port Davey Regatta. With *Eye of the Wind* as flagship, it was an exciting rendezvous of over twenty yachts and fishing boats on a sparkling blue day with a fresh north-westerly. Deny took gifts to the *Eye of the Wind*—flowers, raspberries, parsley and lettuce—and borrowed two crew. *Melaleuca* was 'hopeless at turning for a tack so all the other boats had finished before we had gone one round'. Unfazed, Deny switched on the engine and finished the course in his usual manner.

During summer Deny enjoyed hospitality on yachts from the North-West, Victoria, New South Wales and New Zealand, intrigued by state-of-the-art equipment. He welcomed walkers from South Africa, Finland and Holland, meteorologists from the Hobart and Melbourne Bureaus, and enjoyed yarning with a Tobruk Rat, an impromptu concert by two Bushwackers, and three landings by another Caribou.

In 1983 Deny had admitted to Lynne he was 'losing horsepower'. In March 1984 he found a walk to the Norolds unexpectedly taxing, bashing through thick scrub that had grown vigorously since his venture eight years earlier. He was 'so dreadfully exhausted' he did not reach the dinghy until midnight, dismayed he might be a nuisance to others.

Karina's April announcement that she was leaving for good came as 'a bit of a shock as so much depends on her' and his entry 'one lone swallow still here' echoed his desolation. Feeling unwell, he reduced his tea and sugar intake, a drastic step indicating his anxiety. Then while in Hobart for Anzac Day, he was diagnosed with a heart irregularity.

Back at Melaleuca in May, another unpleasant surprise awaited— a Mines Department letter levying a $1260 environmental bond. After Karina left in June, visits from Snapper, Annie, and Fred Peacock brightened the winter and in August after the 'usual hectic rush' *Melaleuca* sailed with thirty-five bags of tin.

Deny celebrated his seventy-fifth birthday in Hobart, and on a Sunday afternoon at Sandfly found it 'so pleasant lying dozing with the sound of the *Pastoral Symphony* mingled with little children's voices'. He visited Dave Watts' exhibition of bird photographs, some from Melaleuca, and a native plant show at the university, and tried unsuccessfully to buy woollen singlets, finding 'the rotters have stopped making them'. He also discussed a trip to South America with old friends Tom and Helen Coles.

Always concerned about fire hazards, and convinced systematic burning off was vital to maintain the sensitive ecology of the Port Davey hinterland, Deny wrote letters in October to the Australian Conservation Foundation and the Wilderness Society. From forty years' meticulous observation, he had substantial data supporting his claim that the rare *buftonianum* orchid and other species only emerged after fire and that dwindling orange-bellied parrot numbers were linked to an absence of certain plants in heavily overgrown button-grass moorlands. He had frequently noted that other bird species also preferred feeding in burnt-off areas, and native fauna liked regrowth.

In an unpublished article, 'Port Davey '34–'84', Deny wrote:

> Looking across to Mount Counsel we used to see a small waterfall, but now this is hidden by trees. The country in general has grown over with bush and trees along the creeks and rivers. Old photos show how bare it used to be. To preserve these belts and patches of trees the open plains should be burnt regularly every 5 to 10 years.

He resented new Department of the Environment edicts about rehabilitating mine workings, and penned a letter to Karen:

> [They] are on my back to cover small areas that would not be noticed unless someone was trying to find fault. The worst of it is they are trying to tell me how to do it. I have been rehabbing my works long before they were ever thought of. I am supposed to sow all sorts of fertiliser on it and they pick a time when metal prices are low and fuel is sky high.

Back in Melaleuca in time for 'the lovely, lovely month' November, when myrtle tips gleamed pomegranate pink, Deny noted 'OBPs very scarce', and planted sunflowers hoping they would acquire a taste for their seeds. He took Peter Brown and Dave Watts to Bond Bay and Old River on an unsuccessful spotting mission, and sadly reported zero sightings on other searches. At month's end a solitary orange-bellied parrot visited the garden; then in December four were seen.

But fence-crashing wombats and parsley-pruning, cabbage-chomping roos were not scarce and were routinely 'arrested and deported'. One 'most indignant' wallaby put ashore downstream dashed straight back into the water heading for home. 'None of your hard bush tucker for him!' Later after depositing two roos at The Narrows, Deny realised they were the Willsons' tamed pair, so thereafter took 'green tucker' for them on each trip!

When 'rasps were getting red in the face', Deny's best Christmas present was finding an occupied orange-bellied parrot's nest near Mount Counsel, after wading across the flooded plain with Peter Brown. Moreover Peter's observation that these birds were feeding on a burnt area en route to Cox's reinforced Deny's belief in the importance of controlled burning.

January 1985, sweet with leatherwood flowers, was busier than ever. An American birdo came to see the parrots, a Channel 9 crew filmed Deny, a German yacht visited Port Davey, as did *Eye of the Wind* with Lynne crewing. A Launceston Walking Club group painted and maintained the huts. Deny assisted in a nightlong medical emergency. Then on 2 February when aircraft were 'coming and going thick and fast', Deny and Mary flew to Hobart. Another of his lifelong dreams was coming true.

Six days later they left for South America.

CHAPTER 30

Eighty not out

'Long live Deny King!'

Since boyhood Deny had read avidly about Patagonia and Tierra del Fuego, challenged by their wild isolation. Fascinated by Gondwanan theories, he was eager to compare this other land's end with Tasmania, and to see its grand contrasts of glaciers and volcanoes.

In Chile, first impressions were unfavourable. Santiago's smog, noise, heat, bushfire hazards, Valparaiso's crowded beaches, shocked him. The barren Andes to the desolate north, 'lifeless undulating plain with nothing green anywhere' depressed him. Then he was thrilled to see the huge machinery and furnaces at Chuquicamata, the world's largest open-cut copper mine; El Tatio, the world's highest geysers, with their extraordinary walking frogs; and at last, a smoking volcano and lava flows.

He admired magnificent lakes amid snow-rimmed volcanic cones, and delighted in beech forests with 'plenty of good firewood, trees draped with lacy moss as though covered in white blossom', and new and known plant species, including *Lomatia*. On land and sea Deny's binoculars were ever ready for observing wildlife.

As always Deny enjoyed people. He found locals engagingly friendly, 'with good teeth in spite of having twice as much sugar in their tea and coffee as I do'. He particularly appreciated their civic pride, with streets swept by hand twice daily so 'you don't have to watch where you tread'. Passing two dark-haired beauties, his room-mate Don Wright asked, 'How old are you when you stop noticing pretty girls?' Deny replied, 'I don't know yet!'

He enjoyed the hilarity of communicating by mime, and incorporated Spanish words into his diary, indefatigably maintained as usual, to Don's dismay. 'Every morning at two o'clock the jolly light'd go on and Deny'd sit up and write.' With so much to see, Deny didn't waste time shaving, considering every second day sufficient, and while others shopped for exotic items, Deny continued unsuccessfully searching for woollen singlets!

Travelling by cargo barge along Magellan Strait and through Beagle Channel, battling south-west winds and seas in 'foul weather', Deny was reminded of Port Davey by snow-clad peaks looming steeply from the sea, fascinated by the uninhabited shoreline and network of waterways 'which make Bathurst Harbour seem a speck'. He was frustrated, however, that with Spanish-speaking crew, his 'burning questions' remained unanswered. In Patagonia where they visited Puerto Williams and Ushuaia, the world's southernmost settlements, winds almost blew them off their feet, making Melaleuca's seem zephyr-like.

In Argentina the first thrill was a chairlift, whose technology intrigued him, as did viewing the plants below. Visiting Estancia Harberton on Tierra del Fuego, was something 'I've wanted to do for sixty years'. A missionary outpost established in 1877, its history of courage and ingenuity stirred Deny's spirit. Now a ranch, its splendid garden flourished despite the harsh climate. In the original house transported from England, the eighty-three-year-old matriarch welcomed them with tea from a silver teapot and 'three kinds of cakes', sharing her story beside cosy wood-fired heaters.

At Lake Argentino, a corner dammed by glacial action looked 'like a hydro lake with dead trees and bare shores'. Deny was enthralled by the crevassed and pinnacled Moreno Glacier, towering blue and breathtaking above frigid waters, and watched for hours as pieces broke off 'with a sharp report like a plug of gelignite exploding. What a sight—columns like seven-storey office blocks toppling with a mighty roar and splash, then a long rumble of water and ice boiling up for minutes'.

Deny revelled in 'something new and exciting every day', and 'the chance of a lifetime', a flight round Cape Horn by twin-engined Cessna. South of Beagle Channel the country was 'pockmarked with lakes and ponds like spots on a jaguar', and on the mighty Cape itself, 'not as weatherworn as our SW Cape', the northern slope was covered with 'green herbage that looks like button grass'. Flying under cloud with turbulence and thickening weather, seeing a cluster of huts housing radio and weather stations, he yearned for their records.

Returning through the Chilean fjords, Deny enjoyed the roll-on ferry's activities, and magnificent scenery. They skirted heavily wooded islands 'like those in Bathurst Harbour', seeing flowering fuchsias among the ferns, and trees like celery-top pines. He yarned for hours too with Chileans, and with two Australians who had visited Melaleuca the preceding summer!

After he witnessed evidence of the previous week's devastating Santiago earthquake, the full seismic thrill Deny had always wanted came on the last morning. When the hotel began rattling and shaking, instead of retreating to a doorway as Mary prudently did, he rushed to the window to watch.

Back at 'Puerto Davey' Deny was travel-weary but elated. At home where fragrant leatherwood and rare *buftonianum* orchids still flowered, he could 'dream about those places', sharing his slides with visitors from Canada, France and Monte Carlo. Meeting a friend in Hobart he advised, 'Don't go to the Himalayas. All you do is this,' walking round in a big circle lifting his feet high, attracting surprised attention. Asked what he was doing, he explained, 'All you do is pick up your feet over other people's rubbish. South America is much better.'

Annie, Snapper and friends, caretaking in his absence, had rebuilt the garden shed at Melaleuca. In May Fred Peacock came to help for three months. Machinery troubles and repairs brought bills Deny 'was not game to open', and there were days when, unwell, he 'would like to have stayed home'. It was a hard winter. The weather station steps were treacherous with black ice. The jig, hung with icicles, sometimes remained frozen all day, and Deny's chilblains were excruciating as he donned gumboots. Toothpaste, tea and maté ran out, and to 'the birdies' consternation' they had only lentils and sago!

A visit from Mary and Kylie was all too short. For Deny partings, always difficult, were becoming harder and harder. At this farewell, standing with Deny in the rain watching the plane head for a rainbow, Fred noted:

> An incredible silence closed in. There was something very sad to see the ageing, alert but slowly tiring man, who had lived so much of his life separated from his family, going through another separation, wandering back to an empty house—no, a home temporarily without a family.

Despite gales and a record high tide, sluicing finished in late July. Fred checked stores, listing what to buy, and just as important, what not, and in mid-August they sailed. It proved to be *Melaleuca*'s last trip carrying tin. In Hobart Deny hit the bottom of a very low market. So with ever-increasing costs, deteriorating plant, the Launceston smelters closing, worsening arthritis, gout and high blood pressure, and 'bad luck'—his seventy-sixth birthday—Deny decided 'not to go out after it' again.

His mining days were over.

At the end of October he sailed home, greeted at the wharf by Richard, to find it was 'a terrific spring for ferns'. In November the orange-bellied parrot team arrived, bringing seed for a feed tray in the garden, which attracted dapper little firetails in increasing numbers. In December MV *Southern Quest* visited, and Deny enjoyed discussing their forthcoming Antarctic expedition, with Lynne and other crew members. Then at Christmas a special diary entry, 'My family arrived', said everything.

In January 1986 he was distressed when *Southern Quest*, caught in ice, sank in eleven minutes, but thankful Lynne and shipmates were rescued. In February in Hobart he enjoyed the novelty of riding pillion on a motorbike. In March Halley's comet and yet another film project vied for attention, and Deny starred. Karen and friends planned a film about hang-gliding in the wilderness, and Deny was co-opted, as consultant and actor. It was 'almost like a picnic race meeting at the strip' when shooting commenced. With walking crony Jessie Luckman, Deny enjoyed watching hang-gliders on location on Mount Rugby and at Strathgordon, and the excitement of rushes flown to Melaleuca.

In August he accepted an invitation from walker Leonie White to visit South Australia, accompanied by Mary and Kylie. They went to the Flinders Ranges, where Deny photographed Cazneaux's famous gum tree, explored Wilpena Pound and spent part of one night in a hollow tree while rain inundated his tent. Canoeing on the Coorong, an orange-bellied parrot wintering area, they talked with the ranger and spotted a solitary specimen. They travelled by The Ghan to Alice Springs enjoying the profusion of wildflowers, and at Uluru and Kata Tjuta Deny noticed the increase in tourism, as at Melaleuca.

In fine warm weather with light following winds, on 30 October Deny departed for Melaleuca with Mary, Jeanette, Don Wright, Tom and Helen Coles. It was to be the worst voyage in Deny's forty sailing years. A freshening northerly and rising slop overnight at Partridge Island caused him to move to Recherche, where by nightfall fourteen boats were sheltering, as wind strengthened to gale. They waited five days among 'barking dogs and smokers' coughs' from the fishing fleet, now numbering eighteen, one of which nearly rammed *Melaleuca*.

On the sixth day Deny left with the others. The following wind swung then hardened from the north and after rounding South West Cape before sunset, *Melaleuca*'s engine stopped within 450 metres of the jagged Pyramids. They raised sails, but although so close to Port Davey, had to beat offshore to windward, losing sight of Whaler's Light. While seventy-seven-year-old Deny struggled below restarting the engine, both mainsail and staysail jammed.

Landmarks were obscured by driving rain, the dinghy came loose and had to be relashed. Then the gale which had driven them leeward freed the sails. They flogged viciously, throwing Deny to the deck, almost sweeping him overboard as the boat heeled. Helen sighted cloud reflection which Deny recognised as Maatsuyker's flashes over South West Cape Range, so he decided to go with the wind. Returning south, twelve hours later they passed South West Cape in darkness.

Entering New Harbour at dawn, they examined damaged blocks, clips and yards, furled ripped sails and thankfully had warm drinks. Two hours later fishermen woke them from exhausted sleep, shouting that *Melaleuca*'s anchor was dragging and she was almost on the rocks. They 'only just got out of it in time', and re-anchored with stock anchor too. Deny, suffering from bruising and strained muscles and still recovering from flu, slept most of the second day during wind and swell which brought more boats in to shelter.

That night they had another narrow escape when a big steel craft, yawing strongly on her anchor chain, plunged within feet of *Melaleuca*. Unable to make her crew hear, Helen flashed an SOS to another boat, whose men came to the rescue.

The next day Tom and Don, who had to return, left by fishing boat for Hobart. Deny, Mary, Helen and Jeanette prepared *Melaleuca* as well as they could and Deny 'rested his sore sides' before their next attempt on South West Cape. On the following afternoon in a strong squally west-north-westerly and rolly seas they passed it and The

Pyramids again, and 'were very glad to get inside Breaksea, open the hatches and have warm drinks'. At 8 p.m., Deny, giddy with exhaustion, was relieved to reach his wharf, after the eleven-day epic trip.

In December the Minister for National Parks arrived, declaring, 'Meeting you is like meeting a legend!' He invited Deny on a flight to see the devastating fire burning north to the Giblin, south to Bond Bay and up the Davey. Recalling his singlehanded firefighting marathons, Deny was impressed by water-carrying helicopters and other apparatus. Army radio operators set up base in the walkers' hut.

Mary coming home for Christmas and the Fentons' visit in January 1987 brought much pleasure. Deny delighted in Tony's creative ideas, but was sad for his frustration. He often wrote to the grandchildren and loved receiving Tony's drawings and designs. 'What a clever young fella!' He was pleased too when Tony developed an interest in weather. On 26 February, Sally's fifth birthday, Deny recorded it was twenty years since Margaret passed away.

Summer also brought canoeists exploring Port Davey, while Nomads as well as Caribous began using the strip. The Australian Bird Banding Scheme sought Deny's help and Peter Brown banded eighty birds at Melaleuca, but only five were orange-bellied parrots.

Deny and his kingdom were ever more popular with media, and in 1987 he gave ten interviews for TV, radio, magazines and newspapers. Sorrel Wilby, who spent several days photographing and researching her article for *Australian Geographic*, published in July 1988, was particularly congenial. But a TV presenter who demanded a car meet him at the airport found neither car nor interviewee awaiting! Deny simply went bush.

Painting was now Deny's preferred occupation despite deteriorating vision, and he used the summer light to advantage. Artist Anka Makovec on her first visit was spellbound by Deny's landscape, garden, home and art. 'He lovingly portrayed nature as it was. So as an artist he'll have his niche in Tasmanian history. I couldn't believe it when I saw those feather-like brushstrokes come from those gnarled, workworn hands, and the clouds start to emerge so gentle and fleecy on the canvas.'

Deny prepared four entries for the May Royal Yacht Club exhibition, and twenty for his own exhibition at the Wilderness Society two months later. Norton Harvey, photographer and bushwalker, opened Deny's solo show which overflowed with well-wishers and buyers. Deny resorted to holding a glass so he did not have to shake hands. Entitled 'A Love of Wild Places', the collection reflected his feeling for many remote places he had visited.

In August Deny flew by Nomad to Melbourne and returned to South Australia for another Flinders Ranges trip with Leonie, Karen and friends, exploring old mines. Leonie took him to Kangaroo Island too, to see wind-sculpted granite Remarkable Rocks, reminiscent of South West Cape, limestone caves, sea-fretted Admiral's Arch, and lighthouses. In the Adelaide Hills he looked up the Smith family, his wartime billet.

In 1985 the National Parks and Wildlife Service had investigated sites for rangers' quarters. Deny hoped they would use the Mines Department site downstream, but they wanted proximity to his facilities. He was horrified when they chose a spot near his boatshed and managed to persuade them to use a slightly more distant waterfront site near the huts. In November 1987 materials arrived by Caribou, to be ferried by helicopter to the site, and the team finished building in mid-December—a very different operation from Deny's herculean construction labours on the walkers' huts.

The concern of the Royal Australasian Ornithologists' Union, Parks and Wildlife Services of Tasmania, Victoria and South Australia and World Wildlife Fund (Australia) at the drastic population decline from thousands to less than forty breeding pairs of orange-bellied parrots, ultimately led to the orange-bellied parrot being listed as an endangered species. In November ten ornithologists arrived to confer on recovery strategies, further vindicating Deny's early disquiet.

Summer 1988, 'inundated with visitors', including Swedish and Japanese, brought more birdos from overseas, botanists and entomologists, more journalists, French, Italian and Japanese photographers, and American yachties. Deny took a crate of fresh-picked lettuces to walkers in the crowded huts. The Frenchman wrote, 'Receive my respectful homage. You are for me the image of a true sage.'

In January 1988 Deny flew to Hobart for the Tall Ships' bicentennial visit, enjoying the carnival atmosphere, rapt at seeing so many splendid sailing vessels. In April, to Deny's delight, Port Davey was the setting for another bicentennial nautical happening. Eleven First Fleet re-enactment boats and other international craft arrived for three exciting days. Deny went aboard *Bounty*, *Trade Wind* and *One and All*, and entertained captain and crew of the Swedish barquentine *Amorina*. The Hobart Anzac Day dawn service and march was attended by the Duke of Edinburgh, with salute taken by 'Missus Queen'. Deny then participated in the First Fleet farewell, aboard Clyde's boat *Belle Brandon*, which accompanied the ships downriver.

Three days later he travelled to Western Australia to visit Karina and husband, now managing Mount Barnett Station, Kupungari, in the Kimberley. Deny was in his element with three weather reports by radphone daily, abundant bird life, waterholes, waterfalls, gorges and caves to explore and rock paintings to ponder. He went with Aboriginal women collecting bush tucker, and stockmen for a beast. He burned off, gathered wood and improved the creek crossing by smashing boulders with crowbar and hammer. Boab trees and a routine Flying Doctor visit, so different from Melaleuca emergencies fascinated him.

On his return through Melbourne Karina's brother Peter took

him to an orange-bellied parrot wintering ground at Werribee, and a British Museum exhibition of European explorers. Peter remembered that Deny, with his profound respect for early seafarers, silently studied Captain Cook's life-size portrait for a long time.

In August Inspector Heather Innes, who had been flying to Melaleuca since 1970, brought a police group on a day's exercise. While Innes co-ordinated communications she yarned with Deny:

> He was in reflective mood and shared some of his past. He certainly missed his wife very much.
>
> He told me we wouldn't get out, and predicted snow. The weather was deteriorating, squalls kept coming through the valley and the light kept changing. 'Look at the hills,' he said. 'They'll go purple in a minute.' And they did. He saw in the colours what was happening. It wasn't just a colour. It had meaning.

Sitting by the hut fire that night, Deny captivated the weather-bound group with his unassuming manner. They told him of their day's exploits and expertise in bush and survival techniques:

> Deny was very polite and attentive, but gradually questions started him talking about his life. He really held their attention. He not only showed them what a man he was, he also showed he could hold his drink, when they were weak at the knees with their 'emergency medicinal alcohol' cocktail!

In October Deny flew with the family to beautiful Flinders Island, thrilled to explore the scene of his father's earliest working days. In Hobart he anxiously discussed with the Mines Department and Minister for Environment the vexed matter of his lease and continuing residence at Melaleuca, then returned in November for the orange-bellied parrots. Marine biologists, botanists, mycologists, herpetologists and archaeologists came for research during summer.

In February 1989 Deny left to discover more of Gondwana,

spending two weeks touring New Zealand by campervan with Mary, now divorced, and Kylie. Glow-worm caves and beech forests, waterfalls, cataracts through limestone labyrinths and avalanches near Milford Sound, jet-boating on the Shotover, watching the steamer *Earnslaw*'s 'thrilling engines' on Lake Wakatipu, and the dramatic Fox and Franz Josef glaciers left him 'most impressed'. Kauri forests, a cruise round the Bay of Islands on a First Fleet re-enactment vessel which had visited Port Davey, geysers and 'a hot bath' at Rotorua provided a grand finale.

In Hobart on Anzac Day he was distressed that only two other 2/9 men marched.

In May Deny left on what proved to be the last of over 150 voyages round South West Cape in forty years. Hands included Don Wright and the Coles. After the previous ordeal Helen declared she would go anywhere with Deny. But thick cloud obscured the moon and with deteriorating eyesight he had problems discerning landmarks through the sea mist. Tom declared, 'Nobody could've seen anything that night unless they were an owl.' Turning too soon before Breaksea, Deny suddenly saw white water astern and realised the wind was driving *Melaleuca* towards a reef. Feeling 'pretty rotten with a strained muscle and neck', he 'was glad to drop anchor in Bramble', and head next morning for Melaleuca with a rising tide.

Deny's bluewater sailing days were over.

The pleasures and challenges of Bathurst Harbour and Port Davey were enough now, and flying to and from Melaleuca afforded him a more relaxed view of the spectacular South-West coast and mountains.

A most unpleasant shock awaited in the house. A young European black rat was trapped in the storeroom. Deny soon caught three others, and more during winter. He used all his ingenuity to devise ways of exterminating the pests, which he and the Willsons, also invaded, decided had come on a Caribou.

As Deny's eightieth birthday approached he thought everyone had forgotten, but secret preparations long organised by Janet were in progress, with cooking bees at the Memorial Hut and at Willsons', where Barbara and Jeanette made six Swiss rolls for the gigantic cake complete with candles, while Deny groused about inroads on firewood! On 12 September, a brilliant morning, the first plane arrived at eight, followed by several others, as forty friends and family converged to celebrate in the daffodil-decorated house. Greeting, eating, music-making, reminiscing, laughter and bottom-less cuppas were the order of the day, with bumper mailbags adding to the excitement. Kylie and Sally were chief parcel-openers and 'Deny was grinning from ear to ear the whole day'.

But the grin disappeared later that week when floods caused the wharf to collapse and drove *Melaleuca* into the bush; and unresolved lease problems with the Mines Department necessitated his flying to Hobart for more discussions, with 'depressing results'.

Deny took the opportunity to visit Peter Brown's orange-bellied parrot captive breeding program, and back at Melaleuca in October began his own scheme to encourage them to breed. He put up a hollow log specially brought from Hobart, and to exclude predators affixed a Huon pine flap with brass screws. As Brown's colleague Mark Holdsworth commented, 'Nothing was too good for Deny's birdies!' Then he built and installed nesting boxes round the garden. He netted the existing feeder to protect the parrots from rosellas and ger cats, and constructed a new feed tray, buying eighty kilograms of seed several times a season.

Twice a day he put out a scoopful for the orange-bellied parrots now coming in increasing numbers morning and evening, encouraged, Deny believed, by the firetails unafraid of people. Mid-November he counted twenty-two of the parrots on the tray, the most seen for years, and had much pleasure observing 'little flocks wheeling in the evenings'.

He joined a Parks team surveying ground parrots' nests and monitoring their night calls, and flew over The Pyramids with Peter Brown counting seals, looking unsuccessfully for fairy terns at Bond Bay, but seeing at least eighteen orange-bellied parrots. In the garden, bird photographer Trevor Waite was another welcome visitor. Snapper helped build an idyllic open-fronted studio from materials salvaged from the Mines Department base, where Deny could overlook garden and creek to Mount Counsel as he painted.

On New Year's Eve 1989 Deny made his last diary entry, before dropping his lifetime's habit.

In January 1990 Deny told Karina there was 'quite a crowd in our little kennel' and among the multitude of visitors was a vice-regal party. Governor-General Bill Hayden flew in and invited Deny on the luncheon cruise aboard police vessel *Freycinet* round Port Davey and marine explorer Jacques Cousteau was another visitor 'who seemed very taken with the place'.

Less welcome were 'office Johnnies flying in on day trips', imposing unrealistic regulations and constraints on his independence from their distant city departments. Bureaucratic inefficiency, increasing interference, and the prospect of being forced by a technicality from his home of forty-four years caused him much stress. After he ceased mining Deny had continued to pay rent, but had not been advised when the lease expired. He was now told that to renew it he had to reapply and repeg the whole area. It was a task he could not face.

In February Deny suffered a minor stroke. Everyone rallied, the Willsons getting wood, Bob Geeves docking it, Mary, Janet, Jeanette and niece Olive staying in turns, followed for a month by Snapper.

There were two major developments in June. On 27 June 1990 the South-West National Park was proclaimed, but the land around Melaleuca incorporating the mining leases remained a conservation area. The reprieve Deny had pined for also came. The state government granted him and his family a twenty-year lease on his house and garden, subject to relinquishing his mining lease. So at his request the Willsons agreed to acquire it. Deny was immensely relieved. 'I don't want to leave here. Where would I go?'

Media continued to find Deny and his world an irresistible subject. He was interviewed by the Melbourne *Sun*, the Hobart *Mercury*, and filmed for the ABC '7.30 Report' and 'Holiday' programs. He featured in photographer Richard Bennett's exhibition 'Thirty Tasmanians', and wrote the foreword to Bennett's book *South West Tasmania*.

Deny's concern for the plight of the endangered orange-bellied parrots had aroused wide public attention. In October Parks built a hide overlooking a new feeder sited to allow the increasing number of visitors to observe the birds without entering his garden. It enabled many more people to learn about their precarious status and to experience the thrill of seeing them, while providing a base for volunteers monitoring the recovery program. Deny, who would have preferred a more rustic structure, was surprised that the hide was named after him.

In November the Governor of Tasmania, Sir Phillip Bennett, made a special visit to confer on Deny a singular honour, The Governor's Commendation, the first of its kind. The citation reads:

> In recognition of his generous commitment to establish facilities for visitors and bushwalkers in the South-West of Tasmania I commend Charles Denison King for his vision and outstanding efforts over many years in preserving and sharing the unique environment of Port Davey with all Tasmanians and those who appreciate Nature's treasures.

Janet, hastily tidying before the vice-regal visit, was mortified to find Deny's washing, rather grey underwear, draped along the fence beside the porch as was his custom. But Deny was unabashed, and later relished Government House tucker on the cruise aboard police vessel *D'Entrecasteaux*.

A German TV crew in December 1990 was followed by a French in January 1991. Deny, who had found an undescribed species of freshwater crayfish in his mine in 1954 and had assisted a Canberra CSIRO scientist with observations, was in 1991 still providing information on yabbies to an Honours student. British naturalists, CSIRO entomologists, and another orange-bellied parrot conference group also visited Melaleuca that summer.

In March Karina's message on the birth of her daughter 'sent a thrill of joy through Melaleuca'. Then Deny flew out for medical treatment and visited Government House for morning tea with Lady Bennett, delivering a cutting of an old Sunset Ranch rose she had admired. He returned to Melaleuca with Sydney's Channel 9 team. It was to be his last homecoming and fittingly he brought back an orange-bellied parrot treated in Hobart for injury, which he released during filming.

In Hobart again for Anzac Day Deny contracted pneumonia and was briefly hospitalised. He was looking forward to going home to Melaleuca to continue work on his book. But at Norfolk Crescent with Mary, in the home Margaret had given him, he suffered a fatal heart attack on 12 May. At eighty-one, in the autumn of his life, spared the bleakness of protracted illness and disability, he had lived to the full to the last.

The last secret

Deny's ashes were taken back to Melaleuca to be scattered on the waters of Bathurst Harbour. But the weather was unpropitious, so the box was left in the house.

Months later Parks officer Mark Holdsworth and Janet's friend Cathie Plowman, at Melaleuca on orange-bellied parrot duties, were tidying Deny's garden shed where the seed was stored. They had almost finished when Cathie uncovered a small masonite box. She was about to stow it in a corner when she suddenly wondered why it was closed and so heavy. Was it gelignite? Mark opened it to check and found something carefully packed in cloth. Cathie unwrapped it, overwhelmed by what she intuitively knew it would be.

Janet had shared her grief at never knowing about her mother. As the cloth fell away Cathie saw the inscription: 'Margaret, 1967'. She wept as Mark held the ornate pewter urn embossed with a crane. All these years Deny had kept his beloved's ashes with him in the garden they had created together and which had given such joy to her and untold others. Mark closed the box and reverently they carried it to the house. Cathie dusted Deny's box and they placed them together in his room, with sprigs of rosemary on top.

Returning to Hobart Cathie broke the news of their discovery to Janet and Mary.

On 1 January 1993, a brilliant day when mountains were iris blue, clouds billowed white as cherry blossom, wrens twittered in the myrtles and crescent honeyeaters called in the melaleucas, the family rowed quietly down Melaleuca Inlet in *Blue Boat*. In Bathurst Harbour where reflections in the deep dark water shone clear and bright, Deny's and Margaret's ashes were scattered together gently, peacefully on an outgoing tide.

Notes

Main sources for *King of the Wilderness* are Deny King's unpublished memoirs, which cover the period to 1934; his war diaries, diaries from 1950 to 1989 and earlier fragments, and travel diaries; Deny King's correspondence, including his correspondence with Margaret Cadell before their marriage, and afterwards; Margaret King's (nee Cadell) correspondence, including that with Deny King before and after marriage, and Margaret's diaries from 1949 to 1966; Mary and Janet King's correspondence with their parents; some of Janet Fenton's (nee King) diaries and notebooks; Charlie King's papers including correspondence with the Department of Mines; Olive Fieldwick's (nee King) unpublished memoirs, which cover the Sunset Ranch period; Melaleuca visitors' books, Charles King Memorial Hut visitors' books, *Melaleuca* logbooks, and all the other material in the voluminous King collection.

Several interviews with Clyde and Win Clayton (nee King) conducted by Janet and Geoff Fenton are also held in the King collection. Interviews with Deny King by Karen Alexander on 9 April 1991 and Jill Cassidy on 22–23 August 1990 were held by the Queen Victoria Museum, Launceston. Interviews with seventy-two other informants were conducted by the author and are held by her, to be lodged in her collection in the National Library of Australia, Canberra.

Other sources consulted were Deny King's correspondence with Karen Alexander, Annie Ball, Audrey Harrison and Karina Menkhorst, and Karina's correspondence from Melaleuca with her family; Lynne Davies' Melaleuca diaries, Fred Peacock's Melaleuca diary, Cons Lowry's Gunbarrel Highway diary, Peter Willson's logbooks. All these informants retain their documents. Olive King's diaries 1925, 1926, 1928, 1929 are in the possession of her son Dennis Fieldwick. Documents pertaining to the mine are in the Department of Mines archives.

Correspondence with all other informants and notes on conversations are in the author's collection. Photographs remain the property of those who loaned them.

Chapter 1

Melaleuca visitors' book; Nevil Shute Norway to Deny King, no date; Mark Woods to Deny King, no date; Hazel Hassett to Deny King, no date; *Mercury* 17 May 1991; Melaleuca visitors' book entries—Denis Chatelain and Claude Regnier, 9 January 1991, and T. B. Kemp to Deny King, 20 March 1964; Karen Alexander, *Mercury*, 17 May 1991.

Chapter 2

Olive Fieldwick (nee King), unpublished memoirs; Olive Parish (nee Fieldwick) interview, 5 April 1994; Kathleen Skinner, interview with author and Olive Parish, 3 April 1994.

Chapter 3

Deny King, interview with Jill Cassidy, 22 August 1990; Deny King, interview with Karen Alexander, 9 April 1991; Olive Fieldwick (nee King), unpublished memoirs; Olive King diaries 1925, 1926, 1928, 1929.

Chapter 4

Deny King, 'The Weld River Caves' in *The Tasmanian Tramp* no. 17, 1966, pp. 13–14; Olive Fieldwick, unpublished memoirs; D. A. B. Hardwicke to J. F. Douglas, 17 April 1920; *Mercury*, 27 February 1929.

Chapter 5

Deny King interview with Jill Cassidy, 22 August 1990; Deny King interview with Karen Alexander, 9 April 1991; Olive King diaries dates: 3 January 1928, 7 January 1928, 18 May 1929; Colin Bester interview, 5 April 1994; Guy Elliston and Vic Mansfield interviews with author and Janet Fenton, 7 December 1991.

Chapter 6

Deny King interview with Karen Alexander, 9 April 1991; Deny King interview with Jill Cassidy, 22 August 1990; Colin Bester interview, 5 April 1994; Win Clayton (nee King) interview, 16 November 1991; Guy Elliston, Doug Mansfield and Vic Mansfield interviews with author and Janet Fenton, 7 December 1991.

Chapter 7

Deny King interview with Karen Alexander, 9 April 1991; Colin Bester interview, 5 April 1994; Win Clayton interview with author and Janet Fenton, 16 November 1991; Guy Elliston, Doug Mansfield and Vic Mansfield interviews with author and Janet Fenton, 7 December 1991; David Martin, 'The Snowy Mountains' in *The Tasmanian Tramp* no. 6, 1945, pp. 18–21.

Chapter 8

Deny King interview with Karen Alexander, 9 April 1991; Deny King interview with Jill Cassidy, 23 August 1990; Allan Walker interview with author and Janet Fenton, 24 June 1991.

Chapter 9

Allan Walker interview with author and Janet Fenton, 24 June 1991; correspondence, Department of Mines archives 1940–46; Deny King to Charlie King, 1 March 1945; Charlie King to Minister of Lands, 8 August 1946; Tasmanian Tin Smelting Company accounts 6 April 1944, 1 June 1944.

Chapter 10

Deny King, war diary; Gordon Colebatch, interview with author and Mary King, 20 November 1991 and pers. comm.; Arthur Tilly interview, 5 April 1992 and pers. comm.; Keith Heeney, interview with author and Janet Fenton, 11 March 1994; Deny King, interview with Jill Cassidy, 22 August 1990; Richard Drummond, pers. comm. 10 October 1991; Jack Jameson, interview with author, Janet Fenton and Mary King, 21 June 1991; Parker journal, quoted by H. L. Rubinstein in 'Critchley Parker (1911–42): Australian Martyr for Jewish Refugees', in *Journal of the Australian Jewish Historical Society* vol. XI, part 1, 1990; W. J. Reinhold, 'The Bulldog-Wau Road. Brisbane,' (John Thomson lecture for 1945), University of Queensland, 1946; Deny King, New Guinea war diary, 19 September 1943; Deny King, PNG bird notes.

Chapter 11

Deny King, war diary; Gordon Colebatch, interview with author and Mary King, 20 November 1991 and pers. comm.; Arthur Tilly, interview 5 April 1992 and pers. comm.; Keith Heeney, interview with author and Janet Fenton, 11 March 1994; Margaret Cadell to Deny King, 7 October 1946;

Deny King interview with Jill Cassidy, 22 August 1990; Margaret Cadell to Deny King: 6 October 1945, 22 April 1946, 5 September 1946, 7 October 1946.

Chapter 12

D. Martin in *The Tasmanian Tramp* no. 6, 1945; Margaret Cadell to Deny King, 16 January 1947; Elaine Pearce interview, 22 June 1991; Elsie Campbell pers. comm. 31 October 1991; Margaret Cadell to Deny King: 11 June 1947, 17 August 1947, 26 February 1948, 29 March 1948, 27 June 1948, 14 July 1948, 28 July 1948, no date October 1948; Elsie Campbell pers. comm., 31 October 1991; Margaret Cadell to Deny King, 30 November 1948; Deny King to Margaret Cadell: 16 December 1948, 18 December 1948; Clyde Clayton interview with author and Janet Fenton 16 November 1991; Deny King to Margaret Cadell: 26 December 1948, 30 December 1948; Margaret Cadell to Deny King: 29 December 1948, 3 January 1949, 28 January 1949; Margaret Cadell diary: 10 February 1949, 15 February 1949.

Chapter 13

Margaret Cadell diary, 21 February to 9 March 1949; Clyde Clayton interview with Geoff Fenton, 15 June 1998; Deny King interview with Jill Cassidy, 22 August 1990; Deny King pers. comm., March 1991; Margaret Cadell diary 1 March 1949, 4 March 1949; Deny King pers. comm., 1991.

Chapter 14

Margaret Cadell diary, 12 March to 10 April 1949; Elsie Campbell pers. comm., 4 February 1992; Margaret Cadell to Deny King: 6 April 1949, 17 April 1949; Elsie Campbell interview with author, 4 April 1949; Margaret Cadell to Deny King, 10 May 1949, 17 May 1949; Deny King to Margaret Cadell 9 April 1949, 4 May 1949; Margaret Cadell to Deny King, 23 June 1949; Deny King to Margaret Cadell: 11 May 1949, 14 May 1949, 11 June 1949, 26 May 1949, 3 June 1949, 23 September 1949, 14 July 1949, 8 August 1949, 29 September 1949; Margaret Cadell diary, 4 August 1949; Margaret Cadell to Deny King, 9 September 1949, 26 October 1949.

Chapter 15

Margaret King diary: 30 December 1949, 11 January 1950, 19 January 1950, 24 January 1950, 25 January 1950, 3 February 1950, 17 March 1950, 19 March

1950, 22 March 1950, 23 March 1950, 16 May 1950, 21 May 1950, 22–23 May
1950, 16 May 1950, 30 January 1951, 25 March 1951, 17 February 1951,
13 January 1951, 31 January 1951, 9 June 1951, 22 April 1951, 13 May 1951,
11 May 1951, 1 June 1951, 21 June 1951; Deny King diary: 22–23 May 1950,
27 August 1950, 18–19 October 1950; *Melaleuca* logbook: 3 January 1951,
8 January 1951; Mary King pers. comm., 7 April 1998.

Chapter 16

Margaret King diary: 24 November 1951, 9 August 1952, 25 December 1952,
28 December 1952, 1 January 1953, 31 March 1953, 7 March 1953, 14 March
1953, 4 June 1953, 5 November 1953; *Melaleuca* logbook 21–22 November
1951, 12 September 1952, 9 December 1952; Deny King diary: 9 January
1951, 5 May 1952, 12 May 1952; Clyde Clayton interview with Geoff Fenton,
15 June 1998; Alan Hume interview, 10 December 1991; Deny King notes for
'Broad-News', no date; Peter Willson interview, 25 March 1994; Win Clayton
interview with Janet Fenton, 9 and 18 January 1994; Margaret King to Deny
King, 21 March 1952; *Melaleuca* logbook: 12 September 1952, 9 December
1952; Janet Fenton interview: 11, 12 and 20 June 1991, 15 and 17 March 1994;
Mary King interview, 11 June 1991; David Jennings interview, 15 December
1991.

Chapter 17

Margaret King diary: 2 June 1954, 23 April 1954, 10 April 1954, 10 July 1954,
10 August 1954, 17 November 1954, 31 December 1954, 18 January 1955,
4 February 1955, 1 July 1955, 17 October 1955, 26 November 1955,
6 December 1955, 4 April 1956, 5 March 1956, 20 February 1957, 4 March
1957, 7 March 1957, 9 November 1957, 21 September 1957, 1 December
1957; Deny King diary: 9 June 1954, 9 October 1954; Deny King interview
with Jill Cassidy, 23 August 1990; *Melaleuca* logbook: 9 December 1954,
24 September 1957; Kathleen Walker pers. comm., 9 November 1991.

Chapter 18

Melaleuca logbook, 22–23 February 1958; Harold C. Reynolds in Melaleuca
visitors' book, 23 March 1958; Leonard Long in *The Artist's Story*, p. 38. Waite
& Bull, Sydney, no date; Margaret King diary: 13 July 1958, 28 July 1958, 22
July 1958, 18 September 1958, 21 September 1958, 18–19 October 1958; Deny
King diary, 22 October 1958; Margaret King diary: 1 January 1959, 15 January

1959; *Melaleuca* logbook, 18 February 1959; Deny King diary, 9 April 1959; Margaret King diary, 11–12 June 1959; Deny King diary, 25 August 1959; Clyde Clayton interview with Geoff Fenton, 30 August 1998; Margaret King diary, 14 October 1959; Elaine Pearce interview, 22 June 1991; Olegas Truchanas, Joyce Denne in Melaleuca visitors' book, 31 December 1959.

Chapter 19

Deny King diary January 1960 to February 1961; Margaret King diary January 1960 to February 1961; Deny King interview with Jill Cassidy, 22 August 1980; Deny King to Margaret Cadell, 21 August 1949; H. G. Tinkler memo Rural Fires Board, 29 March 1960, Tasmanian Archives; N. J. Scott to Deny King, 21 April 1960, Tasmanian Archives; R. H. Green and B. C. Mollison, 'Birds of Port Davey and South Coast of Tasmania' in *The Emu* vol. 61, part 3, December 1961, p. 223; Sir Edmund Hillary, *Mercury*, 13 April 1960; Nan Butterworth interview, 3 November 1991; *Melaleuca* logbook, 10 August 1960; Margaret King diary, 13 August 1960; Deny King diary, 22–23 August 1960; Margaret King diary, 5 September 1960; Charles King Memorial Hut visitors' book, 26 February 1961.

Chapter 20

Margaret King diary: 3 June 1961, 8 June 1961, 9 June 1961; Deny King diary, 4 September 1991; Margaret King diary, 17 September 1991; Ernest Mills in Melaleuca visitors' book, 17 October 1961; Margaret King diary, 31 January 1961; R. Pettman in Melaleuca visitors' book, 8 January 1960; Janet Fenton interview, 15 March 1994, 11 June 1991; *Melaleuca* logbook, 17 February 1962; Deny King diary: 26–27 February 1962, 15 March 1962; Margaret King diary: 3 May 1962, 7 August 1962; *Melaleuca* logbook, 14 March 1962; N. J. B. Plomley to Deny King, 12 March 1963; N. J. B. Plomley ed., *Friendly Mission: The Tasmanian Journals and Papers of George Augustus Robinson 1829–1834*, Tasmanian Historical Research Association, Hobart, 1966, p. 8.

Chapter 21

Melaleuca logbook, 27 February 1963; Deny King diary, 24 April 1963; Margaret King diary, 22 August 1963; Margaret King to Deny King, no date [October 1963]; Deny King diary 24–25 October 1963, 6 November 1963, 23 November 1963; *Melaleuca* logbook, 3 December 1963; Puck Vaughan pers. comm., 19 October 1997; Deny King diary, 10 March 1964; Margaret

King to Deny, 4 April 1964, no date [April 1965], no date [March 1964]; *Melaleuca* logbook, 8 May 1964.

NOTE: Only authorised collecting of Aboriginal artefacts for research is legal. Aboriginal sites are protected by legislation from public interference.

Chapter 22

Margaret King to Deny, no date [October 1963]; Mary King to Deny, 9 April 1964; Margaret King to Deny no date [April 1964]; Margaret King to Deny, no date [April 1964]; Janet King to Deny, no date [April 1965]; Margaret King to Deny, no date [April 1965]; Winifred Curtis, *The Endemic Flora of Tasmania*, illus. Margaret Stones, six vols, Ariel Press, London, 1967–78, (commissioned by Lord Talbot de Malahide FLS); Leigh Candy pers. comm., 1992; Deny King diary: 22 November 1965, 30 November 1965.

Kings lomatia *(Lomatia tasmanica)*, also known as Kings holly, the oldest plant clone in existence, at least 43,600 years old, is listed as endangered under the Threatened Species Protection Act 1995 and the Federal Act. No specific details of its location are given at the request of the National Parks and Wildlife Service, in order to protect this unique plant.

Descriptions and illustrations of *Euphrasia kingii* and *Lomatia tasmanica* appear in *The Endemic Flora of Tasmania* in part iv, p. 248, plate LXX1X, and part vi, p. 468, plate CLV, respectively. Information on *Lomatia tasmanica* can also be found on Parks and Wildlife Service, Tasmania websites: http://www.parks.delm.tas.gov.au/veg/lomatia/lomatia.html http:/www.parks.delm.tas.gov.au/esl/holly.html

Chapter 23

Margaret King diary, 1 January 1966, 6 January 1966; Margaret King to Deny, no date [January 1966]; Margaret King to Deny, no date [April 1966]; Margaret King diary 1 April 1966; Margaret King to Nan Butterworth, no date [1966]; Margaret King to Deny, no date [26 August 1966]; Deny King diary 5 February 1967, 18 February 1967, 26 February 1967.

Chapter 24

Deny King diary: 18 March 1967, 5 April 1967, 26 August 1967, 29 October 1967, 5 November 1967.

Chapter 25

Mine information provided by Janet and Geoff Fenton, Peter Willson, David Jennings and Karina Menkhorst; David Jennings interview, 15 December 1991; Deny King diary: 8 January 1968, 3 April 1968, 1 May 1968, 2 May 1968; Janet Fenton pers. comm., 17 April 2000; Deny King diary: 23 September 1968, 21 November 1968, 30 April 1969.

Chapter 26

Deny King diary: 7 June 1970, 23 August 1970; Janet Fenton interview, 11 June 1991; Janet King diary: 1 January 1971, 23–24 January 1971; Deny King diary, 3 March 1971, 5 April 1971, 2–3 May 1971; *Melaleuca* logbook, 15 May 1971; Deny King diary: 7 January 1972, 15 February 1972, 19 February 1972; J. H. Willis, *Papers and Proceedings of the Royal Society of Tasmania* vol. 87, pp. 81–82; David Jones to Deny King 23 February 1972; Deny King diary, 8 February 1973, 13 February 1973; Mary King pers. comm., 2 January 1998; Winifred Curtis to Deny King, 15 February 1973; R. H. Green and B. C. Mollison, 'Birds of Port Davey and South Coast of Tasmania' in *The Emu*, December 1991, pp. 223–26; R. H. Green to Deny King, 15 May 1964; Deny King diary: 19 August 1972, 8 July 1972; Kath and Roy Davies interview, 22 June 1991; Deny King diary: 17 March 1973, 26 July 1973; Janet King diary, 6 September 1973; Donald and Sandra Macansh interview, 22 June 1996; Deny King diary: 3–4 October 1973, 19 November 1973, 22 December 1973; Janet King diary, 25 December 1973; Deny King diary, 12 March 1974.

Chapter 27

Peter and Barbara Willson interview, 15 June 1991; Deny King, New Guinea travel diary: 24 July 1974, 1 August 1974; Deny King diary: 9 September 1974, 20 September 1974; Gregory J. Jordan, Raymond J. Carpenter and Robert S. Hill, 'Late Pleistocene Vegetation and Climate near Melaleuca Inlet, South-western Tasmania' in *Australian Journal of Botany*, 1991, pp. 315–33; Gregory J. Jordan and Robert S. Hill, 'Two New Banksia Species from Pleistocene Sediments in Western Tasmania' *Australian Systematic Botany* 4, 1991, pp. 499–511; Deny King diary: 3 December 1974, 26 December 1974, 22–23 February 1975, 12 March 1975; Cons Lowry interview, 30 September 1991; Deny King diary: 10 April 1975, 5 September 1975, 4 November 1975, 18 November 1976; May E. Smith, Charles King Memorial Hut visitors' book, 8 April 1976; Peter Hodgman MLC, CKMH visitors' book, 28 January 1976;

Hunter Lilly, CKMH visitors' book, 14 March 1976; Deny King diary: 14 November 1976, 20 December 1976; Deny King to Mary and Janet, 13 February 1977; Deny King diary: 9 March 1977, 3 September 1977.

Chapter 28

Nick Tanner submission to Inquiry into the South-West National Park, 4 April 1977, reported in the *Mercury* 5 April 1977; *Mercury* 4 June 1977; Deny King, *Mercury*, 19 September 1977; Melaleuca visitors' book 1 January 1978; Roy McAndrew interview, 9 April 1994; Deny King diary: 22 April 1978, 4 June 1978; Karina Menkhorst to parents, 16 December 1978; Deny King diary: 8 January 1978, 20 January 1978; Nick Tanner interview, 9 December 1991; Chris Chandler, CKMH visitors' book, 19 January 1979; Steve Bracks, CKMH visitors' book, 28 December 1977; Bob Burton, CKMH visitors' book, 11 February 1979; Deny King Gunbarrel Highway travel diary: 6 May 1979, 30 April 1979, 20 May 1979; Doug Humann to Mary and Janet, 13 May 1991; Deny King to Karen Alexander, 19 November 1979; Deny King to Mary and Janet, 17 November 1979; W. E. Boud to Deny King, no date; Melaleuca visitors' book, 26 March 1980; Deny King diary, 5 March 1980; Trevor Wilson, *Tasmania Essay*, illus. Lord Snowdon, Banks, Hobart, 1981. p. 26; Karina Menkhorst to Audrey Menkhorst, 1 May 1981; Denis Woolley, CKMH visitors' book 21 May 1980; Deny King to Karen Alexander: 31 October 1980, 3 August 1980; Deny King to Janet and Geoff Fenton, 28 November 1980; Fran Pinkard interview, 10 December 1991; David Pinkard interview, 10 December 1991; John Chapman pers. comm., 1 October 1991; Deny King Nepal travel diary: 28 December 1980, 8 January 1981.

Chapter 29

Michael Monester, Melaleuca visitors' book 28 January 1981; Christopher Lilford, Melaleuca visitors' book 8 February 1981; Deny King diary: 14 February 1981, 9 February 1981; Deny King to Janet 18 February 1981; Karina Menkhorst to Peter Menkhorst, 13 February 1981; Deny King diary: 7 and 10 July 1981, 25 July 1981, 14 November 1981, 24 November 1981; Annie Ball interview, 17 November 1991; Deny King diary, 29 April 1982; Deny King to Karen Alexander, 17 April 1980; Mary King interview 20 November 1991; Deny King diary: 17–18 September 1982, 22–24 November 1982, 30 December 1982, 15 February 1983; Karina Menkhorst to Audrey Menkhorst, 26 February 1983; Lynne Davies diary, 15 February 1983;

Lynne Davies interview, 20 November 1991; Deny King letter to Mary and Janet, no date [1983]; Deny King diary: 18 January 1984, 14 January 1984; Phil Jones interview, 20 November 1991; Deny King diary: 2 February 1984, 21 March 1984, 3 April 1984, 19 August 1984, 5 November 1984; Deny King to Karen Alexander, 23 December 1984; Deny King to Karina Menkhorst, 30 June 1984.

Chapter 30

Deny King South American travel diary: 12 February 1985, 23 February 1985; Deny King to Annie Ball, 2 March 1985; Deny King to Karina Menkhorst: 6 April 1985, 2 April 1985; Don Wright interview, 14 December 1991; Tom Coles interview, 13 December 1991; Deny King to Pippa and Bob Cotton, 5 May 1985; Deny King South American travel diary, 6 March 1985; Geoff Andrewartha pers. comm., 18 November 1991; Deny King diary: 29 June 1985, 21 June 1985; Fred Peacock diary, 12 June 1985; Deny King diary: 12 September 1985, 3 March 1986; Melaleuca visitors' book, 4 December 1986; Deny King to Karina Menkhorst, 18 March 1987; Anka Makovec interview, 13 December 1991; Deny King diary, 7 February 1988; Armand Descaf, Melaleuca visitors' book, 24 February 1988; Heather Innes interview, 11 December 1991; Deny King New Zealand travel diary, 5 February 1989; Tom Coles interview, 13 December 1991; Jessie Luckman interview, 22 June 1991; Deny King diary: 19 September 1989, 16 November 1989; Mark Holdsworth interview, 5 December 1991; Deny King to Karina Menkhorst: 1 February 1990, 15 March 1990; Deny King, *Mercury*, 30 December 1990; Deny King to Karina Menkhorst, 9 March 1991.

Acknowledgments

I thank Deny King for asking me to help him tell his story, and Mary King and Janet Fenton for entrusting me with recording their father's life and unrestricted access to the King family papers.

Special thanks are due to Janet for her fullest cooperation; her meticulous reading of and comments on the manuscript, research and information on a multitude of details, arranging interviews with many informants; locating and helping select photos; compiling a bibliography of over one hundred entries for her father and providing a sketch of Melaleuca and other map references. Her letters from Melaleuca have been a special joy.

I am immensely grateful to Geoff Fenton for technical descriptions and details, and overall support for the project, and for the Fenton family's warm hospitality to me at all times. I also thank Tony Fenton and Kylie McKendrick for their interest in and moral support for the telling of the story of their beloved Gerr.

I thank our son Stephen Mattingley, whose interest in South-West Tasmania guided me to Melaleuca and the serendipitous meeting with Deny, which led to this biography. His patient reading of the manuscript through many drafts, his suggestions, ready help and research on many small details have been deeply appreciated.

Peter Brown and Mark Holdsworth included my husband and me as volunteer wardens on the first orange-bellied parrot survey, thereby creating the opportunity to meet Deny King. Janice Haworth sowed the seed on her visit to Melaleuca by asking if an oral history of Deny had been done. Karen Alexander and Pippa Cotton were helpful in discussion. Our son Christopher Mattingley read the manuscript and advised on sailing matters. Deny's nieces Olive Parish and Audrey Wright, Des and Sheila Hadden, Heather Reid, Lilian Grecian, the Cotton family, Helen Turner, and Joan and Jan Alblas gave hospitality and help in the course of my research and travels.

The following people generously made available their personal diaries and letters from Deny: Janet Fenton; Deny's nephew Dennis Fieldwick who lent his mother Olive's early diaries; Karen Alexander, Annie Ball, Lynne Davies, Audrey Harrison, Cons Lowry, Karina Menkhorst, Elaine and Dorothy Pearce, Fred Peacock, Cathie Plowman. Peter Saunders lent his six autographed volumes of *The Endemic Flora of Tasmania*. Deny's letters to Karina and Peter Willson's logbooks were particularly valuable for the period 1990–91, when Deny no longer kept diaries.

I thank all the people who graciously allowed me to interview them and who shared their knowledge and memories of Deny and Margaret: Denis Alexander, Karen Alexander, Bill Baker, Annie Ball, Harry Banks, Colin Bester, Nan Butterworth, Elsie Campbell, Jimmy Childs, Win and Clyde Clayton, Gordon Colebatch, Tom and Helen Coles, Jeanette Collin, Pippa Cotton, Mark Creese, Barry Croft, Kath and Roy Davies, Lynne Davies, Rob Drummond, Guy Elliston, Geoff Fenton, Janet Fenton, Bob and Suzanne Geeves, Dudley Geeves, Audrey Harrison, Norton Harvey, Keith and Clem Heeney, John Hughes, Alan Hume, Heather Innes, Jack Jameson, David Jennings, Lloyd Jones, Phil Jones, Mary King, Cons and Bob Lowry, Jessie Luckman, Roy McAndrew, Don and Sandra Macansh, Charles McCubbin, Helen MacDougall, Anka Makovec, Doug and Vic Mansfield, Karina Menkhorst, Olive Parish, Elaine and Dorothy Pearce, David and Fran Pinkard, Kath Skinner, Jack Symons, Nick and Cynthia Tanner, Norah Tanner, Margaret Tassell, Arthur Tilly, Bob and Penny Tyson, Puck Vaughan, Graeme von Bibra, Trevor Waite, Allan Walker, Kathleen Walker, Peter and Barbara Willson, Don Wright.

Gratitude is also due to Bob Tyson for arranging transcription of interviews, and to Robyn Annear who did them so meticulously and took such a practical interest in the project. Chris Tassell, director of the Queen Victoria Museum, Launceston, kindly allowed me to use Jill Cassidy's and Karen Alexander's taped interviews with Deny and facilitated use of photos from the King Collection, in which the museum holds copyright.

I am appreciative of others writing or phoning with information: Ken Blackwell, Bob Brown, Leigh Candy, John Chapman, Allan Christian and Sheila Reynolds, Joan Dorney, Malcolm Dow, Dick Drummond, Hilary Edwards, Alan Gray, Chris King, Glenn Murcutt, Shirley O'Halloran, Philip Parkin, Peter Sims, Keith Vallance, David Ziegeler.

For providing photos from which to make the final selection for the book I wish to thank Karen Alexander, Roger Archibald, Richard Bennett, Bob Brown, John Chapman, Boris Clark, Geoff Fenton, Janet Fenton, Sally

Fenton, Helen Gee, Alan Gray, Norton Harvey, Mark Holdsworth, Janice Haworth, David Mattingley, Bob Mossel, Glenn Murcutt, David Pinkard, Joanne Richardson, Denis Rittson, Joe Scherschel, Peter Sims, Jack Symons, Trevor Waite, Dave Watts, David Wilson, Bob Wyatt.

Librarians of the Crowther Collection, in the State Library of Tasmania, and officers in the Tasmanian Archives, Department of Parks and Wildlife, Police Tasmania and Transport Tasmania Libraries were very helpful, as were those in the Commonwealth Archives and the State Library of South Australia. Others who assisted with research or answered queries include Alex Buchanan, Tasmanian Herbarium; Dr Greg Jordan, Botany Department, University of Tasmania; Noel Kemp and David Pemberton, Tasmanian Museum and Art Gallery; Kim Akkerman, Sandy Collin, John Cook, Don Hird, Nick Sawyer and Margaret Tassell.

I thank The Friends of Melaleuca for helping to pay for one of my flights into Melaleuca, and The Friends' School for inviting me to be writer-in-residence, providing another opportunity for me to continue research in Hobart. Chris Wisby of the ABC, Hobart, interviewed me several times, which elicited useful responses. Chris Pearce of The Hobart Bookshop has always been a firm believer in the importance of this book.

Finally I thank my husband David for his loyal support and uncomplaining acceptance of living in a ménage à trois with Deny for over ten years, listening day and night as I talked my way through Deny's story; reading and re-reading drafts and more drafts; annotating thousands of entries legible and illegible in the visitors' books and log books; reading the computer manual again and again; going on innumerable research errands and journeys; acquiring a formidable reputation as gatekeeper of our phone and door; and producing cups of 'cawfee' at critical moments. His contribution has been invaluable.

Index